W9-CEM-789

The Game Rifle

The Game Rifle

Hunter's Information Series ®
North American Hunting Club
Minneapolis, Minnesota

The Game Rifle

Copyright © 1992, North American Hunting Club

Library of Congress Catalog Card Number 91-67533
ISBN 0-914697-42-0

Printed in U.S.A.
10   11   12   13   14   15   16   17   18   19

Caution

Contents

Acknowledgments 1
About The Author 3
Foreword 5
Introduction 9
1 Favorite Guns Past And Present 17
2 Western Rifles And Cartridges 31
3 Selecting The Right Elk Cartridge 45
4 Varmint Cartridges 57
5 All-Around Cartridges And Rifles 67
6 Shooting Big-Game Rifles 83
7 Selecting A Rifle For Alaska 105
8 The Magnums 117
9 Rangefinding Facts And Fallacies 135
10 How Temperature Affects Velocity 145
11 Bullet Performance And Stopping Power 157
12 Big-Game Bullets 181
13 Varmint Bullets 197
14 The Best Shots 205
15 No Magic Involved 219
16 Selecting The Right Ammunition 233
Index Of Rifle Calibers 243
Index 245

Acknowledgments

The North American Hunting Club would like to thank everyone who helped with the creation of this book.

Artist David Rottinghaus provided all illustrations. Contributing photos were North American Hunter Editor Bill Miller, Senior Editor Dan Dietrich, Hunting Information Series Managing Editor Ron Larsen and photographers Leonard Lee Rue III, Len Clifford, Marilyn Maring, Len Rue Jr., Tim Lewis Rue, Irene Vandermolen, Bill Vaznis, Bob Hagel, Judd Cooney, Neil and Mary Jane Mishler, Hal Swiggett and Paul DeMarchi.

We also wish to thank Remington, Inc.; Olin/Winchester, and Federal, Inc. for use of illustrations and photos. And, thanks to Mark Harris at Wolfe Publishing.

A special thanks goes to the Hunting Club's publication staff including Publisher Mark LaBarbera, Editor Bill Miller, Managing Editor of Books Ron Larsen, Associate Editor of Books Colleen Ferguson. Thanks also to Vice President of Product Marketing Mike Vail, Marketing Manager Cal Franklin and Marketing Project Coordinator Laura Resnik.

About The Author

Bob Hagel, born in Wisdom, Montana, has spent most of his life in Idaho. His first big-game hunting trip was with his father when Bob was a young boy. He has been hunting "on his own" over the entire Western United States for decades.

In the early 1930s, Bob took rifle and handgun training under Elmer Keith, who also taught him the basics of handloading. At one time he started making his own rifle stocks, and expanded into custom stock work.

In 1936, Bob's first gun article was published in *Fur—Fish—Game*. A quarter-decade later, an article by Bob on long-range game shooting appeared in the inaugural issue of *Shooting Times*, March 1960. By that time, Bob Hagel's name loomed with the best of the firearms writers.

Bob has written articles for nearly every firearms magazine in the United States; he has also been on several magazine editorial staffs, including *American Rifleman*, *Gun Digest*, *Handloading Digest*, *Rifle*, *Handloader* and *Peterson's Hunting*. Bob has contributed chapters and sections to many published books on the subject of guns and handloading.

People have commented on Bob's writing as "telling it like it is." His analysis of new products—guns, loading components, ammunition, scopes or other accessories—can be relied upon as thorough and honest. Readers know that his opinions, whenever

expressed, are not frivolous and are based on both fact and experience.

Bob's expertise covers a wide range of subjects, including firearms, ballistics, design and functioning, handloading, shooting, hunting and conservation.

Using his vast amount of hunting experience, Bob was a professional guide and outfitter for approximately 12 years. Even though he does not guide professionally anymore, he still guides friends each fall on a non-profit basis.

This book is a compilation of what Hagel considers his *best* columns in over 20 years of writing.

Foreword

North American Hunting Club members prove time and again to be among the most successful and responsible hunters anywhere. Their efforts to promote the shooting sports, foster improved hunter/landowner relationships, conserve game animals and help others enjoy hunting never cease to amaze me.

For most NAHC members hunting is far, far more than simply a seasonal pastime. These dedicated outdoorsmen and, increasingly, outdoorswomen, live their passion everyday, 365 days a year. As president of such a positive and purposeful organization I swell with pride whenever I have the chance to talk about the individual and collective accomplishments of our members.

More than a decade ago, the NAHC was founded on the belief that such sportspeople existed in this country in great numbers and that they were not being satisfactorily served by any existing hunting organization. The success the Club has enjoyed ever since most certainly continues to prove that theory true.

All of our efforts at the NAHC are directed to provide the best, most accurate and most complete hunting information to North American Hunting Club members. In striving for that primary goal we found that few up-to-date, thorough resources existed to guide the serious hunter through the selection and field use of what is generically known as "the game rifle." Some books covered one aspect, others covered another. But very few were complete with all the information NAHC members told us they needed and wanted.

Then we were fortunate to uncover a collection of columns by wizened hunter, handloader and gunwriter Bob Hagel. These magazine items were like diamonds of hunting and gun lore just waiting to be assembled into a jeweled masterpiece! That is indeed what *The Game Rifle* has turned out to be!

The volume which you have in your hands is a compilation the best of 20 years worth of Bob's columns for *Rifle* and *Handloader* magazines. These publications are renowned in the firearms industry and among America's shooting public for their accuracy and technical quality.

Of Bob Hagel's work for his publications, *Rifle* and *Handloader* publisher Dave Wolfe writes:

Hagel "tells it like it is." His manuscripts are borne of hours at the test range and in the field. His analysis of new products— guns, loading components, ammunition, scopes or other accessories—can be relied upon as thorough and honest. Readers know that his opinions, whenever expressed, are not frivolous and are based on both fact and experience. Mighty good reasons why he has amassed such a fan club.

His expertise in firearms, ballistics, design and functioning, handloading, shooting, hunting and conservation may be equaled by someone, somewhere—but not surpassed. And when all that experience is coupled with an excellent command of the English language and an outstanding writing ability, there's only one Bob Hagel. Lucky for us, 50 years ago he chose to be an author—and consequently, to share his knowledge with gun enthusiasts around the world—for decades and decades to come.

The quantity of Bob's experimenting and writing as described in the "About The Author" portion of this book places him as one of the experts when it comes to qualifications to author such a book as this. But it is his special ability to make the complicated understandable and the in-depth readable that made this text such a joy for our North American Hunting Club staff to organize and prepare for you.

Based on Bob Hagel's dedication to a career in guns and hunting, I'm confident you'll enjoy this volume and come to cherish it as a first-class rifleman's resource. Like every publication of the North American Hunting Club it is designed to enhance your hunting skill and enjoyment. You can rest assured it was written and edited by hunters and firearms enthusiasts who are as dedicated and serious about their passions as you are.

But as outstanding and thorough as Bob's writings are, we wanted to give you even more. So in the final chapter ''Selecting The Right Ammunition'' you'll find detailed, up-to-the-minute ballistics charts provide by North America's premier ammunition manufacturers. You'll also have exclusive, collected access to detailed information on game rifle cartridges and bullets of every brand and description.

This addition to Bob Hagel's work, truly makes this the complete reference for enjoying your game rifle shooting and hunting to its fullest. Enjoy.

Steven F. Burke
President
North American Hunting Club

Introduction

What you are about to read may seem like a long-winded, backhanded way to get into this book. Maybe it is, but what follows is the agreement of understanding you and I need to have before we hunt together for common ground in the great world of hunting rifles and cartridges.

Make The First Shot Count

It has often been said that if everyone used a single-shot rifle, there would be fewer shots fired at big game, a reduction in missed shots and less game wounded. The thinking behind this is, of course, that if the hunter knew only one round could be fired without taking time to reload the single shot, a lot more care would be taken in aiming to put the first one in the right place. We could logically carry this even further and say that if only a single round of ammunition were carried, the hunter would make *darn* sure the bullet landed in the right spot! Of course, it must be realized that if only a single round were available, the theory could backfire if something went wrong, and the wounded animal escaped.

While few of us will subscribe to the idea of anyone hunting with only a single cartridge at his disposal, there is merit in the single-shot rifle theory. We don't have to go so far as to dispose of our repeating rifles or carry a single round in the magazine, but it does give us something to think about in making sure, clean kills.

With an elk in this position, a single shot will most likely not drop the elk on the spot. A lot of penetration is required to reach any of the vital organs. Unless a quick, finishing shot is capable of smashing through a lot of heavy bone, don't even attempt this shot.

The point is that if every hunter forgot about the extra three or four rounds he could get off rapidly if the first one failed and concentrated on making that first shot count, many misses and much wounding would be eliminated. The trend is to place entirely too much dependence on "follow-up" shots instead of trying to eliminate the need for them. I can't help thinking about the stories of the advantages of lever, slide and autoloading actions in the whitetail woods because so many shots can be fired in such a short time. If you put a little more effort into placing the first one right, there will be little need to empty the magazine.

I've seen some pretty good snap shooters here and there, and my dad was one of them. But, he usually waited until the running buck gave him a well-aimed clear shot rather than trying to mow down a bushel of brush with several shots in the hope that one would land in the right spot. In fact, he always said that if you could sneak up on the buck and take a "lean" on a tree before the animal knew you were there, you stood a lot better chance of eating liver for supper.

Some hunters seem to have the idea that when you are hunting, it is some kind of sin to shoot from a rest. How often have you heard the expression, ''Stand up and shoot from your hind legs like a man,'' which is, I guess, supposed to show sportsmanship. Very few hunters are good enough to be certain of placing all their shots in the vital area of a deer from the offhand position at anything over 100 yards when they take plenty of time to do it, let alone when they try to see how fast they can get off the first one.

Sure, we all have to shoot from the offhand position at times because there is no alternative for one reason or another. But, when it is necessary, put your best efforts into making it count. The only circumstances I know of where shooting from the offhand position is desirable is at running game at close range, and we don't have any business shooting at running game at long range, even though most of us have been foolish enough to try it. At close range, it is next to impossible to swing with the animal from a rest of any kind, or from the prone or sitting position.

When there is no place to take a solid rest, the sitting or prone position with a good shooting sling is the next best thing. But, it seems few hunters fit their rifles with shooting slings, or know how to use them if they do. And, even if they do have one, they are inclined to shoot offhand, squat, kneel or sit without using it in their rush to get off that first shot.

I've also seen them do the same thing when there was a log, rock or tree to give a steady rest within a few feet. This is usually a matter of excitement where the hunter simply goes into action without thinking about a steady, shooting position. There are times, of course, when the game is alerted and offers little time to find a rest or wrap up in a sling, but there are more instances when there is time if the hunter just isn't too excited to take advantage of it.

Many times I've refused to shoot at an animal because the only position available was not steady enough to keep the front sight or scope reticle within the vital area. Some of these animals either stayed where they were or within sight until I could get into a steady position where I knew the bullet would land in the right place before I fired. Others took off and I never saw them again, but I felt it was better to pass up the shot than to muff it and wound the animal.

This brings up yet another reason for giving a lot of thought to making that first shot count. Many hunters never seem to realize that any shot that may miss the game is even more likely to wound it. This includes close-range snap shots at game in the brush where there really isn't much chance to connect solidly, shots fired from unsteady positions and those fired at long range. They seem to think the bullet will either hit in a vital spot or miss completely. Not so, because if you don't think you and your rifle are capable of hitting the right spot, there is more chance that the bullet will land somewhere around the edges of the vitals rather than being a clean miss.

But, no matter what the circumstances, keep in mind making that first shot count. If you keep that thought firmly uppermost before you see game, instead of thinking that if the first one misses there are several more to go, you'll miss and wound a lot less game. Sure, some may run off while you are trying to make sure the first bullet lands in the right spot, but at least your conscience will be clear and the bitter taste of knowing an animal escaped wounded will not plague you for days afterward.

Avoid Wounding Game

Every year, a great deal more game is wounded than we care to admit or think about. Some of these animals are found; some are not. Some are not mortally wounded and recover, but many die after suffering for hours or days. Many run only a short distance after being hit and die within a few minutes without ever recovering from the initial shock. They suffer very little, but are still lost to the hunter. Both meat and trophy are wasted as far as the hunter is concerned, and the only thing that benefits is some carrion-eating predator.

In such cases, there should also be a lesson learned by the hunter so that he does not make the same mistake again, but I fear it often fails to sink in.

Of course, anyone who has seen much game killed is well aware that some game is unavoidably wounded because of circumstances beyond the control of the hunter: sights knocked out of line, a bullet that does not perform correctly, or an animal that moves just as the rifle fires. But, the largest percentage of game wounding could have been avoided if the hunter had used better judgment. Often, it can be blamed on not knowing when to shoot or when not to shoot.

To start with, a hunter is never justified in taking a shot at an animal if he doesn't think the chances of his putting the bullet

This whitetail deer was found after being shot weeks earlier. Upon decaying, the carcass was scavenged by predators.

where it will do the most good are greatly in his favor. To shoot at an animal that is hopelessly out of range with the hope that a bullet will find it, and perhaps kill it, is *never* sporting or humane. The same thing applies to shooting at running game when you know the chance of a vital hit is very slim. Always remember that if the chance for a solid hit is small, there is a greater chance the animal will be wounded than missed cleanly. Of course, there are hunters who are outstanding long-range shots, and, if armed with the right equipment, can kill animals at ranges the average hunter should never attempt. There are also those who are equally proficient on running game, but this doesn't mean the average once-a-year hunter should attempt the same shot. This boils down to the fact that if you are uncertain of your own ability to make the shot, don't attempt it.

A scoring long-range shot takes a bullet with good ballistic coefficient at high velocity, a flat trajectory, high retained velocity ensuring expansion and enough energy to tear things up when it gets there. If your cartridge doesn't have it, don't shoot beyond its sure killing range no matter how good you are.

When shooting in thick brush—where most running shots need to be taken—remember that a fairly small caliber with a rather fragile bullet may do very well when placed broadside in the ribs, but lacks penetration to reach the vitals of the same animal while it is running at an angle either toward or from the gun. Again, if in doubt, pass up that shot.

And, while we're talking about timber shooting, a great many animals are wounded because the hunter tried to hit a vital spot that was covered because of brush. Regardless of what has often been written and said about the ability of certain bullets to buck brush, don't shoot unless there is a hole in that brush to slip the bullet through. The bullet that will consistently continue on its true course after plowing into even small brush and branches, has yet to be designed. It only takes a few inches of deflection to wound instead of kill.

Finding a clear hole through the bushes is not the total answer, either. Better take a second hard look through that hole, and around it, to make certain it is in line with a vital spot. It is easy to assume the clear spot is over the ribs, when you are looking at the paunch instead.

An equally important factor when looking at an animal where only part of it is visible through a small hole in the brush, is what position it is in relation to the gun. We'll assume the spot seen is

This whitetail's vital spots are hidden behind brush. Unless there is a hole somewhere within the brush, do not even attempt to shoot. Brush often deflects bullets which wound animals instead of killing them.

over the shoulder, and you can see the front leg below it. Is the animal broadside, or quartering to or away from the hunter? If it is broadside, the bullet will go through both shoulders, and probably part of the lungs or heart. If it is quartering to the gun, the bullet will go through the shoulder and into the lungs. Both are good, fatal hits. But, if it is quartering away from the hunter, the bullet will most likely pass through the shoulder and come out through the chest without hitting the lungs. In this case, especially if the shoulder is not broken, the animal will live a long time and, in all probability, go a long way.

If the animal happens to be an elk or a moose, you'd better have second thoughts about trying such a shot with light bullets that are not designed for deep penetration.

Finally, when you shoot at an animal and it runs off as though unhit, don't assume that it wasn't. The great majority of shot game runs from a few feet to several hundred yards after being hit. Mark the place where the animal was when you fired, then go there. If there is blood, follow it; if there isn't, follow the tracks anyway, for several hundred yards if possible. If everyone did this, it is safe to say that at least a quarter of the game lost would be recovered.

Okay. That sets the ground rules for everything else this book is intended to share. Let's get at it!

1

Favorite Guns Past And Present

Ken Waters sized up the situation well, when he stated that it is much easier for the average gun owner who owns only a few guns to pick a favorite or two than it is for the gun writer who has many. This point can be carried even further to differentiate between the gun writers of yesterday and those of today. It comes a lot easier for those who very definitely lean toward certain cartridges or, in some instances, bore diameters.

Jack O'Connor never had any difficulty in picking his favorite. It was the .270 Win., first, last and always. His favorite rifle chambered for his beloved .270 Win. was a little more difficult to pick out of the several in his rack, but my feelings in watching him handle them was that a piece by Al Biesen on a pre-1964, Model 70 Winchester action might be it.

Elmer Keith, my old friend of many hunts and shooting sessions, was never at a loss to let anyone know that he wanted no part of any rifle that was chambered for a cartridge using anything smaller than .338 bullets of at least 250 grains. I suspect that for hunting any North American big game, Elmer would have been completely happy with his .338 K-T and a 300-grain bullet.

Those who remember the days when Warren Page was shooting editor of *Field & Stream* know that while he tested the potency of many cartridges and rifles in many places, his all-time favorite was one of the 7mm magnums—more specifically, Old

Betsy, a custom rifle from Mashburn Arms chambered for the 7mm Mashburn Super Magnum, and loaded almost exclusively with 175-grain bullets for everything from pronghorn to moose; from impala to eland.

Even further back in the annals of shooting and hunting history, Col. Townsend Whelen was partial to the .30-06 for the great majority of his North American hunting forays.

A "First" Favorite

It isn't all that easy for me. Like Ken Waters, I find it hard to narrow down cartridge and gun choices. Ever since I started shooting, which is about as far back as I can remember, I have shot everything I could lay my hands on. During the past 25 to 30 years, I've had samples of nearly every new gun and cartridge that has arrived on the scene. These recent guns and cartridges, as well as most of the older ones, have been wrung out on the range, in the chronograph room and in the shop to see how well they performed and functioned.

But, my interest in guns sprang from my interest in hunting, so nearly every new cartridge that surfaced has been used in hunting some kind of game somewhere. This does not only apply to commercial guns and cartridges. In fact, I have probably killed as much game with wildcat cartridges as with commercial numbers.

When you cover half a century of shooting and hunting, there are bound to be favorite guns and cartridges that have been nudged out by newer, more efficient developments. You still, however, remember with pangs of nostalgia many of those that served you well.

While I cut my shooting teeth on lever-action rifles, my serious big-game hunting started with a Model 96 Krag. The old Krag was issued with 30-inch barrel and full stock. For hunting purposes, the stock was immediately cut back to just forward of the sling swivel, and the handguard was removed. Later, it was stocked in a fairly good piece of Circassian walnut, but I could never bring myself to chop off any of that long barrel. Being young and full of energy, I didn't mind the extra length and weight, either in the brush or on top of the peaks. Much game fell to that .30-40 rifle loaded with 220-grain bullets of various makes, but I soon found that the big, slow bullets did not expand well at much over 100 yards so I switched to 180-grainers.

Then, taking Elmer Keith's advice, I bought a Lyman Number 3 tong tool and started rolling my own, using mostly 172-grain

Favorite rifles change over the years, especially when the itch to hunt bigger game takes the hunter into the more rugged areas of the West. Greater firepower helps overcome range miscalculations in this type of terrain.

Western Tool & Copper Works and cavity-point bullets ahead of all the Du Pont Number 17½ powder the single-lug action would stand.

I had a world of confidence in that old Krag rifle and the .30-40 cartridge. And, even though its performance is below the standards of many rifles and cartridges I've used since, and the rifle has long ago gone down the gun-trade trail, it still occupies a private niche in my memories of favorite guns.

A Powerful Favorite

Cartridges carrying a magnum designation were not often seen or used in this country in the early 1930s, but the cartridges generally used in the West at the time—.25-35, .30-30, .30-40 and .30-06 for shooting mule deer, elk, goats and black bear—stirred up a big itch to own a more powerful rifle, a rifle chambered for a cartridge that would reach the far side of a mountain canyon with

One early favorite magnum is this 1917 Enfield .30 Newton. Its receiver sight later gave way to a scope. With this rifle, many head of mountain game were taken—establishing the author's fondness for magnum cartridges.

less bullet drop and pack more punch when the bullet arrived.

That itch was relieved after I piloted Charlie O'Neil, who later became the guiding light of OKH Rifles, on a mule deer hunt. When Charlie returned to Minnesota, he rechambered a 1917 Enfield for the .30 Newton cartridge for me.

Restocked and scoped, that rifle accounted for many head of assorted big game. I don't recall ever shooting a single animal with it with factory ammunition, which was nearly impossible to get. And, the absence of the slow powders, which we now have, held the potential of the big rimless case down somewhat. But, even with IMR-4064, which was new on the market, it was a true magnum. Trajectory was so much flatter than anything I had used before that when I sighted it 3 inches high at 100 yards with 172-grain WT&CW hollow-point bullets, I came to believe that all I needed to hit an animal at long range was its address.

The biggest problem I encountered with the .30 Newton was a

lack of bullets that would hold together on heavy game under the velocity impact it delivered. It did quite well on deer-size game, but ruined a lot of meat at ranges under 200 yards or so. Any bullet I could find blew up on elk at anything except extreme ranges. Some of the 220-grain bullets in the big case of that day may have done fairly well on big animals, but they were not designed for the flat trajectory I wanted.

O'Neil later rebarreled the Enfield action for the .333 OKH when that cartridge was developed, but the .30 Newton was my first magnum-capacity cartridge. And, while the bullets and powders we had then failed to bring out the full potential of the cartridge, it did impress me with the advantages the big cases had when shooting big game under most conditions. Today, I use magnum cartridges in one caliber or another for hunting nearly all big game. The .30 Newton was the cartridge that started it all, and that cartridge and rifle have to be one of my favorites when my memory drifts back through the years.

Even More Power

The .333 OKH was the cartridge that probably had more influence on starting a trend toward the ⅓-inch bore in American cartridges than any other. It was an excellent cartridge. However, with the powder capacity of the .30-06 case, which it was based on, it was obvious that more powder capacity could be utilized with the then-new, IMR-4350, slow-burning powder. The .334 OKH took good care of this, but because it was based on the full-length .375 H&H Magnum case, few actions would handle it except the big Brevex Magnum Mauser, and, even then, they were scarce and expensive. Then, the .333 OKH Belted cartridge was developed, which is duplicated today by the .338 Win. Mag. The old Enfield action was again used, the barrel rechambered for the more potent .333 OKH Belted.

The new cartridge, based on the .300 or .375 H&H cases using the original body taper, was cut to about .30-06 length and was given a sharp shoulder. The 250-grain Barnes bullet could be boosted along at over 2,700 fps from the 25-inch barrels usually used on rifles chambered for it. With the high ballistic coefficient of the Barnes spitzer bullets, this bullet gave flat trajectory over the longest game-shooting ranges, and the great sectional density delivered deep penetration with the heavy-jacket style I used.

That cartridge and rifle became my favorite for hunting elk under all conditions. The only problem I ever encountered was

An all-time favorite rifle is this 7mm Mashburn Super Magnum, stocked in French walnut with Douglas barrel and FN action. At 400 paced yards, this Alaskan caribou fell to a 160-grain Nosler. This rifle could be considered an ultimate long-range mountain rifle.

For big game that may get nasty if wounded, the .340 Wthby is a favorite. This one is built on a late Winchester Model 70 action with French walnut stock and 4X Redfield in Buehler mount. This Alaskan brown bear was taken with a 250-grain Bitterroot.

finding bullets that performed the way they should at all distances from a few yards in heavy timber to long cross-canyon shooting. The Barnes .049-inch-thick jacket worked very well at close range, but the jacket became even thicker at the point during the swaging process and often failed to expand when initial velocity dropped off. When the .338 Win. Mag. appeared, and Nosler Partition bullets were made in that diameter, I traded off the .333 OKH Belted rifle.

Today's Favorites

Since that time, I've used many rifles in both wildcat and commercial chamberings for cartridges with .338 caliber bullets. The rifle I use mostly for shooting heavy game is built on a post-1964, Model 70 Winchester action made for the .375 H&H cartridge and has a Hobaugh barrel chambered for the .340 Wthby Mag. cartridge. By forming cases from .375 H&H cases and hard W-W brass, it is no real problem to boost the 250-grain bullet along at 2,900 fps from a 24-inch barrel, and the 210-grain Nosler at 3,200 fps. The 250-grain Nosler Partition is my first choice for heavy game like Alaskan brown bear, moose and elk where ranges are not overly long, and the 210-grain Partition bullet for areas where long range may be the rule. That bullet at 3,200 fps shoots as flat as any of the good hunting bullets in the big 7mm or .300 cartridges at 400 to 500 yards, and it packs a lot more wallop and penetrates deeper when it gets there. This rifle is, and probably always will be, a top favorite for heavy game.

Charlie O'Neil also built another rifle for me that held a special place among the best for deer-size game. This one was based on a small-ring 98 Mauser action, and had a 22-inch, pencil-thin Ashurst barrel chambered for the 7x57 Mauser cartridge. I stocked the rifle to hold down weight for use as a light mountain rifle, and it seemed that when I headed for rough country to look for muleys, sheep or goats, that rifle was the one that usually went along. I also killed a few elk with it. While it never failed me, I've used a lot of cartridges that I like better when chasing wapiti.

Mostly, I used handloaded ammunition in the little 7x57mm, and while the velocity was certainly nothing to get excited over, I soon found the .284-inch-diameter bullets had a lot of what it takes to make a versatile big-game cartridge for nearly all classes of big game. This experience led to my use of many 7mm cartridges, both commercial and wildcat, standard and magnum.

I later used a .285 OKH extensively and killed a lot of game with it. This cartridge was nothing more than the 7mm-06 with long-bullet seating for slightly more powder capacity, and was undoubtedly the inspiration of the .280 Rem.

Use of the .285 OKH indicated that even more powder capacity might be needed with the advent of H-4831. After a good deal of correspondence with my friend, Warren Page, who was just then starting to use the 7mm Mashburn Super Magnum, I had Art Mashburn chamber a Douglas barrel for it and fit it to an FN series 300 magnum-length action.

After developing loads to maximum trouble-free hunting pressures for 7mm cartridges ranging in capacity from the little 7mm-08 (Remington's addition to their rather extensive line of 7mm cartridges), to the big 7mm-300 Wthby wildcat, it seems the Mashburn Super Magnum has about optimum powder capacity for the .284-inch bore diameter with available powders. The big over-bore capacity Wthby .300 case gives slightly more velocity with the 175-grain bullet, but shows less with the 160-grain and lighter bullets. The Mashburn offers only about 100 fps over the 7mm Rem. and 7mm Wthby cases. But the advantage lies with the slightly larger case. This, however, has little to do with this cartridge and rifle being perhaps my all-time favorite, big-game rifle. There are other reasons for that.

The accuracy of that rifle with both 160 and 175 Nosler Partition bullets, particularly of the old style, is exceeded by few sporters I have ever owned or used. The French walnut stock is completely stable through all climatic conditions. I cut weight from both the action and stock in the right places to bring it down to 8 pounds, 4 ounces with a Bausch & Lomb 4X scope in Conetrol mounts. It is stocked to fit me perfectly for average hunting conditions, and if its bullets don't go where they are intended to, I know it is not the rifle's fault. But, perhaps of even more importance to a favorite rifle is the miles I have carried it, the places we've been together, and the game that has fallen to its ever-lethal bullets. I am not certain how many head of big game it has accounted for, but there have been antelope, many mule deer and elk, black bear, goats, caribou, moose and grizzly. I'm sure the score will increase before we make our last hunt together.

Few Favorite .30s

The .30 caliber cartridges are the American hunter's choice. I've killed big game with most of them, but somehow, except for the old Krag and .30 Newton and some I've had chambered for .308 cartridges I have had few favorites. For me, the .30-30, .30-06, and various .300 magnums, both commercial and wildcat, have come and gone. I've killed some game with the venerable .30-06 cartridge, and it has served me well. But, neither the cartridge nor any rifle I have ever had chambered for it could be called a favorite.

The .308 Norma Mag. is top-drawer, and I've used it a lot. The .300 Wthby Mag. is certainly right at the top of the 30-caliber-cartridge list, but while I've tested loads in several, I've never owned one. I find that with existing cases for the .300 Wthby with their thin web section and rather soft brass, the .300 Win. Mag. with strong, hard W-W cases delivers as much velocity if you want to reload the cases several times.

As for the .300 Win. Mag., I've hunted with several rifles chambered for that cartridge and owned most of them, and find it a superb long-range cartridge with anything from the 150- to 200-grain spitzer bullets. With the 200-grain Nosler, it gives deep penetration for the heaviest American game.

However, not until recently have I owned a rifle chambered for the .300 Win. Mag. cartridge that is becoming a favorite. That rifle has a Hobaugh barrel fitted to a Remington Model 700 BDL action

This .300 Win. Mag. is stocked with Bastogne walnut. With a 4X Leupold in Leupold mount, it is superbly accurate and relatively light, making it ideal for hunting any American big game in various terrain and cover.

A good combination varmint-and-big-game rifle is this 6mm Remington, a Model 700 with 20-inch barrel. It was restocked in Oregon myrtle and topped with a 2.5-8X Bushnell in Conetrol mount.

and is topped with a Leupold M8-4X scope in Leupold mounts. Stocked in classic style with a piece of Frank Pachmayr's excellent Bastogne walnut, it hovers around the minute-of-angle mark with full-throttle loads and 180- or 200-grain Nosler Partition bullets. And, those full-throttle loads from the 24-inch barrel start the 180-grain bullet at 3,200 fps and the 200-grain at over 3,000 fps. That kind of punch, flat trajectory and accuracy, and weight of only 8½ pounds are making this rifle a definite favorite.

Favorite Varmint Numbers

There has been a varmint and big-game rifle or two in my rack for many years, and the rifle that gave me the most pleasure and confidence for both long-range varmint shooting and on deer-size game, was one of the original Remington Model 700 ADL rifles for the 6mm Rem. It was an extremely accurate rifle with loads it liked, both varmint and big-game bullets and many groups going

These Remington Model 700s are favorite varmint rifles. The sporter is a .22-250 with a 2.5-8X Bausch & Lomb in a Buehler mount; it has been restocked in claro walnut. The Varmint Special is a .222 Rem. restocked in black walnut. (It is usually equipped with a more powerful varmint scope than the 4X shown here.)

well under a minute of angle. It was later stocked with a fairly good piece of Oregon myrtle, and was very light with its 20-inch barrel. Topped with a Bushnell ScopeChief variable 2.5-8X scope in Conetrol mounts, it was an ideal varmint and big-game outfit. In fact, I liked that little rifle so well that I eventually shot the throat out and replaced the barrel with one chambered for the .25-284. That cartridge is a little better on the big-game end, but less desirable as a varmint round. I'm not sure that I will ever like it quite as well as in the original chambering.

If there is a varmint cartridge that I haven't used for varmint shooting, I can't think of what it might be—in commercial form as well as many wildcats. For most varmint shooting, the .222 Rem. does an excellent job. One of my favorite rifles is a Remington Varmint Special restocked to fit me with an outstanding piece of American walnut from Fajen. I use that rifle a lot for testing scopes of varmint-hunting power, so it seldom has the same scope mounted for very long. It is also used extensively for testing the performance of varmint bullets, and with good bullets it stays under the half-inch mark at 100 yards. That kind of accuracy gives me a soft spot for that rifle when I want to shoot ground squirrels out to 200 yards.

Many rifles chambered for the .220 Swift and .22-250 cartridges have been used over the years. To me, these two cartridges are the two top commercial numbers for straight varmint shooting. They may not buck the wind quite as well as the .243s and hot .25s, but if you take a close look at wind-deflection dope, you'll find that there isn't as much difference as some would have us believe. They are cheaper to shoot and do the job on varmints of all sizes just as well as the larger calibers if the right bullets are used.

Fact is, I have a .22-250 Model Remington sporter that I use exclusively for hunting coyotes. It not only has plenty of range for reliably hitting coyotes far across the sage flats, but will usually drop them where they stand. Highly explosive light bullets usually stay inside and leave only a tiny entrance hole in the pelt. The rifle has been restocked from a blank of Pachmayr claro walnut and mounted with a Baush & Lomb Balvar 2.5-8X variable with tapered cross hairs.

It is by now obvious that I have no concrete preferences as to either cartridges or the guns they are used in as far as brands are concerned. It is also obvious that I prefer bolt-action rifles over other action types, but who makes them is not the deciding factor.

Any of the quality brands are reliable, and your preference may not parallel mine for one reason or another.

As for rifle cartridges, there are many that overlap or are too near the same performance level to say that one is superior to the other. Most do very well if used with the right load for the game and terrain being hunted, and if you realize their limitations. While I have given them as favorites in terms of both cartridge and rifle performance, I could be happy with a cartridge giving similar performance, and with an action and barrel from different makers if it was stocked and equipped to suit my tastes and needs. A favorite gun is probably based more on how, where and when it has been used than on strict preferences to minor detail in performance. Even so, I have given some of the reasons why certain guns have become favorites of mine in the past and present. So, even though you may not agree with my choices, you will see the reasons why they gained a distinction.

2

Western Rifles And Cartridges

Earth has few places that can boast a greater variety of hunting conditions than those found in the western United States. If you consider the West as a whole, from the eastern slope of the Rockies to the shores of the Pacific, and from the Mexican border to the Canadian boundary, you'll find an unbelievable variety of terrain and climatic conditions.

Huge areas along the West Coast are covered with rain forests that result in twilight shooting conditions at high noon, and undergrowth so thick it makes the Eastern whitetail woods look like a desert. Within a few miles, the rain forest gives way to true alpine timber types and snowfields on the crest of the various coastal ranges which show some of the highest peaks in North America.

Dropping down on the east side of these ranges puts the hunter in sage and juniper-covered, desert-like country where jackrabbits carry lunches. In the Southwest, you can look up from the sun-seared, cactus-studded floor of the desert to peaks streaked with perpetual snow. And, as you go northward into Colorado, Wyoming, Utah, Idaho and Montana, much of the same conditions prevail, except that the cactus of the wide-open spaces gives way to sage, greasewood and grass. Many of the valleys have an elevation of anywhere from sea level to 4,000 feet, while the peaks surrounding them push their tops 12,000 feet or so into the sky.

And, some of the timbered country of these states can be about as hairy as any woods a hunter can swing a rifle in.

All of this adds up to a great variety of hunting conditions that makes rifle and cartridge choices highly confusing. And, to further complicate matters, there is the great variety of game from antelope to moose. And, if you're really fortunate, you will have the chance to hunt several varieties on the same trip.

To the local hunter who hunts the same country and game year after year, the problem reduces because he knows what to expect. But, the fellow from the other side of the continent doesn't find it all that simple.

Lever Guns Are Out

In the beginning, rifles for Western hunting were thought of in terms of what fitted the side of a horse best, something that was short, light and fast to yank out of a saddle boot. Times have changed, and so have rifles and their cartridges. Also, the four-wheel-drive and other off-road, mechanical transportation for hunting have replaced the horse.

There is also another difference. Hunters once did a great deal of hunting from the top side of a pony in open country where there were lots of game and few other hunters; little hunting of that sort is done today. You may use a horse to get there and back, but will do very little hunting *from* the horse. This makes the short rifle less of a necessity—you may carry it on a horse, but you're not in such a hurry to get it off.

The lever-action rifles like the Winchester Model 94 carbine and the Savage Model 99 were about the top of the heap for true saddle guns, and they were also hard to beat in the thick stuff. But, the cartridges for which they were originally chambered leave a lot to be desired for all-around, Western hunting.

I remember a time when two out of every three horses you met on the trail had an M94 carbine .30-30 hung on its saddle. There was a lot more game around that hadn't seen much hunting pressure, and a lot more country to hunt it in.

The M94 .30-30 can hardly be considered today's answer to the Western hunter's prayer.

The current M99 chambered for cartridges like the .308 Win., the Browning BLR for the same cartridge, and a few others, are much better suited for general Western hunting situations. There are also some slide actions and semi-autos that are chambered for more potent numbers like the .270 Win. and the .30-06, but few if

Lever-action rifles were popular saddle guns when the majority of hunting was done from horseback. However, today, horses are not used to hunt from, instead they are used more for transportation.

any approach the light lever guns for saddle use. Fact is, most of these rifles are no better suited to horse-use than a light bolt-action.

Generally speaking, this all leads to the use of a rifle that is chambered for the cartridges best suited for the hunting conditions and the game. If you insist on a lever-action, you have little choice in cartridges that are suitable for both long-range and heavy game. Sure, Browning and Savage chamber for the flat-shooting .243 Win. which is fine for antelope- to deer-sized game, but hardly considered the ideal elk and moose cartridge. The same thing can be said of the M99 in .250-300 chambering. Savage also lists the .300 Savage. Both chamber the .308 Win., but both cartridges are beaten by many others in both the long-range and potency departments.

Browning's answer to this dilemma is the BLR long-action chambering such potent numbers as the 7mm Rem. Mag., .30-06 and .270. These guns have great potential as Western saddle guns, but haven't

The Model 99 Savage lever-action carbine is strong, light, trim and easy to carry. It is certainly one of the most aesthetic lever actions ever built. But, like the short bolt actions, it is capable of handling only shorter cartridges.

been without a few flies in the ointment. Early on, they underwent a recall for safety problems.

The imported Sako M73 is also chambered for the .243 Win. and .308 Win.

Pumps, Semi-Autos Don't Cut It

Those who like the slide action do not have much choice in rifles, but the Remington M7600 does offer two fine cartridges for all Western hunting in the .270 Win. and .30-06.

For the fellow who leans toward the semi-auto, the choice is wider in rifles chambered for the better cartridges for Western hunting. The Remington 742 is chambered for the .243 Win., 6mm Rem., .280 Rem., .308 Win. and .30-06.

And, for those who want both potency and long-range capability for any class of Western big game, there is the Browning Magnum Auto Rifle chambered for the 7mm Rem. Mag., the .300 Win. Mag. and .338 Win. Mag. These rifles deliver top rate accuracy and function reliability, but they are not especially light, and are a bit on the bulky side.

Single-Shots Limited, Too

For those who yearn for a single-shooter, there are a few that are chambered for suitable cartridges. The Browning 78 is

When you're in a situation that calls for a quick, second shot, you might consider a pump-action rifle. This Remington Model 7600 centerfire pump-action rifle features Remington's famous twin action bar system for fast, smooth ejection and chambering.

chambered for the 6mm Rem., .25-06 Rem. and .30-06 for big-game shooting; the first two are hardly suitable for the larger species, but the .30-06 is a good choice.

The choice of calibers chambered in the Ruger No. 1 is indeed large, and there are some custom actions, barreled actions and full-custom jobs that can be made up in nearly any caliber the customer desires.

There is a good deal of difference of opinion regarding the use of single-shot rifles on game. Some say they tend to make the hunter think twice before he shoots, and do a better job of it when he does. Others think the hunter with a single-shot is asking for trouble because he can't follow up with a fast second shot.

Both sides have valid points. The truth is that if you acquire a case of "buck fever" when you spot game, or are one of those who insists on shooting at everything he sees regardless of range or conditions, the single shot will not cure the problem. If, on the other hand, you are cool and deliberate when seeing game, you'll realize the limitations of slower fire and make that one shot count. The temperament of the hunter controls how he'll react a lot more than the action he uses. One point in favor of the single-shot rifle is that it can have a longer barrel for a bit more velocity and still be short and light for mountain use.

Bolt-Action King Of The West

This brings us around to the most popular of all actions: the bolt. There are so many bolt-action rifles being made that there is no reason to say much about them. Few riflemen will argue against the fact that the bolt-action of good design is the strongest and most reliable of all actions under severe hunting conditions. Neither will they argue against the fact that they are near the top of the pile where accuracy is concerned.

A well-stocked, bolt-action is trim enough to run the best of the lever guns a close second for weight and bulk in all of the more powerful calibers. They are also chambered for all of the cartridges modern gun-bugs have been able to dream up.

There are two things the rifle for Western big-game hunting should have—in fact, they are a must for general hunting. One is a good scope and the other is a sling for carrying and/or shooting.

The scope best suited to all types of Western hunting use is the 4X. It has plenty of field for most situations and enough power for all. The sling can be anything from a plain carrying strap adjustable for length, to a shooting sling. In any event, it should be light and not more than 1-inch wide. The ¾-inch to 1-inch slings hang on the shoulder better than wider straps, and they are lighter. My personal choice for all hunting situations is the Brownell Latigo Sling. Quickly adjustable, it is light and can be used for both carrying and solid-hold shooting.

The Weight Debate

The actual weight of the rifle for Western hunting, as well as the barrel length, is largely a matter of preference and strength and stamina of the hunter who will use it. Remember that if you use one of the big magnum cartridges from 7mm up, and insist on a very light, short rifle, you'll pay for the lack of rifle weight in greater recoil punch, muzzle jump and blast. Only you can decide which is more important. Indeed, the extra weight and a couple of inches of barrel length do hold advantages in steady holding, reduced muzzle blast and velocity gain.

Western Cartridges

The rifle is the lesser portion of the partnership that does the job for the hunter. The significantly larger end is the cartridge for which it is chambered and the bullet loaded into that cartridge.

This basic bolt-action rifle, the Browning A-Bolt, is chambered for the .308 Win. Bolt-action rifles are strong and reliable under severe hunting conditions. They are also extremely accurate.

When John Browning designed the Model 1886 Winchester, there was no repeating rifle that could even come close to it in terms of its strength or the power of its cartridges. But, by today's standards, it is too long and heavy to be ideal for hunting big game in America.

As already pointed out, there are so many variations in the type of country hunted in the West, and the kind of game hunted there, that a cartridge especially suited to one section may be totally inadequate for another. As an example, the .30-30, .35 Rem. or .358 Win. would certainly be good choices for blacktails in the brush of the Pacific slope, or for whitetails in any number of places, but they would be less than ideal for shooting antelope on the Wyoming flats. Actually, the hunter who uses a 6mm cartridge or a hot .25-06 Rem. for hunting antelope is a lot better off if he dives into the thick stuff after deer or black bear than the fellow who tries to use his .30-30 deer rifle for hunting antelope. The .243s and the .25s will do a great job on deer at any reasonable range, but the .30-30 soon runs out of steam on the sage flats.

Sure, I know the .30-30, the .35 Rem., and a lot more of the low-velocity, big-bore numbers are supposed to be capable of mowing down a bushel of brush and go on to punch holes in deer as though nothing had been encountered en route. Someone started this story before smokeless powder became very popular. American hunters still believe and repeat it. I've shot a lot of assorted animals in the bushes with a lot of different cartridges, and I've tried to punch holes in paper under the same circumstances.

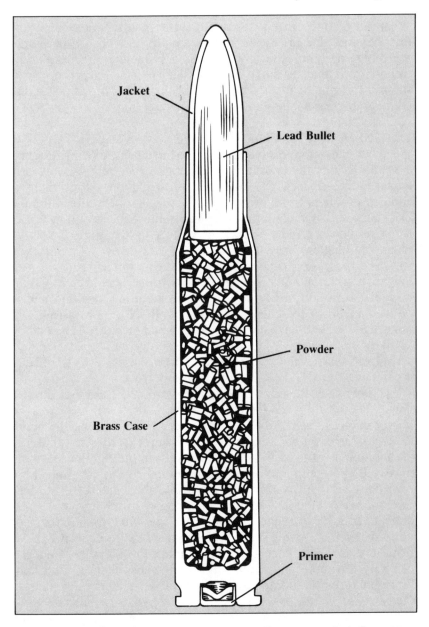

To create an accurate, efficient hunting cartridge, all components including primer, case powder and bullet must be precisely matched. Selecting the right combination is the hunter's challenge. Being able to rely on the research and development of ammunition manufacturers in creating a wide range of loads is the greatest advantage to buying factory ammunition.

What this testing proved was that if the animal is more than a few feet beyond the brush the bullet connects with, it is purely accidental if it hits the animal, and a miracle if it doesn't just wound it. It matters little if the bullet is a fat, slow one, or a skinny, fast one; it just won't penetrate much brush without either coming apart or heading off in another direction.

Western Deer & Antelope Cartridges

What works to the advantage of the hunter in choosing the right cartridge is that if he is hunting antelope or blacktail, he usually knows it in advance and can pick the right one. But, there is another problem he may have to face: elk often mix with the blacktails and whitetails. During the same trip, you may shoot antelope down on the flats and elk up in the high basins or lodgepole tangles. You never know.

Take the case of the deer in heavy cover mixed with elk and maybe moose. Obviously, nearly any cartridge from the .243 Win. up will do the job nicely on deer from about any position with a bullet that holds together reasonably well. Not so with elk and moose. In the first place, the cartridges shown on page 41, and others in the same class, are certainly not to be considered elk cartridges under good conditions where shots can be placed accurately.

I know they'll kill 'em. I've seen it done. But, that doesn't make them ideal for the job. In the brush, these cartridges are even poorer choices because of the limited chance of placing the bullet exactly where you want it, or even knowing exactly what spot you are looking at. It is unusual to have an elk in the right position; he may be end on (either end) or quartering to or from the gun. These cartridges are not capable of driving into the vitals of a big bull through heavy bone and muscle at an angle from long range. You don't need a lot of range capability for this kind of shooting, but you do need a cartridge and bullet that will dig in deep enough from any angle to reach the vitals. Under these circumstances, I certainly am more confident with nothing less than a 175-grain, 7mm bullet or a .30 caliber in 200-grain weight. It is in hunting under these conditions that one soon learns to appreciate even larger calibers like the .338, big .35s and even the .375, and then with bullets that have good sectional density and are built to expand without coming apart upon impact with the first bone.

What about the little whitetail or blacktail deer you were hunting on the same day? The big gun will kill him, too, and

All of these cartridges work well for shooting antelope, deer, goat and sheep, if using the right bullets. The three on the righthand side are outstanding for long-range, flat-shooting ability. However, none are good choices for elk and moose under any circumstances. From the left: .243 Win., 6mm Rem., .257 Roberts, .240 Wthby, .25-06 and .257 Wthby.

probably won't spoil any more chops than the .243 Win.

Cartridges For Larger Western Game

Now, to go back to the antelope, mule deer, sheep and goats, with the elk and maybe a moose (if you're lucky in drawing a permit) on the same trip, maybe the same day. Chances are you won't shoot antelope, sheep and goats in the brush, but you may shoot either elk, muleys or moose in the brush anywhere in the mountains.

The main difference in hunting anywhere in the mountainous, big-game country is that ranges are likely to be on the long side no matter what the game. Antelope will normally be shot at longer ranges than the others, but I've killed more elk and mule deer at long range than all of the others combined. One reason for this is that you hunt them a lot more (no limitation on permits being necessary in many areas), but it is mostly because of the kind of

For hunting Western big game under all conditions, cartridges similar to this line-up are superior to those of smaller caliber and less potency. From the left: .270 Win., .30-06, 7mm Rem. Mag., .300 Win. Mag. and .338 Win. Mag.

places you hunted. A great many elk and muleys are shot from one side of a canyon to the other. Obviously, you can't cut the shooting distance by walking in a straight line toward the animal, and it may be a long way around for a closer shot. Time may not allow that approach, and the wind may be wrong if it does. There may not be any place where you can see the game if you try to stalk closer, or it may wander off while you are making the stalk. So, it's shoot from where you are or not at all.

As mentioned earlier, the 6mm cartridges or the .25s are not ideal elk cartridges, even under the best conditions. When ranges stretch beyond 300 yards, they become even less desirable. So, if you have an elk tag to fill, no matter what member of the smaller species you are looking for, better give some serious thought to the cartridge you use. For this kind of mountain hunting, the .270 Win. is about as small as anyone should consider. If you're going to use it to hunt elk under the many varied conditions, the

150-grain pointed bullet is a better choice than the 130 grain.

The .30-06 will do a good job, but only if elk are on the menu; stick to bullets of 180 grains or more. The pointed 200-grain weight has a great deal of merit.

For this kind of mixed bag mountain- and plains-hunting, the 7mm magnums and the big 30s are the best. The 7mm magnums fire 150- to 175-grain bullets at velocities high enough for the trajectories to be extremely flat at the longest ranges at which big game should be shot. And, they pack a lot of wallop when they arrive. The same thing can be said of the .30 magnums with 180- to 200-grain bullets. Pointed bullets should be used for all hunting situations where the range may be anything from a matter of a few feet to 400 yards or so. The pointed bullet will do the job just as well at close range—yes, even in the brush—as the round point, and do it a lot better at long range.

If you know you are going to hunt only antelope, there is certainly nothing wrong with any of the 6mms, 25s or the 6.5s; in fact, such cartridges as the .240 Wthby, .25-06 Rem., .257 Wthby, 6.5 Rem. and .264 Win. are excellent, being equally good for deer, sheep or goats. Few cartridges show better performance for this class of game shot in the Mountain West than the ever-popular .270 Win.

Bullets: The Crucial Connection

No cartridge, no matter what the headstamp, is any better than the bullet it shoots. Also, advertising for those bullets, both for factory-loaded ammo and bullets from the various bullet manufacturers, is sometimes more lip service than an actual performance indicator. If you want spectacular kills on the smaller species like antelope and deer, bullets with the fragile, quick-expanding jacket that erupt to spew pieces of jacket and core over a large area will give them *if* they hit the vitals. But, don't expect them to get inside on quartering shots on large animals, maybe not even big buck muleys. That kind of bullet will also make hamburger from a lot of good chops if it lands at high velocity. And, it doesn't matter if it is small and light or big and heavy.

For a reliable kill on elk and moose under all conditions, a bullet that will hold together and retain most of its original weight so that it will deliver deep penetration in big bones and heavy, tough muscle is the answer. It must also expand as velocity drops off to be reliable at the longer ranges. Such a bullet will leave a long, but often narrow, wound channel. It will not, as a rule, give the spectacular "drop in their tracks" kills as do the explosive types. It will drive into the vitals of a heavy animal from nearly any angle, and the animal won't make many more tracks after it gets there.

Few factory-loaded bullets can boast of this kind of action; neither can most of the conventional designs from the bullet companies. We might sum up the bullet angle in this way: If you don't intend to hunt anything heavier than mule deer on the Western scene, nearly any of the factory loads or conventional bullets will do if you use the weights suggested for big-game shooting. (The lighter bullets in most calibers are for varmint shooting.)

If you buy conventional design bullets for elk and moose hunting, choose bullets at the heavy end for that caliber. Better yet, the so-called special-purpose or premium bullets will do the job even better under all conditions. They'll also kill an antelope just as dead, but maybe not quite as fast.

Summing Up

The complete summation for cartridges for general hunting of Western big game is simple and brief. The 6mms, .25s and the 6.5s are good choices for all smaller big game from pronghorn through mule deer, but they are far from ideal for the larger species. They can cause plenty of trouble under good conditions and are often complete failures under unfavorable circumstances.

The larger-caliber cartridges from .270 up to .338 will take the heavy stuff in any circumstance under which a hunter is justified in shooting. They'll kill an antelope just as well and just as far away as the 6mm.

3

Selecting The Right Elk Cartridge

Whenever anyone writes about elk cartridges, two things should be considered. First, the subject is always highly controversial. Second, no matter what is said will come under fire from those who have some pet-rifle chambered for a cartridge considered by its owner to be the ultimate in elk cartridges. Much of this criticism comes from those with very little elk-hunting experience, or perhaps from someone who has killed a number of elk under conditions that are not typical today.

The amount of elk hunting experience the hunter must have, and the number of elk he has to kill before he can speak with authority, depends upon his power of observation. Included are the kinds of terrain he has hunted, the amount of time spent hunting, the time of year, his ability to follow the bullet's path after it has hit an elk, the ability to determine where it landed and the bullet's angle of penetration, as well as what it did along the way. He must also be able to analyze the information he is gathering and form an unbiased opinion based on the results.

A good deal can be learned from careful observation of a dozen kills or so, if range, angle of shot, point of impact and the elk's reaction after being hit are carefully considered. But, it is almost certain that even in seeing that number of elk killed, the hunter won't encounter all of the many different conditions in hunting elk in different areas. There certainly will not be a very large variety of

An experienced elk hunter must be able to analyze information from killing an elk in order to be an authority on the subject of cartridges. The information should include things such as terrain type, hunting time and bullet path.

cartridges and bullets involved.

Perhaps to qualify myself to discuss elk cartridges I might mention that I killed my first elk in the early 1930s with an old .30-40 Krag rifle and a 220-grain, soft-point bullet. I have hunted elk somewhere every year since. As a professional guide for many years, and acting as a guide while hunting with friends over the years, I have seen about 200 elk killed. These elk have been taken with everything from the .25-35 to some of the most powerful, modern magnums.

I am not setting myself up as the expert on elk and elk cartridges; others have had even more experience. I am still learning things as elk habits change and new cartridges and bullets appear. But, I have hunted under about every conceivable condition found in elk hunting, and I must be some kind of freak because I am curious enough to enjoy the messy, smelly job of tracing bullets in elk carcasses to find out what they did and didn't do, and why. That is how I learn what I've done wrong or right.

As already indicated, it seems that many opinions pertaining to which cartridges are best suited to hunting elk usually arise from hunters' experience in only one kind of terrain. Often, too, it was many years ago when there was little hunting pressure, and at a time and place when elk were commonly found in open country.

Terrain And Cartridge Selection

As an example of the extreme in the area being hunted and the bearing it has on cartridge choice, there is the correspondence I had with a fellow who was with the U.S. National Park Service at the time of one of the big, wintertime elk-reduction kills in Yellowstone National Park. My friend said that he used a number of different cartridges at various times, shedding some light on their performance. One of the rifles he used a lot was a .264 Win., with various bullet weights. He found it entirely adequate for the kind of shooting he was doing. He said that if an elk was hit properly, it made few tracks. He also used a .300 Win. Mag. and a .338 Win. Mag. at times. He thought that even though the .264 did a good job, the .300 and the .338 did it even better, especially if the bullet failed to land in *exactly* the right place or entered from the wrong angle.

This shooting was done mostly on the winter range in open country with a lot of snow on the ground. The elk were thin and, perhaps of greater importance, were shot at fairly long ranges because the large number of elk made it possible for him to pick the shot with extreme care and pass up anything that didn't look "just right."

This kind of hunting, and what constitutes the best elk cartridges for it, is in sharp contrast with hunting some other areas earlier in the season. Certainly, the hunting conditions would be much different if you hunted Yellowstone's lodgepole pine stands in October with the hunting pressure considered normal for most elk ranges today. This is why elk hunters like Will Hafler, who hunts the heavily timbered, brush-choked elk jungles of northern Idaho, and Elmer Keith, who did a lot of hunting in the same area, demanded big bores and heavy bullets. Range is not overly important because even a 100-yard shot is rare. What is important is a bullet that will get inside from any angle and make a big hole while doing it. I, too, have hunted this kind of country. While I do not necessarily agree with Hafler's and Keith's choice of some cartridges, the big bore/heavy bullet cartridge is ideal, and

When hunting elk in heavily timbered areas, big bores and heavy bullets are essential. A bullet needs to get inside and hit a vital spot from various angles, and make a big hole.

cartridges like the .25-06 Rem. or the .264 Win. which did an excellent job on the winter Yellowstone elk should not even be considered.

Hunting elk under these two widely varying conditions of terrain and season is as different as hunting mule deer in sagebrush-foothill country and whitetail in a second-growth hardwood forest. And, the great majority of elk hunting embraces both kinds of hunting in one location—plus everything between these two extremes. When hunting in open country, the hunter usually sees the elk before the elk sees him, which allows time to pick the place the bullet should land, take a good solid rest and put it there. (Nearly any deer cartridge and bullet will do a respectable job.) In this kind of shooting, a cool hunter can hold his fire until the animal turns broadside, then send the bullet into the center of the lungs. On even the largest bulls, it only takes a few inches of penetration to reach the lungs—an amount most deer cartridges and bullets will provide. And, if the bullet gets into the lungs and blows up, tearing a big, though shallow, hole, the elk is not going to go very far, in spite of what some hunters would have us believe. An elk, or any other animal, is not going to live very long with a jagged hole in its heart or lungs.

Hunting in the thick stuff is an entirely different matter. An elk lying in its bed has the advantage of being still and making no sound while the hunter is moving and making noise. The outcome is that the elk is alerted to the hunter's presence long before the hunter knows it is there, and will nearly always be on its feet and moving before a shot can be fired. Even if the hunter does catch an elk in its bed before the elk sees, smells or hears him, it is unlikely that the entire elk will be visible. And, even if it is, there is even less chance that it will be in the right position for a picture-book broadside, lung shot.

I dislike shooting at a bedded animal because it is so hard to tell what position it is actually in, and where the bullet will go after it hits the target. Once the elk is on its feet, it is very unusual if it stands broadside; usually, it is quartering to the hunter as it takes one last look before taking off. And, if it is already in gear when seen, you are either looking at a yellow rump-patch or a long angle from hip to shoulder. Even if you catch one wandering around or browsing in heavy cover, the chances are about 5-to-1 it will not be standing broadside.

In this kind of situation, you usually don't shoot at the chest, but try to place the bullet where it can penetrate the vital area. With the elk quartering away, the bullet may have to hit the flank and pass through the paunch to penetrate the lungs or heart. Or, you may have to take the option of placing it high on the hip to break the hip joint, pelvis and spine.

For the elk quartering toward the hunter, the bullet will have to plow through heavy shoulder muscle, probably smashing bone as it goes, and still have enough steam left to tear up the lungs and/or heart when it gets there. And, if it doesn't land in quite the right spot, or the elk isn't in the position it appears to be, the bullet will have to tear a pretty big hole, pack a lot of shock-delivering wallop and dig in a long way to be effective. This is why most elk hunters who hunt in the thick stuff like big bores and heavy bullets. They have found that those bullets will usually do the job.

It is this kind of elk shooting—and there is a lot of it in any elk area sometime during the open season—that causes some elk hunters to stay clear of anything smaller than .30 caliber with the

The group of cartridges on the left will all work well on elk when conditions are good and the hunter carefully places his shot. From the left: .264 Win. Mag., .270 Win., .270 Wthby Mag., .280 Rem. and .30-06. The cartridges on the right will take care of all hunting conditions likely to be encountered: the 7mm Rem. Mag., .300 Win. Mag., .300 Wthby Mag., .338 Win. Mag., .340 Wthby Mag., .358 Norma Mag. and .375 H&H Mag.

heaviest bullets. And there are a lot of them who insist on calibers like the .338, .340, the .35 and the .375. It is also one reason why some of them like the .40 to .45 calibers. While you may not care for big, slow bullets, you'll have to admit that they have advantages for this kind of elk hunting.

Changing Elk Patterns

Few big-game animals are hunted under the same conditions that they were 100 years ago. Recently, there has been a lot of change in the hunting of some species. The mule deer has changed its habits so much in the past 25 years, that veteran mule deer hunters can hardly believe they are hunting the same animal. Muleys once fed on the open and semi-open slopes over most of their range during the fall hunting season. This is seldom true today—except in a few places back in some areas where hunting pressure is light, and these areas are growing smaller every year.

The mule deer's larger cousin, the American *wapiti*, or elk as we all know him, has also changed habits.

While originally most elk were plains and foothills animals, few if any living hunters can remember many situations where this was true. A gradual transition has occurred from an animal that loved and fed upon the high open meadows and ridges of the Rocky Mountains during the fall, to one that acts more like a whitetail deer under intensive hunting pressure. Like the muley, there are still places where elk feed on the open grass areas around sunup, and during the last couple of hours before darkness. However, fewer elk are found in these places when there is enough light to shoot.

This change in elk hunting greatly influences the proper choice of cartridges for busting bulls. Until recently, you could depend on getting a shot at elk in open country if you knew elk, had a little time and worked it right. They usually holed up at midday in the thick stuff no matter where they were hunted, especially during warm, early-season days. But, on stormy days and for a couple hours after dawn and before darkness crept up the canyon sides, they fed on open mountain slopes and meadows. A lot of long-range shooting was involved. Regardless of whether it was long range or close-in, there was usually time to pick your shot and take a good steady position to assure proper bullet placement.

There are still a few places where this is possible, including some of the high timberline back-country of Wyoming and the private ranches of New Mexico; however, the average elk hunter will never see them.

Most of what was wild elk country 20 years ago is now cut up with logging roads affording access to virtually every square mile. The subsequent increase in hunting pressure is terrific, and any feeding that elk do in open areas is strictly at night. And, if they do venture out at dusk or dawn, it is for such a short time that the chance of a shot is slim. This situation raises an entirely new problem for the elk hunter as far as choice of cartridge and bullet is concerned. While the elk in these heavily hunted areas hole up like a bunch of whitetails, they are also moved around by that pressure. It makes it necessary for the hunter to go in and dig them out in the hope of at least getting to see one. So, as often happens, you may spot one at long range moving in an attempt to find a hiding place or evade a hunter on its trail.

If and when you see these elk drifting along on the far side of some canyon or basin, or going over the next ridge, it is unlikely there will be much time for a shot or even to figure the range. If the animal is in the position you would like, it is strictly a fortunate accident. Under these shooting conditions, neither a flat-shooting small bore nor one of the big-bore, heavy-bullet, low-velocity numbers is the answer.

It all comes down to the fact that there is no way the hunter can know in advance what kind of shot he will get; whether it will be at 400 yards at an elk that is rapidly expanding the range, or at 40 feet in the brush at a small, obscured part of the elk. These are the conditions that prevail throughout most elk country in the Western mountain states today. It is not so much a matter of what cartridges do the best job under any of these various elk hunting conditions, but which cartridges will do the best under *all* of them.

If you are lucky enough to do your elk hunting in areas where elk still frequent open spaces, there is certainly nothing wrong with the old standbys like the .270 Win. and the .30-06. If you are cool and careful about where you place the shot, you will also do quite well with the 130-grain bullet in the former, and the 165- to 180-grain bullets in the latter. But, for all-around elk shooting under today's hunting conditions, the 150-grain in the .270 Win. and a 200-grain in the .30-06 are a much better choice. And, even then, considering the brush shooting possibility, the bullet should hold together on heavy bone and muscle and still drive on to the vital organs.

The Core Cartridges For Elk

For these reasons, then, cartridges from 7mm magnums up through the .340 Wthby form the core of *the best* elk cartridges. These cartridges all have two things in common that make them ideal for today's elk hunting conditions: the ability to handle heavy bullets of good sectional density and ballistic coefficient at high velocity for extended sure-hitting ranges, and the bullet weight and punch to plow a couple of feet through big bones and hard muscle, and still tear up the vitals.

No cartridge is any better than its bullet. If all shots were at ranges of over 300 yards, a spitzer bullet at high velocity in calibers from .264 up would do quite well if placed in the right spot, and if controlled expansion isn't a must. Conversely, in the thick stuff, any of the big bores that will push a heavy round-nose bullet along at around 2,000 fps will do quite well if the bullet holds together. But, the bullet for hunting elk under all of the conditions must turn in a good performance no matter what the situation. It may be called upon to shoot flat at about 400 yards, making a solid hit without too much guesstimating, and it must expand with certainty at that range and pack enough wallop to kill a big bull. That *same bullet* must have the expansion controlled so that it will penetrate to the vitals of an elk that is quartering to or

Author Bob Hagel used a belted magnum cartridge on many North American hunting trips. Here is a bull elk taken at 300 yards with a 250-grain Barnes bullet.

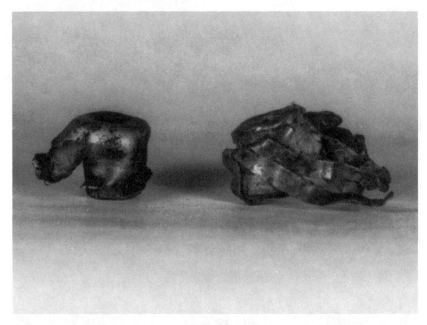

These bullets show that jacket design and bullet construction can be more important than sectional density (SD). The 210-grain Nosler (left), from a .340 Wthby, landed near the back of the rib cage of a five-point bull elk, went up through the top of the paunch and liver, penetrated 6 inches of spine and lodged between the shoulders. The 300-grain steel jacket Kynoch .333 (right) hit a five-point bull broadside behind the shoulder and did not reach the hide on the off-side. Both elk were at about 75 yards. The 210-grain has an SD of .263, while the 300-grain is .376.

from the gun, and normally exit on broadside lung shots. And, it will have to be capable of doing this at very close "timer shooting" ranges at near-magnum muzzle velocity.

This means that the ideal elk bullet should have the high ballistic coefficient that comes from a spitzer or semi-spitzer point, coupled with good sectional density. But, good ballistic shape is not enough. While sectional density is necessary for deep penetration, it does not necessarily assure deep penetration. If structure—a thin jacket and soft core—is poor, the penetration of even a large caliber, heavy bullet will not be good.

Testing Bullet Structure

An example of bullet structure, and penetration of bullets of various weights in the same caliber, is revealed by a series of tests I ran with the .340 Wthby. The test included nearly every .338 bullet available in weights from 200 to 300 grains. All bullets were

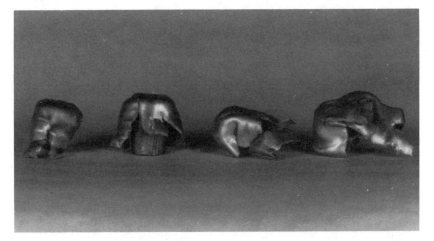

These .338 bullets, fired from a .340 Wthby Mag., were taken from a recovery box. They illustrate the importance of jacket design in conjunction with sectional density. From the left: 210-grain Nosler at 3,200 fps; 250-grain Nosler at 2,900 fps; 275-grain Speer at 2,741 fps; and 300-grain Barnes at 2,536 fps. The very large, frontal area of the Speer and Barnes bullets shows that shock and tissue destruction will be great. However, this doesn't mean much if they fail to reach the vital organs from adverse angles.

fired at 15 feet at near-maximum muzzle velocity into my recovery box which is filled with a mixture of fine silt and rotten sawdust and enough water to give it the consistency I have found best. For those who think that sectional density alone is the criterion on which penetration must be based, the results should prove interesting.

The 210-grain, Nosler spitzer bullet with a sectional density of .263 started at over 3,200 fps, penetrated 28 inches and retained 122 grains, or 58.1 percent of its original weight. The 275-grain, Speer semi-spitzer, with a sectional density of .348, started at 2,840 fps, penetrated only 17 inches and retained only 110 grains, or 40 percent of its original weight. The 300-grain Barnes, with a sectional density of near .370, started at 2,536 fps, did little better than 18 inches of penetration and had a remaining weight of 137 grains, or 45.7 percent.

The truth is that the 160-grain, .270 Nosler bullet, the 175-grain 7mm, and 200-grain .30 bullets of the same make and partition design will deliver nearly as much penetration as the same bullets in the heavier .338 and .375 calibers. They will not tear up as much bone, tissue and nerves. So, they do not have the killing effect of the larger calibers with equal bullet action.

An evaluation of the results seems to indicate that under the great majority of elk hunting conditions found today, cartridges like the 7mm magnums, the big .30s, the .338 Win. Mag. and the .340 Wthby with the heavier bullet weights in spitzer form, and the controlled-expansion design of the Nosler, are the ideal elk stoppers. This certainly does not mean that a hunter can't kill elk successfully with cartridges of far less power and range—cartridges like the .270 Win., .280 Rem., .308 Win., the good old .30-06 and several others. But, it does mean that when using those cartridges, you'll have to choose the bullet just as carefully, and if you don't want to leave a lot of cripples wandering around in the brush, you'll have to pass up a lot of shots and be careful where you place the bullets that you do fire.

Human nature being what it is, as well as most elk hunters only seeing an elk on about every third year they hunt them, few hold their fire when they see one, regardless of where the animal is or what position it is in. Let me repeat: It is not a case of the best cartridge and bullet to kill an elk when everything is right, but the best ones for the job when conditions aren't good.

4

Varmint Cartridges

Varmint cartridges have come a long way since the days of the .22 Win. Centerfire and the .25-20. In fact, it is doubtful if those cartridges were ever really thought of as varmint cartridges as we use the term today. Perhaps they were considered combination cartridges for shooting small game for the pot and plinking a few pests on the side. For this use, they were quite well adapted. They weren't overly destructive of the meat of small-game animals at ranges of 50 to 100 yards or so, and they did a fair job on chucks, ground squirrels, crows and jackrabbits at these same ranges, where most of the pest shooting was done at that time.

A bit later, when cartridges like the .22 Savage High-Power and the .250-3000 Savage came along, varmint cartridges took a giant step forward, but varmint shooting popularity didn't increase much. There was more than one reason for this lack of enthusiasm for serious varminting. First, and most important, ammunition for these rifles was too expensive to be used to shoot something you didn't eat. Second, most of the bullets made for these cartridges were designed with deer in mind and were something less than ideal for small pests. Accuracy of factory ammunition and the rifles chambered for it was not up to consistent, long-range hits, and only a few gun-buffs did any reloading or had rifles built for top-hole accuracy.

The truth is that most of the gun-buffs who were doing most of

Glassing the side of a mountain for woodchucks, this hunter is prepared for solid shooting with a Ruger M77 .220 Swift. No better factory loaded cartridge was ever produced for the majority of varmint shooting; and few, if any, wildcats hold any advantage.

the varmint shooting were doing it with wildcats that, in many cases, became commercial numbers.

There is little doubt that the advent of the .22 Hornet, which was the .22 WCF case loaded to peak velocities in strong rifles, touched off varmint hunting by the average shooter when it appeared in 1932. By today's standards, the .22 Hornet is pretty puny as a varmint cartridge, with its factory loading of a 45-grain bullet at a reputed 2,690 fps. But it had two things going for it that no earlier varmint cartridge ever had. Its bullets were designed as varmint bullets both in the accuracy and expansion departments. And, the first factory rifles chambered for it in this country, the Savage Model 23-D and the Winchester Model 54, both had excellent accuracy.

Apparently relishing the .22 Hornet's success and subsequent sales of rifles chambered for it, Winchester made another bid for the varmint cartridge-rifle market in 1935 when they introduced the king of the high-velocity clan, the .220 Swift. It seems unbelievable that this cartridge, born over 60 years ago, still retains that crown despite the improvement in powders. True, some wildcats may surpass it slightly in velocity, but no commercial round does. Also, it is impossible to boost velocity in the Swift cartridge with the lighter bullets, even with the best modern powders. The 50-grain bullet can be fired at slightly over 4,100 fps with IMR-4064, which is certainly not new either, and the 52-grain at a bit over 4,000 fps with the same powder. Of the newer powders, 760-BR (now 760) and Norma 203 (now discontinued) seem to give the highest velocity with most bullet weights in the Swift. The heaviest of bullets like the Speer 70-grain will, of course, give the highest velocity with the slower powders: IMR-4350, Norma 204 and H-4831 (plus Norma 205 and 780-BR, now discontinued), none of which were available at the time the Swift appeared. Any of these powders will kick the 70-grain along at over 3,400 fps, and this isn't loafing!

Because of the marked success with the Hornet and Swift, Winchester brought out another pair of varmint cartridges chambered in lever actions in the form of the .218 Bee and the .219 Zipper. The Bee had an edge of 200 feet of velocity on the Hornet, firing a 46-grain bullet at 2,860 fps, and the Zipper pushed a 56-grain bullet along at a reputed 3,110 fps, which certainly did not rival the Swift. This time Winchester made a mistake, and sales were never good for either cartridge. Not that there was anything wrong with the cartridges—many single-shot rifles chambered for

For shooting varmints, such as this prairie dog, nothing has been able to surpass the high-velocity .220 Swift cartridge. This cartridge was introduced in 1935.

the Bee and Zipper made excellent varmint rifles—but the lever guns failed to deliver varmint shooting accuracy, and the cartridges weren't suited for reloading several times if high velocity was to be obtained in the lever actions.

Not only did Winchester make a mistake in sales when they chambered the Bee and Zipper in lever action rifles, but they also made a mistake when—almost 20 years later—they discontinued the Swift and chambered the revised Model 70 for the semi-rimmed .225 Win. cartridge. There wasn't actually too much wrong with the .225 Win. except for that silly, semi-rimmed (actually a rimmed case that headspaced on the shoulder) case that required magazine modifications to work through bolt-action rifles. Its only advantage was purely from the manufacturing angle; the rim was the same size as the .30-06 head, allowing a minimum of modification on the production line. Secondly, it allowed Winchester to drop the stainless barrel which supposedly was necessary on the Swift. It develops about 3,650 fps with 55-grain bullets, shoots flat, and is a good varmint cartridge. The M70 varmint test rifle delivered outstanding accuracy with good handloads or factory ammunition. But, it somehow never got off to a good start and, like the .224 Wthby, which has only slightly less velocity, never carried much sales appeal.

Some of this was because Remington had cut in on the varmint cartridge market with the .222 Rem., .222 Rem. Mag. and the .223 Rem. that had been around in military guise as the 5.56mm. The .225 also saw the light of day just about the same time that Remington saw fit to commercialize the .22-250 Rem. cartridge, which was already the most popular of the wildcat .22 high-velocity clan.

As for the varmint cartridges using larger diameter bullets, there had always been an unfilled gap between the .22s and .25s. Many varmint hunters thought that there was a strong need for a high-velocity cartridge to fill this hole for long-range varminting and for such smaller big game as deer, antelope and sheep. There was some wildcatting along this line with .243 caliber bullets, but these bullets were not easy to find. So, not too much work was done.

Almost simultaneously, in 1955, Remington and Winchester announced the .243 Win. and the .244 Rem. This time it was Remington who took the back seat. (This is another one of those cases where it is difficult to fully understand what happened that caused shooters to flock to the .243 Win. like coyotes around a ripe steer carcass, while they backed away from the .244 Rem. as though it were impregnated with strychnine.) As far as a varmint cartridge goes, the fact that Remington M722 rifles had a 1-12 twist that was not supposed to stabilize 100-grain bullets should have made little difference. The 100-grainers were not what you used for varmint shooting, anyway. But, many people wanted the 6mm cartridge for a combination varmint-and-big-game getter, so they picked the .243 Win. when the word got around that the twist was wrong in the .244 Rem. rifles for deer-weight bullets.

This was a case of the rifle being wrong, not the cartridge. The .244 Rem. always was as good a cartridge as the .243 Win.; this was proven with the advent of the 6mm Remington—an identical case with a different name.

While the .250-3000 Savage and the .257 Remington-Roberts never gained any great popularity as varmint cartridges by the average shooter, the advent of the 6mm cartridges finished them

These .25 caliber cartridges have been popular combination varmint-and-big-game cartridges. They have an advantage over the 6mms for big game because heavier bullets are available for the .25s. The .250-3000 (left) and the .257 Roberts (middle) were discontinued, leaving no commercial rifle chambered for a .25 caliber until Remington introduced the .25-06 (right).

off. They were both good cartridges, and still are. And, the .257 is slightly superior to the 6mm numbers for shooting the smaller, big-game animals because of the slightly larger bullet diameter and the heavier bullet that is available.

Finally, sales of rifles chambered for both of these .25 cartridges dropped so badly that Savage discontinued chambering the .250-3000 in their famous Model 99 rifles. The .25 caliber fans didn't like the idea at all.

Considerable pressure was put on manufacturers for the revival of a .25 in some form, and it was assumed that the .257 Rem. would be the cartridge. Remington was the one to bring the .25 back. Seeing the appeal of the high-velocity trend, they commercialized the old wildcat .25 Niedner and called it the .25-06 Rem. Then, with fits of nostalgia assailing the American shooter and pointing toward the rejuvenation of discontinued cartridge-rifle combinations, Savage reintroduced the .250 Savage in the Model 99-A. So, we again had a pair of commercial rifles in .25 caliber.

There have, of course, been many other larger caliber cartridges that gained some popularity as varmint cartridges, such as the .270 Win. But, these cartridges are so clearly in the big-game category that we won't go into their merits here. As varmint cartridges, they are specialized, long-range numbers that are used almost exclusively by those advanced gun-buffs who

While any one of these cartridges can be used for all types of varmint shooting, each is best-suited for a particular situation. The smaller cartridges are the most versatile for varmint use, while the larger ones make good deer-and-varmint combinations. From the left: .222 Rem., .22-250 Rem., .243 Win., 6mm Rem., .257 Roberts and .25-06 Rem.

know what they are doing and what they want to accomplish.

In evaluating varmint cartridges, there is little reason to go below the performance level of the .222 Rem. While we are considering cases in this capacity range, however, there is one that is truly a varmint cartridge with no other purpose. The .17 caliber started life strictly as a wildcat. No commercial bullets were available, and there were many case shapes and sizes. Most of the wildcats were based on .222 headsize cases in one form or another. When Remington brought out the .17 Rem. in 1971, it was on a modified .223 Rem. case. Few cartridges kicked up more controversy than the .17. Some attributed mystic killing power to the tiny bullet that was sudden death to anything it hit, from mice to Kodiak bears; some maintained it wasn't worth anything!

Perhaps the .222 Rem., .223 Rem. and .222 Rem. Mag. are the most ideal, all-around varmint cartridges. True, the .222 is a 200-yard varmint cartridge (and you can add another 50 yards for

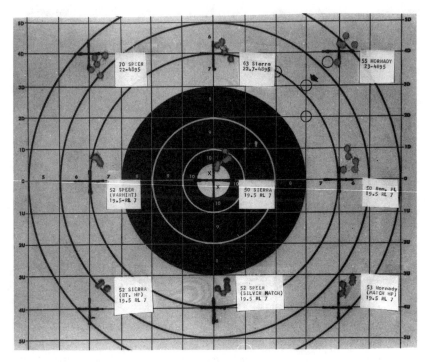

This target is about average for a 20-inch barrel rifle with various hunting and over-the-counter match bullets. All of these groups are five shots at 100 yards.

the two larger cases), but most varmint shooting is within this range. These cartridges are extremely accurate, easy on barrels, give long case life, and they kill well within the 200- to 250-yard range on everything from ground squirrels to coyotes. I once shot three coyotes one afternoon with a .222 Rem. Mag. from 50 to 150 yards, and none of them moved from where they stood.

I've used both the .224 Wthby and .225 Win. for a great deal of varmint hunting. Both are excellent varmint cartridges that can be loaded to high velocity with all bullet weights.

The advent of the .22-250 did much to hold down sales of the .224 Wthby and .225 Win. rifles. Actually, the .22-250 offers little advantage in velocity. It is entirely possible to get 3,700 fps from a 55-grain bullet in the .22-250, but these loads are not mild by any means. I have always received the best accuracy at around 3,500 fps.

As we said earlier, the .220 Swift is still on top of the heap where velocity in .22 cartridges is concerned, and it is also at the top of the pile as a varmint cartridge for extremely long ranges. It will blow a 52-grain bullet along at over 4,000 fps at full throttle, and give its best accuracy at nearer the top velocity than most other .22 cartridges. I have killed chucks out to 500 yards with the Swift, and the bullets still expanded well. While this is stretching the point a bit, it is a 350- to 400-yard varmint cartridge on any quiet day. I have also killed chucks at 400 yards with a .22-250, but this is about the limit of effectiveness for this cartridge.

This takes us up to the 6mm cartridges that have taken over much of the long-range varmint shooting from the .22 hotshots. The .243 Win. and .244/6mm Rem. are the most widely used, and, perhaps, the best as far as varmint hunting is concerned. For varmint hunting in this caliber, the 70- to 85-grain bullets are the ones to use. Some advocate the heavier bullets because they think they buck wind better, but there isn't that much difference at varmint hunting ranges, and the heavier bullets do not expand violently enough at the longer ranges on small varmints to be effective. I've done a lot of varmint hunting with the .243 Win., 6mm Rem. and the .240 Wthby, and I actually could never see that it was any easier to hit a chuck or jack at long range with any of them other than with a .22-250 or a Swift. The 6mm, 75-grain Hornady bullet traveling at 3,600 fps and sighted for 200 yards, has slightly more drop at 500 yards than the Hornady 53-grain traveling at 3,700 fps. And, it's easier to get 3,700 fps out of a .22-250 with a 53-grain bullet from a 24-inch barrel than it is to get 3,600 fps from a 75-grain, 6mm bullet from a 6mm Rem.

The big difference is that for shooting the larger varmints, like bobcats and coyotes, the 6mm packs a lot more authority at long range. The most deadly and explosive bullets I have found for the 6mm rifles are the Hornady 70- and 75-grain weights, with the edge going to the 70-grain, if you don't want any part of the carcass.

When we go to the .25s we are obviously looking for more punch at longer range and thinking in terms of less drift in stiff winds. With this in mind, the .250-3000 is good, the .257 Rem. is a bit better and the .25-06 is best. I've actually done little varmint shooting with the first two, but a lot with the .25-06. I've made some pretty long-range chuck kills with the latest Remington quarter-incher, but it doesn't seem to do a lot more damage on varmints up to the size of chucks than a Swift at the same range. The most destructive varmint bullet I have ever used in the .25-06 is the 75-grain Hornady. I have had this bullet tear small chucks into two or three pieces at ranges out to 300 yards or more. And, it's no wonder, when you consider that 59 grains of IMR-4350 will drive the 75-grain hollowpoint spitzer at 3,770 fps.

Summing Up

For the average varmint hunter, hunting the average run of varmints under average conditions and shooting ranges, one of the .22 centerfires is the answer. If most of your shooting will be at under 200 yards—and an honest 200 yards is a ''fur'' piece—the .222 Rem., or one of the slightly faster cartridges on the same case headsize, is impossible to beat. If, however, you live where a great deal of your shooting is at 200 to 400 yards, the .22-250, or one of its close cousins, is the best bet.

5

All-Around Cartridges And Rifles

Interesting food for thought was raised by the writer of a recent letter. It was in the form of an inquiry regarding a technical problem. The writer believed I was doing a good job, but we did not agree on one point. His opinion was that the .270 Win. is the best all-around cartridge for hunting American big game. He was, of course, aware that the .270 Win. is not necessarily one of my favorite cartridges under all hunting conditions for all species of North American big-game animals, and that I thought it has definite limitations.

This brings up the question of what it takes to qualify as an all-around cartridge for American big game.

To determine what would be the all-around cartridge, we have to ask a few questions. The first question that occurs to me, when someone says that a certain cartridge is *the* best for all-around hunting of American game, is how much game has he killed or saw killed with it, and how does it compare with the many other cartridges available to the average hunter? Is this experience based on hunting game that the average American hunter looks for each fall—antelope, deer and black bear—or does it include the larger species like elk, moose and grizzly? And, under what conditions has most of the hunting been done? Has he hunted all kinds of terrain from the deserts of the Southwest to the timberless tundra of the North to the broken mountain country that lies between, as well

This bolt-action Remington Model 700 Mountain Rifle is chambered for the .270 Win. which is an excellent cartridge for shooting deer-sized game. If the right bullet is used and put in a vital spot under ideal conditions, it will kill any North American game animal cleanly.

as the thick stuff in between where 50 yards is long range?

The answers to those questions can and do change opinions on what it takes to be the ideal all-around cartridge. To form a completely candid and objective opinion, the hunter has to be thoroughly familiar with hunting all game under all conditions he is likely to encounter in all areas of the country. In addition, the hunting must be done with not just one or two cartridges, but with the many calibers and cartridges of various sizes and ranges of potency available.

For example, take the letter writer's opinion that the .270 Win. is the top all-around cartridge for hunting American big game. For the fellow who hunts pronghorn on occasion, black bear when the opportunity presents, deer of any kind under any conditions (and especially mule deer wherever they are found), sheep, and goats, as well as caribou (if he happens to hunt on their range), the .270 Win. is hard to beat. For animals in this weight class, it is an ideal all-around cartridge, but certainly no better than several others—the .280 Rem. being one and the .30-06 another. Also, the .270 Win. cleanly kil's any game animal in North America, or anywhere in the world for that matter, if the right bullet is used and put in exactly the right spot under ideal conditions. But, that

For animals in the same weight class as this pronghorn, the .270 Win., .280 Rem. and .30-06 are ideal cartridges. However, the right bullet needs to be used and conditions need to be good.

doesn't make it the best choice for an all-around cartridge for all American big game.

No one who does much hunting or shooting needs to be told what my old friend Jack O'Connor thought about the .270 Win. as a big-game cartridge. However, when he hunted Alaskan brown bear on Admiralty Island many years ago, he did not use one of his favorite .270 Win. rifles; he used a .375 H&H Magnum.

One criterion for an all-around cartridge for American big game is that it handles bullets of various weights that are not only suited for shooting pronghorn weighing 100 pounds or so, but for Alaskan-Yukon moose, weighing as much as a ton, as well as brownies that are close up in the brush and can rough you up if not put out of commission with the first shot—all within reasonable hunting ranges. It should also be able to do the job under conditions in which the animal is not posing in picture-book broadside position. And, let's not be seduced by the oft-repeated saying that the good, experienced hunter does not shoot unless everything is exactly right—because 98 percent do!

For these reasons, I would personally prefer either the .280 Rem. or the .30-06 to the .270 Win. for an all-around cartridge for hunting American big game. The .280 Rem. shoots just as flat with the lighter bullets for long-range work on smaller species and offers heavier bullets for deeper penetration on the big ones. The .30-06 is almost as flat as either one with light bullets (just as flat if loaded to the same pressures) and has the advantage of the real heavyweights like the 200 and 220-grain for heavy game at close range. It also has the advantage of a larger frontal area that does more tearing along the way.

That's not to say that any of these cartridges is the ideal all-around cartridge. There are cartridges that not only shoot the lighter bullets in their respective calibers flatter, but also shoot the heavier bullets just as flat as this class of cartridges does the light ones. For this reason, they are much better suited for shooting elk and moose at the longer distances that are often necessary. The various 7mm Magnum cartridges shoot 150- or 160-grain bullets at about the same velocity as the .270 Win. does the 130-grain, and the .300 Magnums do the same thing with the 165- to 180-grain bullets. The big sevens and .30s also carry the heavyweight 175-grain, 7mm and the 200- and 220-grain, .308 bullets for the big stuff at any distance within range.

Going up the caliber ladder, there is also the .338 Win. Mag. and the .340 Wthby. On the heavy end, bullets from 250- to

An all-around cartridge for American big game should handle bullets of various weights. It should handle bullets for shooting game the size of pronghorn, as well as bullets needed for game the size of this bear.

300-grains are available for adequate bone-shattering penetration—bullets that will quickly put a moose down. Even these heavy bullets move along fast enough to make fatal shots on larger animals fairly easy at practical ranges. For the flattest trajectory when shooting the smaller species like pronghorn, sheep, goat and deer at long range without too much guesswork, the 200- and 210-grain bullets in the .340 Wthby drop no more than the 130-grain from the .270 Win., and the .338 Win. is not far behind.

Sure, I know the .340 Wthby is not an ideal pronghorn cartridge, and that the .270 Win., .280 Rem., .30-06 and a host of other cartridges are better choices. I also know that the .340 will surely kill the pronghorn. If you think it is "overkill," I can't see it as a bad fault. But, I wouldn't be overly happy trailing a wounded brownie (or even if he weren't wounded) into the thick stuff along an Alaskan salmon creek with a .270 Win. If you polled Alaskan guides on the cartridges used on brown-bear hunts, you'll find most would agree. But, if you think I firmly believe the .338 Win. Mag. and .340 Wthby Mag. are the best all-around cartridges, that isn't correct, either.

Considering the various species of big game hunted in North America, the conditions they are hunted under in various places and times, the sizes and temperaments of those animals, and the fact that the hunter may have only one opportunity to take a certain animal on a very expensive trip, it is not hard to arrive at the conclusion that there is *no single best* all-around cartridge. I've shot game with most of the commercial numbers and a lot of wildcats, but when I make a hunt that requires a lot of time, effort and dollars, I pick a cartridge that I feel will do the best job for the kind of game being hunted in the area where it lives. And, I don't worry much about whether it is considered an all-around cartridge. I do, however, prefer "overkill" to "underkill."

The Ideal Big-Game Rifle

With the advance of technology in all lines of endeavor since this country was first colonized, it would seem that life would steadily become less complicated with decisions easier to make and greater opportunity to attain the ideal answers to our needs, but it doesn't always work out that way.

Take hunting with firearms, as an example. Our forefathers lived off the land by necessity, and hunting was at least as important as any other aspect of living. But, the choice of firearms was simple because the only guns were muzzleloaders that were

Although heavy and cumbersome, the Winchester Model 1895 rode well in a saddle scabbard and was considered the ideal, all-around, big-game rifle of its day by many big-game hunters. It was chambered for some of the most powerful and flat-shooting cartridges that were popular then, such as the .35 and .405 Win., the .30-40 Krag and the .30-03 (later .30-06).

This .300 Win. Mag. (top) with 24-inch barrel on a long Remington Model 700 action weighs 8 pounds, 8 ounces with a Leupold 4X scope and mount. The Winchester Model 70 Featherweight (below) is a .270 with 22-inch barrel, weighing 7 pounds, 11 ounces with 4X Weaver in a Redfield mount. Most of the 13-ounce difference is in the Remington's longer, slightly heavier barrel. For all-around, big-game shooting, the heavier rifle's more powerful cartridge holds a strong advantage.

about as long as a fence post and almost as heavy. The diameter of the balls that they fired varied, but most were large. These rifles were cumbersome by any standard, but people of the frontier were used to doing things for themselves with whatever they had at hand. The settler's hunting rifle was no exception.

The American hunting rifle remained about the same until the advent of the metallic cartridge. That is, the rifle was loaded from the front and was long, heavy and ungainly. Of course, some improvements in ballistic performance came with the introduction of rifled bores and conical bullets like the hollow-base pointed Minie ball.

When the first metallic cartridges did appear, and repeating rifles like the Spencer and Henry were designed to handle them, the hunting rifle took a new turn in portability. But, while the new repeaters were lighter and shorter than the muzzleloader, making them a lot easier to pack in the hand or on the side of a horse, the cartridges that they fired were rather puny against the larger, big-game animals of the Western frontier. The repeater's advantage in firepower was more than offset by the lack of effectiveness in killing larger game like elk, moose, buffalo and grizzly bear.

With lever-action repeaters chambering only cartridges of inadequate power for larger big game and capable only of close-range shooting of smaller species, big-bore cartridges holding large charges of black powder behind long, heavy bullets became more popular, even though the single-shot rifles that fired them were often long and heavy. The big-game hunter, who was often a market hunter for hides or meat, needed a rifle that he could depend on to give sure kills at both short and long ranges. He was a tough and hardy realist who preferred a cartridge with sure killing ability to a light, short and handy rifle. His livelihood depended upon accuracy and killing power, not on the ease of packing the rifle.

It was not until the 1880s that the repeating rifle started to take over as the ideal, all-around rifle for hunting American big game. When John Browning designed the action that became the Model 1886 Winchester, it not only set a precedent in lever-action design, but allowed the chambering of black-powder cartridges which were effective on all types of American game.

The Model 1886 was followed by other Winchester lever actions of similar design, including the famous Model 1894, which is still going strong over 100 years later. Two factors added to the popularity of the Model 94: The light, short carbine fit so well on the saddle that you hardly knew it was there; and it was chambered for the new small-caliber cartridges charged with smokeless powder.

Marlin produced similar, lever-action rifles chambered for some of the same or similar Marlin cartridges. Savage came along with the Model 99 with its rotary magazine that eliminated the magazine tube under the barrel and improved the aesthetics.

By the early 1890s, smokeless-powder cartridges were becoming popular, and the lever actions of 1870 to 1890 vintage were either not strong enough or too short to handle some of the modern cartridges. This probably influenced the development of the Browning-designed, 1895 Winchester lever action with its in-line magazine under the receiver. This rifle was chambered for some of the most powerful, smokeless cartridges of the day: the .30-40 Krag, .35 Win. and .405 Win., and eventually the .30-03 and .30-06, as well as other smokeless and black-powder cartridges.

The Model 95 was made in several versions with barrels of different lengths and styles. And, while it was heavy and a bit cumbersome with the magazine protruding under the receiver, it

Cartridge length governs the suitability of rifle actions for their cartridges. In the first group (left): the .243, .284 and .308 Win. function in lever-action and short-bolt-action rifles. Standard-length cartridges in the second group: the .270 Win., 7mm Express Remington and .30-06 require longer rifle actions; so do the short magnums in the third group: 7mm Rem. Mag., .300 Win. Mag. and .338 Win. Mag. The longest cartridges: the .300 and .340 Wthby Mag. and the .375 H&H Mag., are suitable for only the longest actions.

was considered by many experienced hunters as *the* ideal all-around, big-game rifle. Teddy Roosevelt considered it the best big-game rifle that he had ever used, and it became very popular in the Alaska-Yukon, gold-rush country. The cartridges that it fired were probably more responsible for its popularity and reputation as an ideal big-game rifle than the rifle itself.

This period saw the popularity peak of the lever action as the ideal big-game hunting arm. The development of the strong bolt action and the high-pressure cartridges that followed ruled out the use of the weaker, rear-lockup lever action as a base for the ideal big-game rifle.

The first bolt action rifles that could be considered anything like ideal big-game rifles sprung from military actions—the Krag, Mauser and Springfield. In some cases, the stocks were simply worked over by removing the excess wood and sometimes inlaying extra wood to form a pistol grip and raising the comb. Other rifles were restocked to give dimensions more suited to the bolt action and to the use of the telescopic sights that were starting to appear in sizes and weights that could be used for hunting big game. Custom gunsmithing shops sprang up all around the country and turned out many rifles that were considered ideal, all-around, big-game rifles.

Most of those rifles had 24-inch barrels, while some had 22-inch barrels. Weight was held down to 8 pounds or so with iron sights. These rifles handled and carried well, and were chambered for high-velocity cartridges ranging from the .250-3000 Savage to the .30-06.

The hunting-rifle situation didn't change much until the 1920s when Remington updated the old 1917 Enfield action into the Model 30 and 30S, and Winchester came along with the Model 54. The Model 54 Winchester was seen by many big-game hunters as the ultimate big-game rifle, and that thought carried over to the Model 70 when it replaced the Model 54 in 1935. The Remington Model 721 also had many fans who remained loyal until the Model 700 arrived and became one of the most popular big-game rifles made anywhere.

About the only change that had much effect on rifles ideally suited to hunting American big game until World War II was when Winchester chambered the Model 70 for the .300 H&H and .375 H&H Magnum cartridges in 1937. These two British cartridges not only became quite popular with American hunters, but paved the way for later American developments of magnum cases. The thinking then (just as valid today) was that if using a magnum cartridge, a long barrel was necessary to efficiently burn the big powder charge. Also, the barrel's extra length added weight which reduced muzzle jump and muzzle blast, making felt recoil less objectionable.

Then, things started to change in the early 1950s with a trend of ultra-light, short rifles. It is hard to say whether the American big-game hunter suddenly lost the stamina to carry anything besides himself through the woods and up mountains, or whether modern living created the impression that nothing should require any physical exertion and discomfort that could be avoided—no matter what the cost in efficiency.

In the frenzied search for lighter and shorter rifles, any barrel length over 22 inches was a major sin, and an action long enough to handle anything longer than the .30-06 case was to be avoided completely. From this sprang a line of short magnums including the .264 Win., .338 Win. and .458 Win. and, a bit later, the 7mm Rem. Mag. and the .300 Win. However, all of this turned out quite well, because these short-belted cases with their minimum body taper had as much powder capacity as the much longer H&H cases.

In fact, the howl for even lighter and shorter rifles became so loud that Remington developed the 6.5mm and .350 Rem. Mag.

cartridges especially for the Remington Model 600 with its very short action and 18½-inch barrel. The rifle's total length was 37½ inches, and it weighed just over 6 pounds.

The short, fat cases actually have about the same powder capacity as the .30-06, but not when bullets for the 6.5mm and .350 cartridges have to be seated to fit the short action and magazine of the Model 600. Many bullets would not hold in the short neck of the 6.5mm when handloaded to fit the magazine, and the heavier bullets cut into powder capacity greatly. This, coupled with the short, 18½-inch barrel, dropped ballistic performance so much that even the hunters who were obsessed with shorter, lighter rifles could see that it had gone too far. Of course, Remington was the loser, as the Model 600 and the later Model 660 were discontinued.

Meanwhile, Winchester discovered that while the Model 70 Featherweight sold very well with its 22-inch barrel in standard calibers, it was a classic flop when chambered for the .264 Win. Mag. With 4 inches chopped off the barrel, the high-velocity, flat-shooting .264 Win. Mag. was not far ahead of the .270 Win. with the same barrel length and kicked up a lot more muzzle blast and jump, along with giving a harder punch to the shoulder.

It would seem that the failure in sales of short-barreled, light rifles when chambered for magnum cartridges would have taught big-game hunters a lesson in cartridge efficiency vs. rifle portability. But, if my mail, phone calls and personal contacts mean anything, it didn't. Some of the older hunters either have short memories or never used the big cartridges. Many of the younger hunters apparently haven't looked very far back into the history of big-game rifles and cartridges. Something worth considering is that few, if any, commercial rifles with magnum chambers are sold today with barrels shorter than 24 inches. In fact, some have 26-inch barrels as an option.

The short, light rifles are fine if you prefer to use the so-called standard cartridges in the power range of the .270 Win., the 280 Rem. or the .30-06. The 22-inch barrels that are so popular on today's rifles in these calibers do not give as much velocity as the 24-inch barrels, but they lose only about 50 fps, which isn't overly important. If you want to reduce weight and length to even lower levels, you can always settle for the cartridges made to function through the short actions designed for the .308 cartridge length. You will, of course, have to settle for cartridges like the 7mm-08, .308, .358 and a few others. The rifle will be short, light and easy

A long-action rifle, such as this Remington Model 700 Mountain Rifle (top), will weigh about 3 ounces more and is 1 inch longer than a short-action rifle, such as this Remington Model 700 CS Camo Synthetic (bottom). However, the major difference will be in the chambering for cartridges.

to carry up a mountain, but few hunters consider any of these cartridges ideal for all-around hunting of American big game.

The old adage, "You can't have your cake and eat it, too," is as true with rifles as anything else; you have to compromise, and the ideal rifle-and-cartridge combination requires sacrifice.

As far as rifle design is concerned, there are several angles to consider for what *you* consider the ideal, all-around, big-game rifle. First, there's the rifle's action. Regarding the very short and light action that will be chambered for the short cartridges just mentioned, the Remington Model 700 short action weighs about 3 ounces less than the long action that can handle everything up to, and including, the .375 H&H and Weatherby magnums, and it is ¾ inch shorter. So, assuming that you use the same barrel length and weight, a rifle made on the short action weighs only 3 ounces less and is less than an inch shorter than one with the long action. This isn't really a lot of saving with a light, short rifle. The major difference is in the chambering for cartridges. The short action handles only cartridges that are minimal for all-around big-game shooting, but the long action handles all the standard-length cartridges like the .30-06, as well as the short and long magnum cases with the exception of the .378 and .460 Weatherby case which is too fat, but not too long. Obviously, the short action is not the ideal base for the ideal, all-around, big-game rifle—this applies to all short actions, not just Remington's.

So, the long action is chosen for the ideal rifle. It doesn't necessarily have to accept the long magnum cartridges, as the long Remington Model 700, Winchester Model 70, Sako magnum-length, and some others do, but it should accept .30-06-length cartridges and the short magnums up to the .300 Win. As we've seen, this action is a bit longer and heavier, so to make it light and short, the barrel must be chopped to no more than 22 inches and thinned as much as possible. The action can also be lightened by milling and drilling here and there, and the stock can be hollowed out in the front and in the butt. This drops the weight a pound or so and makes the rifle reasonably short. If you want to go all the way, you can put on a fiberglass stock and drop the weight about another pound. In fact, the High Country rifle made by Brown Precision uses only a 20-inch barrel that has a muzzle diameter under ½ inch and weighs just over 6 pounds, complete with a light scope and mount when built on the long Model 700 action and chambered for the .270 Win.

A lot of hunters will ask what they have really given up if such a rifle will handle the standard cartridges, as well as the very efficient short magnums. The answer is that they won't give up too much, as long as they stick to the standard-capacity cases. The .270 Win. loses very little velocity in a 22-inch barrel, as compared to a 24-inch barrel, and not a great deal more from a 20-inch barrel. The .280 Rem. and .30-06 do not do as well in short barrels as the .270 Win. for some reason, but they still do quite well in velocity.

However, a lot of hunters today lean toward magnum cartridges that shoot flatter and pack more punch at long ranges and some that use heavy, large-caliber bullets that take care of the heavy game at all ranges. Short, light rifles and magnum cartridges don't mix very well. Not only does velocity go down with big cases that burn a lot of slow powder when barrel length drops below 24 inches, but recoil becomes unbearable for many shooters. If you want a short, light rifle, you don't want it chambered for a

For those who insist on having the lightest, shortest rifles for hunting big game, the fiberglass stock and ultra-light 20-inch barrel of the Brown High Country rifle should meet with approval. But, while this barrel does well when chambered for the .270 Win., it is questionable when chambered for a short magnum.

magnum cartridge, and if you prefer a magnum cartridge, you don't want it chambered in a light rifle with a short barrel.

When thinking about the ideal rifle for all-around, big-game hunting, which should be as light as possible while still being efficient, think about the scope. I've seen dozens of hunters climbing mountains with the lightest and shortest rifles available, yet mounted with a scope nearly as long and heavy as the rifle. These scopes are, of course, big variables of at least 3-9X, and some are even larger. These fellows apparently don't realize that they have undone most of what they tried to accomplish with their ideal hunting rifles. The big scope is so bulky and heavy that it is prone to lose its zero when subjected to hard, rough use. It adds much weight and cumbersome bulk to the rifle, is difficult to carry, and its higher power range isn't needed for hunting big game. A scope of no more than 4X and as short and light as possible, is the best all-around, big-game scope available. If you can't see a big-game animal well enough to hit it with a good 4X hunting scope, that animal is too far away to shoot at.

Summing Up

In summing up the discussion of the ideal all-around, big-game rifle, I have rifles with barrels from 18½ to 26 inches, and some with .500-inch-diameter muzzles and some that mike .700 inch. Some actions are short, some are long, and some rifles have been skeletonized here and there to cut weight while retaining efficiency. But, the cartridge is always suited to the rifle. So, in reality, it becomes the best-suited combination for hunting big-game animals.

6

Shooting Big-Game Rifles

There's more to hunting with a firearm than the mathematics and theory of cartridge and rifle selection. Picking the right gun/load combination is certainly important, but knowing how to best use the combination is a vitally important part of the equation.

Sighting In

It's a safe bet that 50 percent of the big-game rifles that go into hunting country each fall are not correctly sighted in. It is also a safe bet that half of the 50 percent that are at least roughly sighted in, are not sighted to give the hunter the full advantage of the cartridge used in the rifle.

Let's start by considering some of the rifles that find their way into the hills every fall without being sighted at all. First, there is the fellow who goes into a sporting goods store and buys a new rifle, assuming that the rifle was sighted in at the factory and will lay any bullet he fires exactly where he wants it to go. If he doesn't assume this, he may ask the salesman to bore sight or collimate it. Then, he sticks it in a case and heads for the deer woods with the firm belief that it will put bullets in the 10-ring at 100 yards. This may sound far-fetched to hunters knowledgeable about such things as sighting rifles and ballistics, but I am convinced it is true. I've talked to hunters who moaned about missing the biggest buck they ever hoped to see at point-blank range. They didn't think their rifle

It is extremely important to sight in a rifle prior to a hunting trip. Sighting in at a bench such as this one can help prevent the loss of a "once-in-a-lifetime" trophy.

could be shooting off because they hadn't dropped it and the sales clerk assured them it was sighted in when they bought it.

Assuming the rifle had been sighted in at the factory, it would have been done with only one bullet weight; any one cartridge may be loaded with a combination of bullet weights and style. Then, there are the differences within the various brands of ammunition. It would be no less than a miracle if that rifle puts any two loads or brands in the same group. Having it collimated is not much help unless you fire the rifle to check the adjustment. Some barrels collimate closely at 100 yards, but I've seen others that did not fall on the paper of a standard 100-yard target. Even if it does shoot near a 100-yard zero with one bullet weight or brand of ammunition, it certainly will be off with another load.

Then, there are those who shoot one or two rounds on the 100-yard range and feel it is "good enough for huntin'" if they land on the paper. They are well pleased if one cuts the edge of the

6-inch bull. Worse is the nimrod who takes old Betsy out and throws a couple shots at a rock of unknown size on a hillside at an unknown distance. If the dust shows a hit, he's completely happy, and if the dirt boils near the rock, he can "allow a little for the difference."

Then, there is the rifle that was correctly sighted in before last hunting season, or was it two or three hunting seasons ago? Some rifles can change impact from Tuesday to Friday, and most will change some from spring until fall—let alone a couple of years. If you check and find it's still shooting where you want it—fine. But, if it isn't, it's too late when a buck shows up.

The point is that *all* rifles should be sighted in just prior to a hunt. But, so many casual hunters don't know that. We need to tell them, or better yet, show them at Sighting-In-Days held by many of the sportsmen's clubs across the country just before the season opening. Few hunters who would go into big-game country without sighting in their rifles are good shots—despite their opinions to the contrary. If we fail to educate and encourage them to sight in their rifles, we can be sure that they are more likely to wound game than to kill cleanly. Anyway, hunters who go into the field unprepared give the rest of us a bad name.

Even hunters who should know better often fail to make last-minute checks of their rifle's zero. Just because a rifle has held a consistent point of aim back home doesn't mean that it will hold zero after being transported to a totally different climate. Going from the humid East or coastal areas into dry, mountainous country of the West, or from the dry West to the drippy rain forests in Canada or Alaska can make a big difference.

After a long trip into hunting country by plane, car, boat, horse or whatever, try your rifle before you start hunting with it. There is always the chance the sights got whacked during the trip. Or, something else could cause it to change impact—like altitude, for example, which can have a noticeable affect on long-range zero. This can usually be done at base camp where no game is likely to hear the gunfire, but even if you have to do it in a hunting area, it's better to take a chance on spooking an animal or two than missing or wounding one you've worked days to get a shot at. One shot or two doesn't usually spook game anyway. And, if it does, it is only temporary.

Where To Zero

When I started hunting big game, 99 percent of the hunters

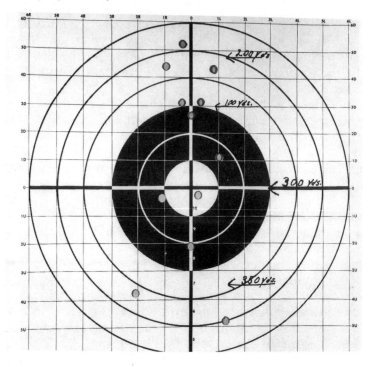

Sighting a rifle to give the longest "point-blank" hold possible without shooting too high at mid-range can be done with a target like this one. Three inches high at 100 yards should be the goal.

sighted their rifles to zero at 100 yards. Any deviation from that tradition was akin to knocking motherhood. There are times when this sighting is in order, but not many, or with many cartridges. Nearly all modern cartridges start their bullets at over 2,500 fps. For these cartridges under average hunting conditions, especially in the West and North, there is a better way—and it isn't the frequently recommended 1½-inch-high, 100-yard point of impact, or the 200-yard zero, both of which amount to about the same thing with most modern bullets in scope-sighted rifles.

Although a 200-yard zero is commonly used by "savvy" hunters, it still requires accurate range estimation at longer distances. Few of us, particularly those who spend 99 percent of their time in urban areas, are very good at estimating range in unfamiliar terrain. A better way is to sight the rifle to give the longest "point-blank" or "dead-on" hold that is possible without shooting too high at mid-range. And, with most rifles and bullets, that means 3 inches high at 100 yards.

I don't know whose idea it was to sight the rifle 3 inches high at 100 to bring out the cartridge's maximum potential, but whoever it was, all serious big-game hunters owe that person a debt of gratitude. A different principle was applied to sighting for hunting than that used in target shooting, where the bullet must be on zero at a particular, known distance. Like all hunters, this innovator was concerned about getting the shot within the vital area of the game being hunted. Unlike the target shooter, he didn't care if the shot was high at shorter distances, so long as it wasn't too high; nor was he particularly concerned about the distance at which the bullet would print precisely upon point of aim, because in the field he could not determine that distance exactly, anyway.

As an example, let's use a 7mm with a 160-grain bullet in good pointed form at 3,100 fps, or a .30 caliber with the pointed 180-grain at the same velocity. Sighted to print 3 inches high at 100 yards, the bullet will land about 4 inches-plus high at 200 yards, and be almost on the nose at 300 yards. It will be down no more than 4 to 5 inches at 350 yards and less than 10 inches at 400, a range which in the field is easily judged ''mighty far'' and can usually be shortened by stalking. If you hold on the center of a buck's ribs anywhere from the muzzle out to 350 yards, which is as far as most prudent men will attempt, the bullet will land in a vital area. And, if he *is* 400 yards you can still hold on the top of his back and hit him near center. At a mid-range of 175 to 200 yards, the bullet still will be below the spine with a center hold. If those same cartridges were zeroed at 100 yards, bullets would land about 3 inches low at 200 yards, over 10 inches low at 300 yards and down more than 2 feet at 400. With the 3-inch-high, 100-yard sighting, you have a point-blank range of at least 350 yards with no figuring whatsoever from a center hold. With the 100-yard zero, you start undershooting the vital area at less than 250 yards.

This same sighting method will also bring out the most range from such cartridges as the .30-30, but you'll have to start holding higher for a vital hit at about 175 yards.

The only time that the 3-inch-plus-high sighting at 100 yards is less desirable is in heavy cover where ranges are seldom over 100 yards. If you see only the head or neck of an animal at 100 yards or beyond, the bullet will be too high if you hold center. I have used the 3-inch-high, 100-yard sighting so long that I hold low without consciously thinking about it. However, if you forget, you'll shoot over, or only crease, the buck's neck. If you hunt in this kind of

Maximum range for shots at unwounded, big-game animals depends upon many factors, including the type of game, type of shooting position, rifle power and accuracy, the hunter's ability to precisely judge the range and his skill in analyzing conditions to get the first shot into a vital area.

country where you may not get to see the whole body of the animal, and seldom get a long-range shot, then the 100-yard zero is probably better.

But, regardless of the method, make sure the rifle is sighted where you want it to group at a known range. Do your sighting just before hunting starts—ammunition is a lot cheaper than hunting trips.

Long-Range, Big-Game Shooting

Some pretty tall tales of long-range, big-game shooting are mixed with the campfire smoke in nearly every hunting camp. Even taller tales drift back and forth over the rims of tall glasses in hunting lodges and hunting country taverns. Unfortunately, many novice hunters absorb a lot and try to apply it at the first opportunity in their own hunting.

This brings up the question: If we can't believe 90 percent of the tales of long-range, big-game kills, what is long-range, big game shooting? And, if the tales we hear are highly improbable, why is this so?

In more than 50 years of chasing big game in the Mountain States and on the tundra of interior Alaska, I've done a lot of long-range shooting at big-game animals ranging in size from antelope to moose, and I've seen other hunters do a lot more. Also, I've made my share of mistakes like muffing a shot and having to trail an animal to finish the job. It is by our mistakes that we learn. In this case, the learning consists of many factors, factors that add up to the limitation of ranges beyond which we should never shoot at any big-game animal. If we cut it finer, and we certainly should, we'll put shooting range limits on some species that are far shorter than for others, and we'll limit those ranges more accordingly to the conditions.

In some circles, nothing under 500 to 600 yards is considered long range, and 800 to 1,000 sounds a lot better. It seems that bragging about 1,000-yard kills is a great boost to the ego of some hunters, and some advertising people seem to think it is a good selling point for certain products. Either someone has stretched the point, made a terrific mistake on range estimation or had one of those fortunate accidents that most true sportsmen would hesitate to tell about for fear that someone else would try to duplicate it.

Strangely enough, many hunters believe that long-range, big-game shooting is limited mostly by the hunter's ability to hit the animal in a vital spot. This is only partially true. Even if he does hit it, there are other reasons why it is extremely unlikely that he will recover the animal. But, let's take the man behind the gun first and go from there.

The average "deer-sized" animal will be about 18 to 22 inches broadside on the rib cage, but this is an overall outline, not the vital area. The vital area on a buck muley or bighorn ram standing broadside in the lung-shoulder area is no more than about 14 inches square; in any other position, it is far less. True, there is a lot of area on both ends of this square, but little of it is vital. If your bullet lands there, you are almost certain to merely wound.

This means that your rifle will have to be capable of less than 1½ MOA in order to hit the buck's vital area at 1,000 yards. Even if you do have a rifle that will deliver 1¼- to 1½-inch groups at 100 yards, few hunting bullets will hold that accuracy level out to 1,000 yards, or even 600 yards. Without this kind of accuracy, the finest long-range rifleman living can't hope to connect more than part of the time. Fellows who win 1,000-yard matches put most of their shots in just such small areas (the V-ring of a 1,000-yard target is 20 inches across), but remember they are not using hunting equipment, and are not firing under hunting conditions. Further, they know the exact range, have a fairly good idea of what the wind is doing, and are sighted perfectly for that range. Last, but not least, they are the pick of literally hundreds of thousands of riflemen!

Even the better-informed rifleman doesn't know how much his bullet will drop at all ranges. And, at a range of 1,000 yards, elevation and humidity can cause a miss, to say nothing of the wind that may be blowing at 5 miles per hour from the buck's left, while whipping off your right cheek at 20. Even if the wind is steady from one direction, you don't know how fast it is, or whether it will cause the bullet to drift or make it strike high or low. These things can cause the hunter to make mistakes.

Even the best long-range hunting bullets with the flattest trajectory when fired from today's magnum cartridges will drop around 30 feet at 1,000 yards. This drop is, of course, cut down somewhat by the range for which the rifle is sighted and the height of the sights over the bore. Even so, if you misjudge the range by as little as 25 yards, you are unlikely to hit the vital area. Even if you estimate the range correctly and know your exact bullet drop, can you really be certain of where to hold in order to allow for a drop of exactly 19 or 23 feet? Do you also know how much to hold into the wind?

Along with drop estimation, the sight picture is another factor that can cause a miss at much less than 1,000 yards. Assuming you have a good average scope for most big-game rifles—a 4X with standard medium cross hairs—the reticle intersection will almost cover the vital area of the buck. (Many reticles cover much more.) The fairly popular 3-inch dot, or a post of the same diameter, will almost blot out the entire deer. If you are shooting over fairly flat, open land on a sunny day, heat waves and the resulting mirage will make accurate holding almost impossible. The more power you have, the worse it will be. Now, visualize dropping 18 to 25 feet or so of holdover to the last few inches for a vital hit.

Another factor that will cause a miss under 1,000 yards is not checking the actual drop of the load in your rifle out to that range with the last 300 yards in 50-yard increments. This mistake results in no way of accurately calculating the amount of actual drop. The reason is that if you do calculate it from factory ballistic

While hunting in Montana, this hunter stops to glass distant game. Long-range shooting requires extremely accurate range estimation.

charts—even though you use the same factory ammunition—you are almost certainly not getting the same velocity quoted or, therefore, the same drop. For instance, factory ammo is supposed to give the 130-grain .270 Win. bullet a muzzle velocity of 3,140 fps, but I chronographed bullets from a lot number of one brand that clocked in at 2,977. The highest velocity recorded from that load in *any* brand was 3,040.

If you use a different bullet shape, the difference will be much more. A .30 caliber, 180-grain, round-nose bullet starting at 3,000 fps will drop about 100 inches more at 1,000 yards than a spitzer form. That is over *8 feet* (and this is not calculating for extreme bullet shape in either direction).

Time of flight also must be considered. It will take the high-velocity, high-ballistic-coefficient bullet at least 1¼ seconds to get there. If the buck decides to move about the time you squeeze the trigger, it won't land close enough to scare him. None of this allows for the less-than-ideal shooting positions usually found in hunting country, or even one slight tremble or a poor trigger let-off.

Placing the bullet in the right spot at ranges well under the 1,000-yard mark is almost impossible for an expert rifleman with many long years of hunting experience. But, for the average once-a-year hunter, placing it in the right spot is completely accidental. Even if you are lucky enough to put a bullet into the right spot at an extreme range, don't forget that the velocity and energy it has at that range is a far cry from what it started out with. Using the 180-grain, .30 caliber bullet as an example, we find that if it starts at 3,000 fps, it will arrive at 1,000 yards at only half that velocity. This is for the highest ballistic coefficient, and many pointed 180-grain bullets will be down to around 1,200 fps. Energy would drop to only 600 to 1,000 foot-pounds, depending on the bullet used, or about the same as that delivered by the old .32-20 cartridge at the muzzle. But the .32-20 actually had the advantage because its bullets were designed to expand at lower velocities, allowing the bullet to kill quickly when it gets into the lungs or heart. No .30 magnum bullet is designed to expand at anything close to 1,500 fps.

It is doubtful that any big-game bullets made for high-velocity cartridges will expand properly at under 2,000 fps, and few at that velocity. In fact, few will expand on thin hides and soft meat at velocities that low, and meat is what you have to figure on because it may not hit a bone.

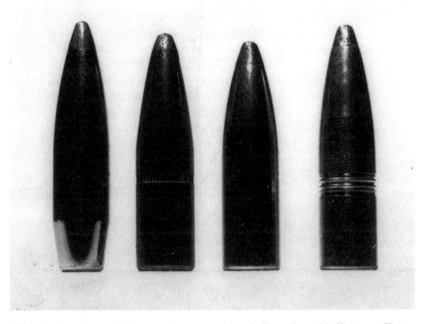

Effective long-range, big-game shooting requires bullets of good ballistic coefficient designed to expand at low velocities, such as these .30 bullets. From left: the Sierra 180-grain BT, Hornady 180-grain Spire Point, Nosler 180-grain .300 Mag and Speer 180-grain spitzer.

Even with the more potent magnums that start 160-grain, 7mm bullets and 180-grain, .30 bullets at 3,000 fps or even a bit more, those bullets will not reliably expand at more than about 500 yards. Neither will they deliver enough energy to be effective at ranges over 500 yards. The same 180-grain bullet that started out with close to two tons of energy will arrive at 500 yards packing only about 1,800 foot-pounds (fp). This is less than the .30-30 cartridge starts out with. Expansion of a bullet designed to stand up under magnum muzzle velocity will not be nearly as great, or cause nearly the damage, as a bullet fired at close range from a .30-30.

One factor favoring the bullet fired at long range sometimes affects killing power. The more rapid and the greater the expansion of the bullet, the less penetration it will give. But, a bullet traveling at the velocity retained at 500 yards, or even 300 yards, will penetrate deeper than at its 100-yard velocity. One possible exception to this is the Nosler. Long experience indicates that

Noslers also penetrate deeper after a drop-off in velocity delivered by the highest velocity cartridges.

At this point, another foreign object appears in the soup. The smaller the animal, the less power you will need to kill it. But, smaller animals provide less resistance so that the bullet is less likely to expand well, if at all. The vital area is also smaller. With larger animals such as elk or moose, the extra resistance will cause the bullet to expand better. Also, a larger animal is easier to hit, but it takes more punch to kill it quickly—punch that is pretty puny beyond 500 yards with even the hottest cartridges.

An antelope buck is not only a lot easier to kill than a bull elk, he is almost certain to be in open country so if you wound him he shouldn't be hard to find in most situations. The elk, on the other hand, is just as certain to be near some kind of cover. Wound him and there is the possibility that you will *not* recover him if he makes it to the brush.

As an example of what you can expect in the way of killing ability, we'll take three popular bores that start bullets at 3,000 fps. The .270 bore with a 150-grain bullet has a remaining energy of 1,318 fp at 500 yards, a .30 caliber, 180-grain kicks up 1,556 fp, and a .338 bullet of 225 grains will deliver 2,038 fp. All bullets have about the same ballistic coefficient and trajectory. (These figures are taken from the Hornady ballistic table from bullets of the same design.) Velocity of all three is within less than 50 fps, so expansion will be about the same. The large bullet will deliver by far the greater shock and disruption. In other words, the .338 bore (In this case, we are using .340 Wthby velocity.) is adequate for elk or moose at 500 yards if you can shoot it well enough to hit the vital area, but you might have second thoughts about using the .270 at the same range. (Of course, some of the magnum .30s will push the .338 if used with heavy handloads at 3,200 to 3,300 fps.)

The big bears stand in a class by themselves as far as long-range shooting is concerned. (Here, we refer to mountain grizzlies and Alaskan brown bear, because polar bears are hunted under completely different circumstances.) Even though these animals get quite large as far as weight is concerned, the vital area is not nearly as large as that of either elk or moose. This is because the bear's body is much more compact, with a great deal of the weight in the legs. The body is also rounder in shape and not nearly as deep. The lungs and heart are much smaller in a bear.

The big bears are hard to kill cleanly with a single bullet. If

Big bears, such as this grizzly, get large in weight, but their vital area is small. Because they are difficult to kill with one bullet, you should try to break up bone in the shoulder or spine.

you want to put one down and keep it there, it is best to break up a lot of bone, either in the shoulder or spine. This cuts the vital area down even more. This is especially true if the bear is near timber, brush or rough, rocky areas. If he doesn't go down and makes the bushes, you've got a sticky mess on your hands. It is of little comfort to *think* that first shot was *probably* right when you are parting the alders with your rifle barrel looking for him. If he isn't dead when you find him, you may not have long to regret the error of a long-range shot!

The small vital area of even the largest bears (the larger the bear, the harder it is to kill), their tenacity for life and the bear's tendency to fight back all add up to the fact that you need a lot of punch in the right spot to do the job. This leaves little room for error in aim or hold. It also dictates that the bullet should still have a lot of authority when it lands. All of which rules out shooting at distances that would be long range for any hoofed American game. What is long range for the big bears? I'd say 250 yards. And, then, only with cartridges and bullets that still have a lot of bone-smashing energy at that range—if the hunter is capable of putting that bullet in a 10-inch circle at that range and cool enough to do it with a bear in his sights.

Sensible Long-Range Shooting

We've seen that many problems prohibit shooting at any game animal at ranges anywhere near the mythical 1,000 yards. But, what, then, is sensible long-range shooting? It is obvious that many high-velocity cartridges are capable of bullet expansion (if correctly designed) out to 500 yards or so, and that these bullets still have enough energy to kill antelope and deer-sized game. But, assuming your rifle is accurate enough to put the bullet in the right spot every time and that you are also a good enough shooter to do it, there is still a terrific chance for a miss because of poor range estimation.

Few hunters, even those of long experience, can estimate the range at 500 yards, within 50 yards on either side. To misjudge the range by 50 yards at 500 will result in a miss on smaller animals and, perhaps, only wound larger ones. Also, during normal sighting with the flattest-shooting cartridges, you will have to hold *above* the back line on the smaller animals by quite a margin, and maybe leave some daylight between hair and reticle on the larger ones, too.

You don't have to look into a crystal ball to see that even

There are many reasons why few hunters are ever justified in shooting at game like these bighorn rams at more than 400 yards. For the average hunter, 300 to 350 yards is long range. Never is anyone justified in shooting at the mythical 700 to 1,000 yards so often talked about.

500-yard, big-game shooting should not be attempted by anyone who is not an expert rifleman with a lot of experience in judging range under various hunting conditions. Your ability can, however, be increased by the way your rifle is sighted as discussed earlier.

For the good shot who doesn't get buck fever and shoots only from a steady position, this should be about the limit for long-range shots. If he can't keep all of his bullets within a 6-inch bull at 200 yards from various hunting positions, or from the position he is using for the shot, he had better not attempt even the 350- to 400-yard shot.

What's Right For You?

What distance should *you* consider long range for big-game shooting? A few simple deductions, and your ability to abide by them when you are looking at game can help determine your answers. First, are you reasonably sure of the range to within 25 yards or so? Second, do you know the exact drop of the bullet with the load you are using at that range. Third, do you have the ability to hold all of your shots well within the vital area from the position you have to use? Fourth, is your rifle accurate enough if you have figured everything right? Fifth, will the bullet you are using expand sufficiently at that range? And, finally, will that bullet retain enough authority for a clean kill on that particular animal if it lands in the right place?

This is what it takes to decide what is long range for you and your equipment for the game you are hunting. And, remember that if you can't place that *first bullet* in the vital area, you are more likely to wound the animal than miss it cleanly.

Why You Missed

Standing near the end of a rocky bench on the mountain's face overlooking the beautiful, alpine meadow far below was a big ram with heavy horns that curled up past the bridge of his Roman nose. He was looking at something along the slide in an absent-minded manner, and he stood broadside to the hunter who was behind a rock outcrop at the ridge's crest 250 yards up the steep slope.

It was a perfect setup for a one-shot, clean kill, one that should drop the ram where he stood. There seemed to be little chance of him plunging off the bench and tumbling down the cliff-studded slope in a bouncing, horn-breaking roll. The hunter had time to estimate the range as being 250 yards and be fairly sure he was right. The bullet would be right on point of hold at that range.

There was no wind, and the cross hairs were rock-steady at the rear of the ram's shoulder with the rifle resting solidly in the hunter's cupped hand on the rock. Gently, the hunter squeezed the trigger and the shot's blast bounced from peak to peak and died away. The big ram jerked his head even higher; with a startled glance up the slope, he dashed over the edge of the bench.

The hunter stared in disbelief; he couldn't believe he had missed—but he had. When the ram appeared again it was climbing the far side of the basin, in good health and untouched.

Why had he missed a shot that should have been comparatively easy? Could his rifle be shooting somewhere other than where the reticle centered? In camp that evening, the bullets landed exactly where the rifle had been sighted at the start of the hunt. Why, then, the miss?

This happens to dozens of hunters every year in rough country hunting. The shot is fired at an animal well within the cartridge's sure-hitting range, but at steep, downhill angles. The bullet cuts a path through the clear mountain air just over the animal's back, perhaps shaving the hair and maybe a little flesh from above the spine. Why does this happen, what causes it and how can these misses be avoided?

These questions draw many answers, and some are pretty wild. Others, while technically correct, are of little use to the hunter. I have heard many hunters who overshoot downhill claim that the rifle actually shot higher when shooting downhill. This is true only to the extent that the bullet does not drop as much when range increases at steep angles as when fired on the level. Obviously, if the bullet was fired straight down, or up, there would be no change in trajectory. So, if your bullet fired from a level bore drops 24 inches at 300 yards (with no sight compensation for trajectory drop), the amount of drop will decrease as the downward angle is decreased. If you shot straight down from the top of a cliff, the bullet would land exactly on bore line at any range. However, if the distance from the muzzle to the target with level bore is 250 yards, the rifle's sight compensates for the pull of gravity on the bullet. With the compensation for a horizontal shot, the bullet will strike higher at that range as the angle of fire decreases. This difference in drop is not large enough to greatly affect your hunting hold until the angle of fire becomes quite steep, from about 45 degrees and below.

Theoretically, the drop of a bullet is exactly the same when fired on the level over a given distance as it is if it is fired at a

Overshooting on steep, downhill shots causes many misses during hunting season. Although the trajectory is flatter on such shots, most of the problem is caused by holding too high.

steep, downward angle at a longer distance. For example, if the bullet fired from a level bore drops 20 inches at 250 yards, it will also drop exactly 20 inches if the downward slant range is 300 yards. For most hunters, this is of little value because in order to use it successfully, you would need to measure the slope angle, the exact range and be able to convert the information to level distance.

Two other points to this overshooting-downhill-business are much more important to hunters, and they may be considered optical illusions.

First, if you are looking down at a steep angle at an animal at any great distance, it appears farther away than it would at the same distance on the level, or if it were uphill from you. Try it sometime. Look down from a steep mountain at an object on the flat valley below; then, go down and look at the same object from the valley bottom.

But, mostly the error lies with the way you see the animal, and not in the change in bullet drop at steep angles. When you look down at an animal from above (say 45 degrees), you not only see its side in full, but you also see the full width of its back with a little of the downward body slope on the far side. Okay, so what? The ''so what'' is that when you hold where the center of the body *appears to be*, you are actually holding very near the line of the back as it would be seen from the level. Now, combine this with the fact that your bullet does not drop quite as much as you expect it to at that distance, and that your rifle may still be shooting a little high at what may be midrange in the bullet's trajectory path, and you have a wonderful setup for overshooting!

The answer? When shooting at steep, downhill angles where the animal is within the range where holdover becomes necessary, hold very near the bottom of the *chest outline*. This way you overcome both the overestimated bullet drop and the optical illusion.

Also, remember that this same thing can and does happen on steep, uphill shots but to a lesser degree because you see more of the animal's underside than its back, and the legs help to dispel the illusion. The bullet may go high, however, if the animal is at the midpoint of the bullet's trajectory.

Probably the greatest number of misses at the longer ranges are caused by misjudging distance. There isn't much anyone can tell you about this that will help, except that the best solution is to estimate the range of objects whenever you are out in a field, then measure it as close as possible to check your accuracy. Certain conditions make judging distance more difficult, and knowing what they are and how to compensate will solve some of the problems.

Assuming the terrain is similar, an animal seen under poor lighting conditions, such as during a rain- or snowstorm, or in heavy haze, will appear much farther away than one viewed in bright, clear light. An animal against snow or other very light background stands out so well that it appears nearer than it actually is, while one in deep shadow under trees seems farther away. If shooting cross-canyon at an animal in sunshine and the hunter is in the slope's shadow, the animal will seem nearer than it is. Put yourself on the sunny side and the animal on the shaded slope, and it seems farther away. A light-colored or white animal such as a mountain goat often seems nearer than it actually is because of its sharp contrast with the darker background, while dark animals against equally dark backgrounds are indistinct, and seem far away. Even animals seen through long, open lanes between the trees seem farther away than they actually are. The outcome in all these situations is obvious.

Another situation where range estimation can be tough is in northern Canada and Alaska where game is found in relatively open country where there is low brush, but no trees. This situation is especially true of bears. If the brush is higher than you think and the bear is smaller than you estimate, you are inclined to assume the range is longer than it is. Conversely, a big bear in short brush appears closer. This also leads to misjudging the bear's size even when you do guess the range right!

Another condition that causes many misses by lowland, urban dwellers is a sudden change to higher elevations where the air is free of smog and dust. The animal on the far side of a canyon stands out in the thin, clear air in such sharp relief that it seems much nearer than it actually is. Thus, the ram that looks to be 300 yards away gets squirted with rock dust from a bullet fired at 400 or 450 yards.

Not knowing the exact load drop used in the cartridge that your rifle is chambered for at various hunting ranges is another mistake that results in many misses. By this, we mean the load you are actually using in your rifle. Factory ballistic tables are highly misleading at times. If you go strictly on this information, you'll have many unaccountable misses. This is not to say their calculations are not correct for the bullet and velocity quoted, but therein lies the trouble. It is highly unusual for any factory ammo to give the velocity in your rifle that it did in other rifles by the same company, so your velocity is probably much lower. It also varies greatly between ammunition brands.

Even the hunter who determines the best sight setting for his rifle and conscientiously sights it in to that point may forget an important fact: A rifle shot from bench rest is quite likely to group at a different point when fired from field positions. For instance, many hunters use a sling for stability with longer hunting shots. Yet, they may not have determined how much effect the sling's tension on the forend has on the point of impact. To know what your rifle is going to do, sight it in from the bench; then, check the point of impact when the rifle is fired from the kinds of positions you're most likely to use—prone, sitting, over an impromptu rest, with and without sling—when a long-range shot presents itself.

Another reason for misses, although it isn't likely to present

After sighting a rifle in from a bench, check the point of impact when the rifle is fired from positions you will most likely use, such as this improvised field rest.

itself except on extremely long shots, is that some variable-power scopes shoot to considerably different points of impact at different power settings. Try your scope at different powers and sight in at the power you're most likely going to use.

Another problem is the length of time the hunter takes in sighting in his rifle. The barrel is likely to be both well-fouled and quite hot. Most lightweight hunting rifles will shoot to a considerably different point of impact when the barrel is cold and clean, as it usually is during hunting. The solution is to clean the barrel after sighting it in—if it will be clean while you hunt—and let it cool. Then, see where that all-important first shot goes. You may be surprised.

While we are talking about sighting, one other point should be stressed. How often have you heard or read about some hunter falling with his rifle, dropping it, or having his horse fall and roll on it? He is afraid that the scope has been knocked out of alignment, but he is equally afraid to check it for fear of scaring all of the game out of the country. So he continues on hunting, finds the trophy of a lifetime, but the bullet from the banged-up rifle misses the mark.

Let's look at this with a little "horse sense." First, game that is not looking right down your shirt collar is not going to be spooked much by a few shots. Second, if you hunt for days with a rifle that is shooting off into the brush somewhere, and you at last find the animal you are looking for, you'll miss and spook the animal for sure. If you think your rifle is not shooting right, take it back to camp and try it. Or, go on the other side of the mountain from where the game is and test it there, especially if you banged it up early in the morning and want to continue the hunt. It's far better to take a chance on spooking an unseen animal by taking a sighting shot or three, than it is to shoot at the same animal and miss or only wound it.

Another way to assure yourself that your rifle is right is to carry an optical collimator *and* written notes on where your rifle points when properly sighted in for a given bullet and load. It's not a substitute for actual test firing, but it can be used to regain the same setting if the scope has been knocked out of kilter. Admittedly, a collimator is not likely to show the different forend pressure effects or bedding changes since the rifle was sighted in, but it is better than worrying about your sight's accuracy if you don't want to risk firing a test shot.

Any time you miss your target on an animal for any reason, you stand a good chance of wounding it, and this is much worse. Most of us, being human and subject to error, miss shots that we should not miss. We also occasionally wound an animal. But, if we know some of the reasons for those unaccountable misses, we can surely eliminate many of them.

7

Selecting A Rifle For Alaska

Caribou—40 or 50 of them—were feeding on the level tundra of a high plateau, perhaps one-and-a-half miles from where we rode along the rim of a little creek. We headed down into the creek bed and rode halfway to the herd before running out of cover for the horses. Tying them to an arctic willow, we started the final stalk across the tundra in an attempt to close the distance to within shooting range.

From this point on, there was no cover larger than moss-covered, frost humps that were too small to hide anything but a ptarmigan. If we were to get within even long-rifle range, we'd need a lot of luck. With guide Johnny Porter in the lead, we stooped low and pressed close to the ground trying to look like some four-footed critter out for a midday stroll. We wandered erratically in the general direction of the caribou, stopping often but always working closer to the slowly moving herd. Every few minutes, a small band would break off from the main herd and come out toward us to investigate. We managed to look innocent, and they would return without "winding" us—thanks to the stiff breeze blowing in our faces.

Finally, we were within what later proved to be just over a 400-yard range. The caribou seemed to be getting nervous. Although still feeding, they started moving along faster than we were going. Johnny asked if I thought I could do it. I nodded

Because bull caribou are not extremely large animals, cartridges less potent than the 7mm Mashburn Super Magnum can kill them cleanly. However, the range should be 400 yards or less.

affirmatively and started looking for a frost hump high enough to lay my packsack on for a prone shot.

A half-dozen mature bulls were with the herd, but only two held our attention. One of them moved around to our side of the herd, eliminating any doubt as to which one of the two to take. I estimated the range at 400 yards so the 160-grain Nosler from the 7mm Mashburn Super Magnum would drop 6 inches below point of aim. As the big bull quartered toward me and slowed to a walk, the cross hairs touched the point of his shoulder two thirds of the way up. The bullet landed just at the rear of the shoulder and was found at the forward edge of the off-hip.

Now, a big bull caribou is not an especially large animal, and much less potent cartridges than Art Mashburn's big seven will kill one cleanly. There are also other cartridges with much less energy that are flat enough to land the bullet where you want it at 400 yards. At this range, however, even a 160-grain, 7mm bullet which starts at 3,250 fps with some 3,750 foot-pounds of energy is getting pretty puny. What would you have left with some of the smaller cartridges?

I had traveled nearly 3,000 miles to look for that bull. A cartridge with much less long-range potential could have cost me the trophy—which stands high in the Boone & Crockett listings. On the same trip, I could have killed several good caribou with a handgun, but we knew this big fellow with the mammoth double shovels was there somewhere. We had spent many days looking for him, and when we found him, there was no chance of getting any closer. Success depended on the efficiency of the cartridge I would use.

Alaska Is A Mixed Bag

Another point to remember in hunting different species in Alaska is that not all game is in the caribou-size class, and not all are friendly if you don't kill them with the first shot. You may start out in the morning hunting caribou or sheep; then come around a boulder or alder clump and find yourself within spitting distance of a big hunk of cantankerous grizzly. Or, maybe you spot nearly a ton of bull moose with a 70-inch-plus spread of paddles adorning his brow.

On this sample trip, I wanted a decent moose, but the way things turned out I didn't have a lot of time to look for one. One usually thinks of moose as being shot on the edge of some pond or lake, or in some meadow where you can get within close range. For Alaskan moose hunting, this isn't necessarily true. A lot of old bulls hang out on the hillsides in timberline country where you may find the range on the long side whether you like it or not. Remember that when you are hunting for horns you may find the one you want is not an ideal shot, but you have little choice.

So it was when we found this old buster of a bull feeding in little openings in 10-foot alders on a steep hillside near timberline. The shot had to be taken at 300 yards from a rocky ridge. If we dropped lower to get closer, the alders would be in the way, and we couldn't circle above him because the wind would be blowing toward the moose. The 175-grain Nosler from the Mashburn took him in the shoulder exactly where the cross hairs rested and left a silver-dollar-size exit hole on the far side. It could have been done with a .270 Win. or .30-06, but neither one would have had much energy left at impact. I'm sure the extra power wasn't wasted, and I never doubted the outcome.

When hunting in Alaska, not all game is caribou-size. You may start hunting caribou in the morning and come across a large brown bear like this one. Hopefully, you'll have something powerful enough to take him down if he gets angry.

These incidents are not cited to sing the praises of the 7mm Mashburn Mag. There are others that are about as good in the same caliber: The 7mm Rem. Mag and the 7mm Wthby both deliver almost as much velocity with good handloads and the same bullets. There are also the big .30 cartridges like the .300 Win. Mag., .308 Norma Mag. and .300 Wthby, as well as the potent and long-range .338 Win. Mag. and .340 Wthby. Neither is it implied that you need a magnum cartridge to kill Alaskan game. What is important is that these and similar cartridges are the ideal answer for Alaskan hunting where the trophy hunter is looking for something big and has limited time to get it.

The local hunter looking for his winter meat, with more time to hunt and more suitable animals to pick from, may find that less-potent cartridges fit his needs just as well. If he can't get within range of a given animal today, maybe he can tomorrow. If the angle of the shot is such that it is doubtful if the cartridge and bullet he is using will do the job, then he can wait for a better shot or look for another animal. If he jumps an irate grizzly off the moose he killed yesterday, or bumps into one in the thick stuff and it runs the wrong way, he can do his best with what he has. If he lives to reminisce, he may use a larger cartridge in the future.

The point is when you are hunting in most of Alaska you don't know what game may turn up when, or under what conditions. By the time you think about it and decide your rifle is chambered for the wrong cartridge or that the cartridge is loaded with the wrong bullet, you may have already lost his hide or your own!

Few places on earth have more diversified hunting conditions than Alaska when you compare the tangle of huge trees, undergrowth, and downed timber in the rain forest of southeastern Alaska to the tundra and scanty brush of the arctic, or the moss and grass-covered plateaus and rock and ice spines of the interior ranges. On the one hand, you are lucky to see an animal a few feet away, and, on the other, you can spot him as far away as a good binocular or spotting scope can pick him up. Yet, there are exceptions to both cases. I've seen big brown bears that could be stalked for a mile in open country on Admiralty Island tide flats, and I've climbed up game trails padded down with mountain grizzly tracks where you could run into one close enough to shake hands.

I remember starting out one snowy morning to look for a Dall ram in the Alaska Range. We didn't find any sheep that day because we ran into a grizzly that my hunting partner smacked in the neck with a .30-06, and the 180-grain bullet blew up. I finally stopped the bawling bear 5 feet from the toes of my boots with a .300 Win. Mag. loaded with 180-grain Noslers. I've always been happy that I wasn't using a .243 Win. to hunt sheep that morning!

On that same trip, I hunted sheep most of the time for nearly a month before I found the ram I was looking for. When I shot him—at a little over 100 yards—I could have done it with a .30-30 just as well, but I never felt that the .300 Win. was overkill. If my only chance at him had happened to be from a quarter-mile away, with no way of getting closer, I had the rifle to do it.

Alaskan Guns To Consider

For general Alaskan hunting, I'd rule out the 6mm caliber cartridges. Not because they will not kill sheep, goats, black bear and caribou cleanly, and at fairly long range, but because they are not moose cartridges, even under good conditions and with the best

The 6mm caliber cartridges are good for killing game the size of this Dall ram. However, they are not ideal for moose or grizzlies that may be encountered on the same hunt.

This mountain grizzly was killed in prime caribou country in interior Alaska, and within five miles of a good sheep area. The .300 Win. Mag. shown here did well on all Alaskan game.

bullets. And, if you bump into a grizzly where you can't back off, you may find your 6mm shrinking until it seems like a .22 pistol. I know they'll kill both moose and grizzly, but this doesn't make them ideal for the job.

When you get up to cartridges like the .270 Win. and .264 Win. Mag., more depends on the bullet you use than on the killing power of the cartridge. On all classes of Alaskan game, only the heavier bullets should be used in either cartridge, and then only those that are designed to hold together for deep penetration—bullets like the 150- and 160-grain Nosler in the .270 and the 140-grain Nosler in the .264.

I don't get carried away thinking of the .308 Win. as being ideal for all-around Alaskan hunting. True, it will deliver well if the range isn't too long. But, long, heavy bullets cut down on the already minimal powder capacity, and velocity drops off quickly. Velocity isn't high enough with the 180-grain bullet to make the cartridge any great shakes for long-range shooting. It is not easy to get a hit at long range, and it doesn't pack much authority when it gets there.

There is little doubt that the venerable .30-06 is good on any Alaskan game, with the proper bullet weight and design. It has accounted for many grizzly, brown and polar bears at close quarters with 180- to 220-grain bullets, and is fairly flat at the longer ranges with lighter bullets. With good handloads and the right powder, it will send a 180-grain bullet on its way almost as fast as the factory 180-grain load for the .300 H&H Mag. However, factory loads in hunting-length barrels show less than the claimed 2,700 fps.

Cartridges For Southeast Alaska

When hunting shifts to southeastern Alaska, or to any part of the Gulf of Alaska region, the situation changes drastically. Near the coast, it is more difficult to choose a cartridge for all-around hunting than choosing one for the interior or the arctic. In the Southeast, you will be likely hunting game the size of goats, Sitka blacktail deer or black bears, none of which requires a very potent cartridge. Complications arise because almost any time you are hunting these animals, you are either in, or passing through brown bear country. You won't need a lot of killing power for the little stuff, but meeting a big bear in the alders and devil's club close enough to rub noses with can mean big trouble if you only have a small-caliber deer rifle.

I once hunted Sitka blacktail in high, open country at timberline on Admiralty Island. We backpacked from the beach and it was a long, steep way up through tangled blow-down and typical rain forest. I carried a 6mm Rem. because it was light and handy—plenty of gun for the little deer. Fortunately, we didn't meet any brownies going in or out, and the open country at the top made it unlikely to surprise one without knowing he was there. Also, my friend, Carl Jacobson, packed a .358 Norma Mag. for insurance, but I've sometimes wondered if I was very bright when I could have used a 7mm Mag. or big .30 that would have handled either situation.

When hunting the big coastal brown bears, there is a wide difference of opinion as to what is the best medicine. Many local hunters who have clobbered brown bear with everything from .30-30s to .30-06s with good results will argue that there is little need for anything bigger. But, a lot of this depends on where you find the

When hunting in southeastern Alaska, most game will be the size of this blacktail deer, which requires a less potent cartridge. However, you should have something along that is powerful when passing through brown-bear country.

This line-up of belted cartridges can be considered ideal for various types of Alaskan hunting. The 7mm Wthby, 7mm Rem. and the wildcat 7mm Mashburn Super-Magnum (left) will take any Alaskan game under good conditions. The .300 Win. and .300 Wthby (middle) are "all-purpose" Alaskan cartridges; while the .338 Win., .340 Wthby, .358 Norma and .375 H&H (right) are ideal for moose and all big bears, especially brown bear in coastal jungle.

bear and whether you feel you are obligated to follow him into the thick stuff to finish the job if you wound him. Most of the guides who hunt brown bear use rifles chambered for cartridges from the .30 belted cases on up, cartridges like the .338 Win. Mag. and the reliable .375 H&H Mag.

Sitka-based brown bear guide Ben Forbes, who has either guided hunters to or killed some 160 of the big bears himself, uses a .450 Watts Mag. He says he doesn't always need it, but it sure is nice to have along when he does.

A brown bear was killed in its bed with a 7mm Rem. Mag. from about 150 yards. The bullet was a 175-grain Nosler that took the small brown bear in the center of the back and came out the chest. This doesn't prove the 7mm magnums are ideal brown bear cartridges, but they will do the job on any of them with the right bullet under the right conditions. For beach hunting where the bear is in the open and the shot can be chosen deliberately without the hunter being nose-to-nose with the bear, they are excellent, as are the various .300 magnums.

If you hunt the salmon streams in the fall where the shots may be unexpected and at only a few feet, then the big bores with well-constructed bullets are mighty attractive. For all-around brown bear hunting close-in on small, grass meadows or along a salmon creek, or at a fairly long range on the beaches or tidal flats, my preference is one of the .338, .35 or .375 cartridges. They are ideal for the longer shots, and plenty of gun for the close shots if the right bullet is used.

Rifles For Alaskan Hunting

Little can be said regarding the rifle you should use that wouldn't fit most other hunting in similar terrain. The light, short rifle may be badly overrated for mountain hunting. It's nice to have a short, light rifle when you start to the top of a high, rough mountain, but use of this same rifle may place limitations on the cartridge, reducing its effectiveness—the reason you bought it in the first place.

This is especially true of magnum cartridges. You buy a magnum because you want flat trajectory and a lot of punch when the bullet reaches the game. You also have to hit the animal somewhere near the right spot for it to be effective. Chop a 24- to 26-inch magnum barrel down to 20 or 22 inches, and, in most cases, you've lost several hundred fps in velocity. You also have added to the muzzle blast. And, if the barrel is turned down to lighten it, that likely didn't help accuracy any. Worst of all, if recoil bothers you, the lightened rifle adds plenty of that.

One thing for sure, you don't need a light, short rifle for normal hunting of brown bears in southeastern Alaska; most of the hunting will be done by boat where weight and bulk are of little consequence.

Scopes For Alaskan Hunting

Perhaps a few remarks on scopes for Alaskan hunting are in order. Not that scopes for Alaska are necessarily any different from those used for the same kind of hunting elsewhere, but you do hunt under somewhat different conditions. First, don't go power-happy. For big-game hunting you don't need more than 4X. If you miss an animal from the size of a deer on up, it wasn't because you couldn't see it well enough with a 4X scope or because a good hunting reticle covered too much of the animal. If that is the case, he was too far away to be shot at, anyway. In fact, for average shooting in the Southeast, 2.5-3X may be better because of the wider field of vision.

Be sure to check your scope for moisture proofing. Dunk it in water heated to around 135 degrees; if a stream of bubbles appears

When choosing a scope for Alaskan hunting, you will not need anything more powerful than a 4X for big game. This scope, manufactured by Leupold & Stevens, Inc., is available in 2.5X and 4X.

from any part of the scope, don't take it. If you're not hunting in the rain much of the time, it is strictly accidental. And, I've seen the weather just as lousy in the interior as on the coast. Better take an extra scope along just in case yours goes sour. And, it is wise to have an extra rifle.

8

The Magnums

Only one reason exists for using a magnum case: to squeeze more velocity from it than is possible with standard-powder-capacity cases. But, this recommendation must be modified based on the bore diameter. A case that is "magnum" for the .22 bore may be substandard in capacity for a .30 caliber, so pay attention to the bore diameter.

This applies not only to belted cases, but to those on the standard .30-06 head size. The standard .30-06 case is certainly of magnum capacity for any bore up to, and including the .25. When used in its many "blown-out" versions, it can be considered magnum in cartridges of somewhat larger bore diameters.

This coin has two sides, however. Many cartridges dubbed "magnum" are not true magnums in case capacity. For instance, the .222 Rem. Mag. has far less case capacity than the .225 Win., .224 Wthby, .22-250 Rem. or the good old .220 Swift cartridges. Remember to keep your eyes open.

Then, consider Remington's additions to the magnum line—the 6.5 Rem. Mag. and the .350 Rem. Mag. Both cases have roughly the same powder capacity as the standard .30-06 case. For the 6.5 with its .264 bore, this short-belted case may just possibly deserve the magnum tag, but the .350 is not in the magnum class.

In this chapter, we'll stick mostly to the big cases—the true magnums.

As far as 6mm magnum cases go, the choice is limited to only one commercial offering, the .240 Wthby Mag. Here it is shown with the standard 6mm Rem. (left) and a wildcat 6mm OKH on .300 H&H case (right).

6mm Magnums

Personally, none of the .22 calibers should be considered suitable for big-game hunting, so we'll skip them and start with the .243 or 6mm cartridges. The field of magnum cartridges in commercial form is very small, with only the .240 Wthby Mag. filling this gap as far as domestic cartridges are concerned. The .244 H&H is a true magnum, but was never chambered in commercial American rifles so it is known little here. The big .244 H&H is probably over bore capacity even with our modern slow powders, and will not give much higher velocity with the same bullet weights than the .240 Wthby or some of the wildcats that preceded it.

When the stubby .284 Winchester case hit the market, it was immediately pounced on by wildcatters and was necked up and down all the way from .224 to .357 (with one of the most popular diameters being the 6mm). The 6.5 Rem. Mag. was also necked down by half a millimeter. Both cartridges produced velocities superior to the standard .243 Win. and 6mm Rem. Both cases are adaptable to short, .308 action lengths, and both have somewhat more powder capacity than the .240 Wthby. There is, however, little difference in velocity between the two wildcats and the commercial Weatherby cartridge.

The advantages, if any, of the magnum 6mm cartridges as

compared to the standard Remington and Winchester offerings, are a definite increase in velocity and, therefore, flatter trajectory for easier hits at long range, and more energy upon impact. For example, it takes a fairly stiff load to push a 100-grain bullet at around 3,150 fps from the 6mm Rem. case out of a 24-inch barrel, while the .243 Win. will not do quite as well. The .240 Wthby will kick this same bullet along at better than 3,350 fps, using 55 grains of either H-4831 or Norma 205, or 56 grains of W-W 780 BR (and from the same 24-inch barrel).

While I have never killed any big game with either the 6mm-.284 or 6mm-6.5mm, I have killed a lot with the 6mm Rem. and some with the .240 Wthby. It was perhaps unfortunate that both the mule deer and the black bear killed with the .240 Wthby, while I was testing it, were at a range of less than 100 yards. I would have liked to compare it with long-range results produced by the 6mm Rem., because that's where extra punch would show up. I might say that all kills with the Weatherby cartridge were one-shot affairs, and the Nosler 95-grain bullet did an excellent job in all cases.

On long-range chuck shooting, there was a definite advantage in the flatter trajectory of the Weatherby. In fact, I was inclined to overshoot at longer distances until I got used to the .240. However, for the kind of shooting the average hunter will do with a 6mm caliber rifle, including many more rounds fired at varmints than at big game, I'm not sure that I would choose the big cases if I could have only one rifle of that caliber.

Barrel life, accuracy, economy and availability of ammunition are factors to consider. Also, there are less recoil and muzzle blast from the standard cartridges. Another consideration is that big cartridges heat up barrels many times faster than small ones. This can be a critical point when varmint shooting, both from the standpoint of barrel erosion and sustained accuracy after the first two or three shots.

.25 Magnums

The .25 caliber has been neglected for many years, much to the dismay of fans of the quarter-inch bore, and magnum cases are no exception. Again, Weatherby makes the only commercial magnum.

Here is a comparison of the various case sizes of the commercial .257 caliber cartridges (now that Remington has adopted the .25-06 as a factory cartridge): The old .250-3000

If we consider the .257 Rem. Roberts cartridge (left) the standard case, it is just possible that the .25-06 Rem. (center) leans on the magnum side. The .257 Wthby Mag. (right) is certainly magnum from belt to bullet.

Savage would drive 117- to 120-grain bullets to around 2,800 fps, the later .257 Roberts would propel the same bullets close to 2,900 fps, the .25-06 will kick them along at about 3,100 and the big-jugged .257 Wthby Mag. will spit them out at some 3,350 fps. All these figures are for 24-inch tubes (except Weatherby, which does its best from a 26-inch barrel). These cartridges should not be used in shorter barrels if you want magnum velocity.

It isn't hard to see that the .257 Wthby not only shoots flatter at long range, but packs a lot more punch at any range than the smaller cartridges. All this combined makes it superior to smaller cartridges for shooting big game. With the heavier bullet weights, it will give a good account of itself on game up to the size of caribou, and it is ideally suited to long-range shooting of deer-size animals. There is little doubt that the big Weatherby .25 also is effective varmint medicine, but few varmint hunters will care to shoot this cartridge for anything except occasional long-range work. Cases and powder for loading in varmint shooting quantities are rather expensive, and the serious varmint hunter would burn out a tube every now and then.

6.5mm Magnums

When we look at the metric 6.5, we find an unusual situation. The only cartridge for the 6.5mm bullet that was ever made in this

In 6.5mm, there are two cartridges with the magnum headstamp: the 6.5 Rem. Mag. and the .264 Win. Mag. With only .30-06 case capacity, the Remington case is certainly borderline between true magnum capacity for the .264 bore and a standard capacity case.

country for an American rifle was the .256 Newton, which was based on .30-06 brass. It was loaded by Western Cartridge Company until about 1938. However, several foreign 6.5mm cartridges have been used in this country in imported or custom rifles, the most popular being the 6.5 Mannlicher and the 6.5x55 Swedish military round. Both left a good deal to be desired by modern standards.

The first 6.5 cartridge to come along in recent years, factory-loaded and chambered in an American factory rifle, was the .264 Win. Mag. And, magnum it is in every sense of the word. It requires big doses of the very slowest burning powders like Hodgdon H-570 and H-870, while H-4831 is on the fast side with the heavy 140-grain bullet. The .264 Win. turned out to be one of those cartridges that kicked up a lot of smoke from various gun-buffs.

When it first appeared on the hunting scene, some who used it sung its praises, while others condemned it with equal vigor. This is nothing new for small-bore, high-velocity cartridges. Perhaps the main reason is that many hunters think that because of the high velocity delivered, bullet action and performance have little to do with killing effectiveness, and that shock caused by the ultra-high velocity will do the job. This is a big mistake when hunting heavy game because the bullet still has to get to the vital organs. Often, it has to plow through a lot of heavy bone and tough muscle to do it.

Another factor affecting the .264 cartridge was that many rifles chambered for it carried 22-inch barrels. Originally, the Model 70 rifle had a 26-inch tube. With this barrel length, attaining the 3,200 fps claimed by the factory ballistic sheets for the 140-grain bullet was not too difficult. In fact, the Speer manual shows velocities of about 3,300 fps attained with three different slow powders from a 26-inch barrel. However, Winchester eventually chambered the Featherweight M70 with its 22-inch barrel for the .264, resulting in a velocity drop of some 200 fps, to about .270 Win. levels.

Muzzle jump and muzzle blast went up, and with most of those who used it in this stubby barrel length, popularity went down. Today, I know of no commercial American rifle with a 26-inch barrel chambered for the .264 cartridge. Both Winchester and Remington now use 24-inch barrels as their longest tubes.

Not until 1966 did Remington get on the .264 caliber bandwagon with the 6.5 Rem. Mag., which is a necked-down version of the .350 Rem. Mag. case. Actually, it is doubtful if the Remington cartridge can be called a true magnum, even though it sports a belt on the case. Powder capacity is very similar to the nearly 60-year-old Newton, and, with modern powders, velocity is about the same.

The main advantage, as some hunters see it, is that the 6.5 Rem. is a very short case designed to work in the short Remington Model 600 action. The Remington cartridge would step a 120-grain bullet along at nearly 3,000 fps from the little carbine's 18½-inch tube, with good IMR-4350 or H-4831 handloads. It didn't do so well with 140-grain bullets, as the top velocity was about 2,800 fps. Then, in 1969, Remington decided to chamber the Model 700 rifle for the 6.5 using a 24-inch barrel. This was the best move they had made in some time, and the cartridge took on new vigor. My own loading for the 6.5 in the M700 with the 24-inch barrel shows 3,125 fps for the 120-grain Speer bullet without excessive pressures, although lighter loads gave somewhat better accuracy. A maximum load of Norma 205 gave the Speer 140-grain bullet a velocity of 3,072 fps, but accuracy was very poor with any load.

All this shows that the 6.5 Rem. Mag. is a pretty potent package from a 24-inch barrel and is ideally suited to shooting antelope, deer, sheep or similar-size game at all ranges. But, there is one problem: When Remington chambered the M700 for the 6.5, they used the short action designed for the length of the .308

In .270 caliber, we have only two commercial cartridges: the venerable .270 Win. (left) as the standard case and the .270 Wthby Mag. (right). There are no foreign cartridges made in that caliber; it is strictly American with not too many American wildcats.

cartridge. So, it is impossible to change overall factory cartridge length, allowing bullets to be seated out farther. This definitely proves to be a downfall when using the M700.

.270 Magnums

It seems a little unusual that the .270 caliber was never wildcatted on the magnum side more than it was. Maybe most gun-buffs thought the .270 Win. was good enough as is. Consequently, there is only one known commercial magnum cartridge in that diameter, the .270 Wthby Mag. The .270 Wthby is on the same case as the .257 and 7mm Wthby Magnums—not an especially large-capacity case as magnum cases go. Perhaps one reason the .270 was never wildcatted more, especially in magnum jugs, is because many thought burning that much powder behind a .270 caliber bullet was a waste when a 7mm would do anything the .270 would do and better. Also, for many years there were no suitably heavy bullets for the .270, so hunters of heavy game didn't get too excited about it.

The .270 Wthby is, however, a good cartridge; with bullets of 150 grains and over it is adequate for any North American hoofed game. It will drive the 150-grain bullet some 300 fps faster than the .270 Win. will, but, again, it should not be used in short barrels if you want velocity and efficiency.

Forerunner of all 7mm cartridges, the 7x57 Mauser (left), is followed by the recent .284 Win., which gives higher velocity, but is not in magnum class. Next is 7x61 Sharpe & Hart, 7mm Wthby Mag., 7mm Rem. Mag. (all commerical), and the wildcat 7mm Mashburn Super Magnum, which gives higher velocity than any of the commercial numbers.

7mm Magnums

With the possible exception of the .30 caliber, no bullet size has been subjected to more experimentation than the 7mm, especially with the big cases. The original 7mm cartridge, the 7x57 Mauser, came along in about 1892, gaining popularity both as a military round and hunting cartridge throughout the world. In about 1907, the British firm of Rigby brought out an almost identical rimless cartridge. Five or six years later, Holland & Holland unveiled what was probably the first 7mm magnum, the .275 H&H head size. It is a smaller case, more on the order of the 7x61 Sharpe & Hart or the 7mm Wthby Mag.

It seems that the 7mm Wthby Mag. was the first American-made 7mm magnum to attain commercial status. It was followed by the 7x61 S&H which was imported into this country in the Schultz & Larsen rifles, with ammunition loaded by Norma. There have been many custom rifles also chambered for the 7x61. In the meantime, everyone was busy designing 7mm cartridges with big cases—Ackley, Barnes and Mashburn being among the best known. Some of these were made on short brass from the .300 H&H case. At the same time, a number of 7mm cartridges were developed on smaller .30-06 brass—the .285 OKH or 7mm-06 which were one and the same, and a few blown-out versions of the same case.

So much smoke curled up around the various big sevens that Remington finally joined the group with a commercial 7mm magnum loaded in their own brass and chambered in Remington rifles. They simply took the .264 Win. Mag. case and necked it up to 7mm, something that was done by wildcatters as soon as the .264 was born. Why Winchester didn't do this originally, instead of making it a 6.5 is hard to say. Anyway, the 7mm Rem. Mag. has become one of the most popular American big-game cartridges.

There is little doubt that the 7mm magnums in general, the Remington in particular, deserve this popularity. Not that the Remington is so far ahead of the other two commercial big sevens, but all the big American ammunition manufacturers, as well as most foreign companies, load ammo for it. There is also a great variety of bullets available to the handloader, bullets ranging from the 110 grains for varmints up to 175- to 180-grain sockers for deep penetration on heavy game. With the advent of these many bullets of various shapes and designs, the 7mm magnums have acquired an enviable reputation for sure, quick long-range killing of big game of all sizes. It's a reputation that is well deserved.

I long ago lost track of the number of big-game animals I have taken with various 7mm caliber cartridges. I have used four different 7mm cartridges extensively for hunting, and tested many others on the rifle range.

Everything considered, the 7mm magnums—be they commercial or wildcat—are among the best cartridges for taking all kinds of American big game under all conditions. However, I should modify this somewhat in regard to hunting the big Alaskan brown bears. Even with a 175-grain Nosler bullet, the 7mm is not ideal for hunting in some of the dense brush of coastal bear country. But, for open-country hunting, mountain or plains, where long shots are the rule rather than the exception and for all hoofed game, they are supreme. Some of the big .30s are almost as flat and pack more wallop, but they also kick harder in the same weight rifle; that's something to think about in precision long-range shooting.

Time-tested .30-06 (left) is compared with magnums in commercial form, past and present. Next is the old .30 Newton (perhaps the first commercial Magnum .30 caliber ever produced), the .300 H&H, the .308 Norma Mag., the .300 win. Mag. and the .300 Wthby Mag., which has the velocity edge on all the others.

.30 Magnums

The .30 caliber magnums are, without doubt, the most popular of all the big-jugged cartridges. And, nearly all other magnum cartridges, no matter what the caliber, are based on the .300 H&H case. However, our own American .30 magnum, the .30 Newton, preceded it by some seven years, and it was not until 1925 that the .300 H&H was loaded by Western Cartridge Company. No commercial American rifles were chambered for the .300 H&H until Winchester brought out the M70 in 1937.

It seems the .30 Newton was actually the first .30 caliber magnum produced on a commercial basis anywhere in the world. For those not familiar with the Newton cartridge, the capacity was about the same as that of the .300 H&H but the case was shorter, rimless instead of belted, with a body size just ahead of the extractor groove of the same diameter as the belt on the .300 H&H. The shoulder diameter was also much larger than that of the fast-taper .300 H&H, measuring about .491.

In 1937, Winchester chambered the Model 70 for the .300 H&H. Of course, custom rifle makers, such as Griffin & Howe, had long been chambering for it, and imported rifles using the cartridge were also coming into the country in ever-increasing numbers. Several magnum cartridges were made up on the full-length, .300 or .375 H&H cases that were blown out by fireforming to give greater powder capacity, but Roy Weatherby's .300 was to become the only commercial version.

Little doubt remains that the .300 Wthby Mag. is the most potent of the big .30s in commercial form, and perhaps is as widely used today as even the time-honored .300 H&H. Anything the old .300 H&H will do, the .300 Wthby will do better. It is not only easier to hit an animal on the far side of the canyon, but it hits him with a lot more punch. That's what counts.

The .300 Wthby went commercial in about 1948 when ammunition appeared under the Weatherby label. The .308 Norma Mag. from the Swedish firm of Norma made its debut in this country in 1960 in what might be called a semi-wildcat, by way of unprimed Norma cases. I believe that Kodiak was the first firm in this country to offer rifles chambered for the cartridge that could be considered commercial, although Norma didn't deliver loaded ammo until nearly two years later.

Early in the summer of 1961, Kodiak agreed to have a rifle chambered for the .308 Norma ready for testing on an Alaskan hunt I was making in September. I got a couple of boxes of brass and dies from RCBS, a supply of Nosler 180- and 200-grain bullets to work up loads, and was ready to give the new, short .30 magnum a wringout on heavy Alaskan game. But, the gun did not arrive until a week after I had left for Alaska. Maybe I was lucky because it kicked its way through the recoil abutment later that fall. However, I did find it very accurate, flat and powerful with the loads I worked up. And I knocked off a bull elk and a muley buck before it shot loose.

Most gun-buffs assumed that Winchester would come along with a big .30 on the .338 Win. Mag. case soon after that cartridge made its appearance in 1958, and that it would be simply a necked down version, like the wildcat .30-338. This was not the case. When the .300 Win. Mag. finally appeared on the scene in 1963, it was built on the same basic case as the .338, but it was considerably longer from head to shoulder—about halfway between the .338 Win. and the .300 Wthby. The .300 Win. case holds six more grains of IMR-4350 when filled to the base of the neck than the .338 case does. However, in order to hold the .300 down to about the same overall loaded length as the .338, bullets were designed to be seated with their bases far down in the case below the shoulder, especially those from 180 grains and up.

Like the 6.5 Rem. Mag., the .300 Win. Mag. has such a short neck and overall loaded factory cartridge length, that to load for normal factory throating, the bullets must be seated so deep that many will not hold in the case.

Even so, the .300 Win. Mag. is a good cartridge, giving close to the same velocity as the .300 Wthby from the same barrel length. I used one extensively and killed deer, sheep, elk and grizzly with it. Performance with both 180- and 200-grain Noslers was excellent in all cases.

Many hunters consider the .30 magnums the most versatile of all the magnum cartridges. In many ways, they have an argument that is hard to refute. The big .30s will shoot just about as flat over all hunting ranges as will the magnums of smaller bore—if bullets of 165 to 200 grains are used and are the correct shape for long-range work. It has also been proven many times that a big .30 is just as accurate for long-range work as the best of the smaller cartridges. So, if you can handle the recoil, you'll have no trouble putting the bullet where you want it. And, with 200- to 220-grain bullets of correct design, it has plenty of penetration and wallop for the heaviest North American game—most Asiatic and African game, too.

Like the big cases in smaller calibers, the .30 magnums do their best with slow powders. For the lighter bullets, IMR-4350 (or other powders of similar quickness) is about right for obtaining the highest velocity at lowest pressure. With bullets of 150 grains and up, either IMR-4350 or H-4831 is top-drawer. For the heaviest bullets of 200 to 220 grains, H-4831 or Norma 205 have the edge. In the .300 Wthby, or its equivalent in powder capacity, the very slowest powder like H-870 or H-570 will give top velocities with the heaviest bullets. H-870 is probably the best because it does not need to be compressed as much, since it is more dense. However, H-870 and H-570 will beat H-4831 by very little.

.33 Magnums

One of the most popular magnums for heavier game, across North America, Africa and Asia, is the .338 Win. Mag. It's a comparatively new number unveiled in 1958. As a magnum, the

The .338 caliber is one of the most versatile for shooting heavy game under nearly any condition. The first .33 cartridges were of British origin and of true .33 diameter, as were most of the American wildcats. Some famous wildcats were the .333 OKH on .30-06 case (left), .333 OKH Belted and .334 OKH, both on .300 or .375 H&H cases. Next, is a wildcat by the author: a .338 on the .300 Win. case; then, the .338 Win. Mag. and the .340 Wthby.

.338 caliber was new; as a bullet diameter, it was not. In about 1902, Winchester brought out the .33 Win. cartridge for the Model 86 Winchester and, despite the .33 headstamp, the bullet diameter was actually .338. No other commercial cartridges of this caliber were made in the U.S. until the .338 Win. Mag. appeared. Newton did make a .338 Newton on the .30 Newton case that was supposed to deliver a 200-grain bullet at 3,000 fps, but this was, I believe, of .333 caliber rather than .338. It apparently was never loaded or chambered on a commercial basis, even in Newton rifles.

The British made at least three .33 caliber cartridges—the .333 Jeffery rimmed and rimless and the BSA Belted. These were true .333 diameter bullets, and British loading sent a 250-grain bullet along at 2,400 to 2,500 fps. Even though not what we would call magnums by today's standards, the .333s won great praise from hunters for shooting medium-sized African game.

Probably because of a lack of suitable bullets in this country, little if anything was done with the .33 caliber until 1936 or 1937 when the .333 OKH was developed on the .30-06 case and the .334 OKH on the full-length .375 H&H case. These were both true .333 cartridges, and the first bullets were imported from Kynoch in England. Later, Fred Barnes made bullets in this size, as did Speer. In fact, Barnes also designed a couple of cartridges for his .333 bullets, and several others also go on the tailgate of the .333 wagon.

When the .338 Win. Mag. first appeared, it was advertised as giving the 250-grain bullet 2,750 fps. Later, these velocity figures were dropped to 2,700—exactly why I do not know. Maybe pressures were a little above those desired by Winchester; maybe accuracy was better at the lower figure. Anyway, it is possible to get around 2,800 fps from a 24-inch barrel with a 250-grain bullet in the .338 case with reasonably good accuracy and pressures that are not prohibitive. So, it would seem that the 2,750 figure can readily be attained with the right powder.

The 200-grain bullet is listed at 3,000 fps by Winchester. You can beat this by about 50 fps with heavy doses of IMR-4350 and still get good accuracy. The 300-grain bullet is not particularly desirable in this caliber, except on very heavy game at close range in the brush. The big round point and rather low velocity of about 2,450 fps takes much of the long-range potential away from the cartridge. I prefer the 275-grain Speer with its better shape that can be loaded for a velocity of 2,650 without undue pressure symptoms, even for close-in work on heavy stuff. Actually, my observations indicate the 250-grain bullet with a decent point and controlled expansion, like the Nosler or the better-shaped Bitterroot Bonded Core, is the ideal weight in this caliber for all-around shooting. The 225-grain Hornady with its outstanding long-range potential is another good bet for long distances, but I have never fired one into a heavy animal to find out how well it holds up.

One of my favorite bullets for long-range shooting in either the .338 Win. or the .340 Wthby is the excellent 210-grain Nosler. This bullet has about the same velocity as the 200-grain, but will hold up much better on heavy muscle and bone. I have found that with elk, unless the bull is quartering or end-on, the bullet is seldom found in the animal.

The .340 Wthby is basically the same as the .338 Win., only more of it. Chronograph checks on my own .340 with its 23½-inch barrel shows better than 2,900 fps with a 250-grain Nosler bullet and H-4831 powder. You can get another 50 fps by using Norma 205 with apparently the same pressure level. One would think that a very slow powder like H-870 would be ideal with 250- or 275-grain bullets in the big Weatherby case, but this isn't true. Even this very dense powder fills the case to where bullets can no longer be seated. A 98-grain charge gave too much compression and very light pressure, providing a velocity of only 2,729 fps with the 250-grain Nosler.

For heavier American game, like elk, moose and grizzly or Alaska brown bear, at long range, there are no better cartridges than the .338 magnums—if the hunter shoots well. They have no peers on any heavy American game under almost any condition if the right bullet is used. Properly constructed, 250- to 300-grain bullets will give more penetration than the same bullet weights in the .375. If you want long range with a lot of punch on the far end, the 200- to 225-grain will do as well as anything. A drop test I made out to 400 yards with a .340 Wthby and 210-grain Nosler bullets which were loaded to 3,125 fps—a rather mild load for this rifle—proves this point. Sighted 3 inches high at 100 yards, the bullets landed 4 inches up at 200 yards, 1-inch high at 300 yards and only 7 inches low at 400 yards. How many cartridges can top this? Not many.

.35 Magnums

While .35 caliber cartridges have always been prevalent on the American gun scene, magnums in this caliber have never been particularly popular or numerous. Again, it was a Newton cartridge that was the first .35 commercial magnum made in this country. For that matter, it was the only one, because the later .358 Norma Magnum is not an American cartridge, is not loaded here and American firms do not chamber rifles for it on a production basis. True, the .350 Rem. Mag. has the name, but it certainly is not a true magnum cartridge as far as velocity or case capacity is concerned. It will not do anything the .35 Whelen will not do, being of about the same case capacity as the .35 Win. of the early 1900s. Increased velocity results from the actions in which it is used rather than in the cartridge.

If you want to shoot a true .35 magnum today, and not a wildcat, you will have to settle for the .358 Norma (which is indeed a potent package that delivers a 250-grain bullet at around 2,800 fps). I have done some load testing with the .358 Norma, but no hunting. It has potential on heavy game with correctly designed

We have a choice of three .375 caliber magnum cartridges in commercial offerings: the .375 H&H Mag. (left), which is considered by many as the finest all-around cartridge for all game dimensions in the world; the .375 Wthby Mag. (center), which is no longer chambered by Weatherby, but has ammo still available; and, the power-house .378 Wthby Mag. (right).

bullets. The lack of many good .358 caliber bullets may be one reason why the .35 magnum has not become more popular. Also, many hunters do not think they need this much bullet diameter for any American game, and it does churn up a bit of recoil. Personally, I feel that if a .35 magnum is needed for hunting the game at hand, a bullet of at least 275 or 300 grains is required to have enough sectional density for deep penetration. If you don't need deep penetration, you don't need a .35 Mag.!

.37 Magnums

If there is one magnum cartridge that can lay claim to being the most popular magnum for game of all sizes from deer to elephants, that cartridge is the .375 H&H. Originally made in England in both belted and rimmed versions for use in bolt-action and double rifles, the old .375 is still considered the ideal cartridge for all medium-sized game, whether the feet are hooves or pads. Hunters also swear by it for the heaviest game found in either Africa or Asia, as well as those who use it for everything found in North America from pronghorn to polar bear. These .375 fans think that if there is an all-around cartridge for use on all game sizes anywhere in the world, the .375 H&H is that cartridge. They do have a strong point.

The .375 H&H shoots quite flat with lighter bullets, and digs in

While there have been many wildcat .45s, there are only two commercial cartridges available: the .458 Win. Mag. (left), and the most powerful, American, commercial cartridge, the .460 Wthby Mag. (right).

deep with heavier ones. It packs enough wallop to be lethal on nearly anything and has enough diameter with solid, non-expanding bullets to do a good job on the big stuff.

The .375 Wthby, which is a blown-out version of the same case burning more powder and giving somewhat higher velocities, is more of the same. The newer .378 Wthby Mag. is a little different story. It's an entirely different case with much more powder capacity—which we might consider as a belted .416 Rigby with about the same capacity.

Comparing the three commercial .375 cartridges using a 300-grain bullet, the .375 H&H will boost it along at 2,550 to 2,600 while the .375 Wthby is 100 to 150 fps faster, and the big .378 Wthby goes over 2,900 fps, with a muzzle energy of over 5,600 foot-pounds.

My own experience with the .375 H&H is that for the best results in both accuracy and velocity, powders of a burning rate of 4064 to IMR-4350 are the best choice. The larger .378 case should do its best with the heavier bullets with IMR-4350 or H-4831 burning rates.

.45 Magnums And Up

The next and latest step in commercial, big-bore American magnums comes in the form of the .458 Win. Mag. and the .460

Wthby Mag. Both use the .458 diameter bullet of 500 and 510 grains. But, while the Winchester cartridge pushes it along at a bit over 2,100 fps, the big Wthby that is built on the .378 case gives it 2,700 fps plus.

This last group of big bores, like the .40 calibers, have little use in American hunting. They were designed to be used on the heaviest African and Asian game. I know of a guide or two who packs a .458 Win. when hunting brown bear. When you have to trail a wounded brownie in heavy alders where 20 feet is long range, this gun gives you a little extra confidence. On average, though, these big-bore cartridges are not needed, nor are they desirable for the average hunter. He doesn't need this kind of power, and he can't handle the recoil and put the big bullet where it should go.

9

Rangefinding Facts And Fallacies

Range estimation and projectile drop have given hunters fits ever since our cave-dwelling ancestors first discovered they could send a flint-tipped stick to longer distances by using another stick bowed by a thong tied to each end. Soon, they found that while the stick with the sharp rock point would penetrate and kill animals at rather long distances, the hunter still had to figure out how high it had to be pointed above the intended dinner to find the mark. They surely didn't visualize at first the range in yards or meters, but it could be that this is when the value of pacing off distance took root.

With the invention of gunpowder, guns and the round ball, the range at which animals could be hit and killed started to increase. As the accuracy and killing power of the round ball increased, so did the desire to shoot it at longer distances. The accuracy to hit an animal, and the punch to kill it at longer ranges is of little value if the hunter can't figure out how much the ball will drop below point of aim at the extended range, or, in fact, what that certain range actually is.

As the years passed, the round ball was replaced by the conical bullet, and the smoothbore muzzleloader gave way to the rifled tube. The metallic cartridge soon followed. Soft lead-cores were clad in copper jackets, and smokeless powder backed them up for greatly increased velocity to afford even flatter trajectory and

This horizontal wire reticle system indicates that this pronghorn is 300 yards distant, if the buck measures 18 inches from back to belly. Because of the difficulty in precisely bracketing an animal, and size variation, such devices should be used for estimation only.

longer-range killing power. This should have made sure hits at longer ranges much easier, and it did. But, as rifles and cartridges became more lethal at longer distances, exact estimation of distance became even more critical. Anyone with a little practice can learn to judge range to within a few feet at 100 yards, and with a bit more practice out to maybe 200 yards, but at distances beyond that point it gets complicated.

But, tough range-judging conditions are not of any great concern to an experienced hunter if the animal is no more than a couple of hundred yards away. Even if it is farther away, say 300 yards, he is still in good shape with today's flat-shooting cartridges on big-game animals if the rifle is sighted in properly. He also isn't hurting too badly with most of the hot varmint cartridges if the guns are also sighted in correctly. Of course, there still are a lot of hunters and far too many guides who can't tell the difference between 200 and 400 yards. Beyond 100 yards, they are in trouble most of the time. For these fellows, rangefinding devices should be beneficial at any range beyond 100 yards, whereas many of us don't need one until the range extends to 300 yards or more.

For hunting use, rangefinders come in two categories: the kind that are built within the hunting scope and are part of, or linked to, the sighting reticle, and the various instruments made for range estimation that are carried as part of the hunter's equipment.

Rangefinders Within The Hunting Scope

Rangefinders found within hunting scopes depend entirely on game size for range estimation, while most of the instruments made especially for rangefinding use the split-image rangefinding approach—the same system used in many cameras based on the triangulation principle. As far as the hunter is concerned, the principle on which any rangefinding device is made is of little importance—it is how well it performs that counts.

First, let's take a look at the reticle rangefinders found within hunting scopes. The first rangefinder, of this design, is the Weaver double cross hairs arrangement. There are two horizontal wires spaced to give a six-minute angle gap between them. This spacing is fixed and remains constant at all times, and at all ranges: 6 inches at 100 yards, 12 inches at 200 yards, etc. When using this instrument, you must know the approximate depth of the animal's body from back to belly. Hold either the top or bottom wire to ride the back or bottom of the chest, and see how much of the body is left over, or how much it lacks filling the space between the wires. Then, assuming you know the animal's body depth, you can estimate the distance by doing quick calculations in 6-inch increments. As an example, a buck deer is supposed to be 18 inches from hairline to hairline. If he fits snugly between the two wires, he will be 300 yards from the rifle muzzle.

This all sounds quite simple and suggests quite accurate range estimation, but a number of bugs can contaminate the broth. As range increases it becomes more difficult to know how much daylight there is between the buck's back or belly and the corresponding crosshair. By the same token, it also becomes more difficult to hold the reticle steady, keeping it in perfect alignment with the back or chest line while estimating the amount of daylight seen in comparison with the animal's broadside view. Last, but not least, deer, like hunters, come in various sizes. There is a lot of difference in the body depths of various deer species and subspecies. Take mule deer as an example: Many young bucks are

According to most information on deer body depths, an average buck is supposed to measure 18 inches from back to brisket. While this whitetail could well be considered average, he is certainly not in the trophy buck class, and much smaller than a big mule deer buck. Small bucks may not span more than 16 inches, while a big one may measure more than 22.

shot that will not measure more than 16 to 17 inches, while some old bucks that are really in the trophy class will go in excess of 22 inches. Remember, we are not concerned with the vital area or the actual body depth, but with what we see from hairline to hairline. There will also be a difference of 2 to 3 inches in the same big buck from September, when he has just put on his fall, gray coat, to late November when that coat grows to winter length.

The picture becomes even more confusing when the average hunter, or even the long-time professional, tries a rangefinding reticle on other game: goat, elk, caribou, moose and bear. Not much published information is available to tell you how deep these animals are through the rib cage. The information that does exist normally shows greater error than that for deer. Some of this information gives the depth of elk at 24 inches. If the fellow who made that measurement read his tape correctly, some areas must have elk that are a lot smaller than any I have ever killed. I've

One difficulty with reticle-type rangefinders is that they are dependent upon the "average size" of various animals. According to some sources, an average elk will run 24 inches from top of shoulder to bottom of chest, hairline to hairline. This one will run 32 or 33 inches, and some will measure a full 3 feet.

measured a number of mature cows that spanned more than that, and a lot of old trophy-class bulls that went 34 to 36 inches. If you misjudge an elk's body depth by a foot, the best rangefinding reticle ever made is of no use whatsoever.

Sure, there have been rangefinding reticle advances since Bill Weaver first produced his simple model, but they are still no better than the hunter's body depth estimation of the animal he is hunting. Take the stadia wire system as used in some Redfield models and some other scopes. I've tested most of them on objects of known size at various unknown ranges and then measured it off. They are very accurate if you have *plenty of time* and a *steady rest*, but you still have to depend on your knowledge of the animal's size to make use of that accuracy.

The advantage of the stadia wire system is, of course, that if you do have the time and can perfectly bracket the animal, it will tell you almost exactly what the range is. (That is, *if* you peg the hairline-to-hairline depth correctly.) Systems like the Redfield Accu-Trac give the range reading on the reticle setup, while older models used a cam arrangement that raised the elevation the right amount for the range. (That is, if the cam fit your particular load, including bullet ballistic coefficient and muzzle velocity.) But, for a number of reasons, even these more sophisticated arrangements become increasingly more difficult to use when ranges extend beyond 300 yards or so.

With the stadia wire system, you don't have to guess the difference between what the two wires cover and the animal's depth ranges over, or under, the range where the fixed system brackets the animal. You can adjust the wires to bracket an animal of any depth at any range, and they either read that range or have it set automatically, whichever the scope provides. But, there is a little more to it than that. Even assuming you do know the animal's depth, you will still have to adjust the stadia wires to perfectly bracket it.

The first problem that occurs is the animal needs to be stationary and broadside (or nearly so). If the animal is facing toward or away from the hunter, it is extremely difficult to know when you are bracketing the body depth perfectly. If the animal is lying down, it is impossible to get a correct reading. It is also difficult if the animal is standing facing steeply either up or downhill. The second problem, and perhaps the most frustrating one, is finding a position where the rifle can be held steady enough for a perfect bracket while adjusting the stadia wires. A fellow testing one of the stadia wire scopes said that after a little practice he had no problem adjusting the scope from the offhand position. He either had more than his share of arms and hands, or would make a great Metallic Silhouette shot!

I don't seem to be able to do it accurately even on a cardboard box with straight lines, unless I have a steady rest and plenty of time. And, speaking of time, this is often a commodity there is precious little of. While you are doing all this fidgeting and adjusting, the buck, bull or ram may just start moving around or disappear. If it is already moving, either just meandering along or taking off, forget trying to estimate range with any kind of rangefinder.

One more point that has never endeared any of the stadia wire scopes to me is that they are all made in variable models, which usually means more bulk and weight. Although some hunters don't mind the "extra" load, these scopes can be quite cumbersome.

Rangefinding Instruments That Hunters Carry

Now, let's take a look at rangefinders that are made for the hunter to carry along while hunting. There have been a number of these over the past few years, most of which I have tested, and few of them still being marketed—which should tell the hunter something.

As mentioned earlier, most of these rangefinders are designed along with split-image range focusing systems similar to cameras without through-the-lens focusing. Accuracy depends on the distance between the two viewing windows at the instrument's ends. The greater the range, the wider this spacing must be to retain accuracy, as well as the ease and speed in setting it. There is little reason to go into the several makes and models that have cropped up from time to time, because they are similar in principle and nearly all have the same failings as a useful tool to either the varmint or big-game hunter.

The best one I have tested to date is the Ranging Rangematic 1000, which uses a 6X monocular. One reason it is superior is because it is quite long with the windows nearly a foot apart. Of course, being long, it is pretty bulky and not especially light for a sheep or goat hunter to pack up a mountain. And, the main problems I found in testing it were some of the same prob-lems found in scope reticle rangefinders. True, you do not need to know the animal's size, because you twist a dial until his various parts fit tightly together, which is one up for the Rangematic. But, you'll find that you do have to hold the instrument quite steady to accurately bring the two images together. As range increases, steadiness becomes ever more critical. After checking objects of all sizes and shapes, including many animals at various ranges, I found accuracy was good out to about 300 yards. After that, it became more difficult to obtain an accurate reading. It also became increasingly slower because you had to allow the needle to go back and forth past the reading a number of times to make sure you were correct. Even then, the range indication proved to be off more times than on (when checked against measured distances). After the range reached 500 yards, my best efforts were normally off by 50 to 100 yards, far too much to be of value on an antelope or deer.

Perhaps the biggest problem with this type of rangefinder is light. If looking across flat land with bright sunlight, the heat waves make it impossible to focus accurately. Also, if the animal is in shadow or blends in with the background, it is difficult to know

For top accuracy, any rangefinder will require the use of a steady rest when used at the longer ranges. Here, a fallen tree stump is used to steady the Ranging "Rangematic 1000."

when the image is in perfect focus. (Close isn't good enough at long range.) Mist, rain and snow will give you fits also. Under any of these conditions, or at the longer ranges, it is time-consuming to take an accurate reading. And, even the specs on the instrument admit errors at ranges over 500 yards. By the time you feel fairly certain that you have an accurate reading, the animal you intended to shoot may no longer be in sight. Actually, this type of rangefinder is much more useful to the varmint hunter than to the big-game hunter for several reasons. For most varmint hunting, the extra weight and bulk matter little. Time is of little importance on ground squirrels, chucks and sod poodles. But, because of the lack of time, these rangefinders are useless on jackrabbits and coyotes. Another reason they are more valuable to the varmint hunter is because they are accurate up to about 300 yards, which will cover the big-end of most varmint hunting.

But, one point that should be remembered in varmint hunting is that you'll hit few ground squirrels at 300 yards with the best varmint rifle and cartridge. And, with the hot numbers that are capable of killing cleanly beyond that range, you'll have to do very little guessing to hit a chuck at 300 yards with proper sight settings. This means that if you sight a hot .22-250 load to impact 1.5-inch high at 100 yards, you can hold center of a feeding chuck and kill him every time out to about 275 yards. You can also kill him with a hold on the top of his shoulder at 300 yards. You'll find it hard to perfectly focus a rangefinder or a rangefinding reticle on a chuck at 400 yards.

In big-game hunting the same situation holds true, only more so. With cartridges in the range of the .308 Win. or even the .30-06, rangefinding equipment accurate up to about 300 to 350 yards could be quite useful if the hunter has time to use it. But, with the flattest shooting numbers it is of little value within ranges that should be considered by even the most qualified riflemen. There are three reasons for this. First, with cartridges that develop velocities of over 3,000 fps with bullets of good ballistic coefficient, and sighted to impact 3 inches high at 100 yards, you can hold in the center of the ribs and get a vital hit on a buck deer or ram at 325 yards or so, depending on the bullet's actual velocity and ballistic coefficient. You don't have to do any range guessing, take any time adjusting stadia wires or other rangefinding apparatus, or try to figure the animal's correct size; you just hold dead center and touch it off. Second, not too many hunters can regularly hit a deer's vital area every time at more than 300 yards, anyway. And, third, if your cartridge isn't flat enough for this kind of sighting and holding at that range, it is not packing too much wallop when it gets there. This may cause the cartridge to not expand its bullets well enough at over 300 yards, which, in turn, prevents the tearing effect for killing shock.

If you use the right cartridge for shooting at long ranges where a rangefinder might prove handy, you probably do not have much use for the rangefinder, depending upon the limitations of your load and your own ability. Also, considering that the practical accuracy of either the reticle rangefinding scope or special rangefinding instruments falls off badly at longer distances, as well as the often vital time consumed in using them, it seems they are of little value to the hunter.

Perhaps the greatest value of rangefinders, whether part of a scope or a separate instrument, is their ability to help the hunter who can't tell 150 yards from 400 yards. But, even then, he is better off using a flat-shooting cartridge and sighting it for the longest range possible without the bullet's path being too high at the midpoint in the trajectory, about 3 inches high at 100 yards. Then, just hold center and forget about judging range. If the animal is so far away that the bullet lands low, chances are that the hunter couldn't hit the vital area if he did know the range and where to hold on the target. The hunter's judgement is important, with or without range-estimation devices. If your first instinct tells you that the animal looks too far away to hit in its vitals, then do not attempt the shot. A lot of wounded animals could be saved.

How Temperature Affects Velocity

Periodically, inquiries arise from hunters wanting to know what affect temperature has on rifle ammunition velocity. Usually, questions are somewhat more specific than that, regarding a certain cartridge and load. Normally, the questions refer to temperatures below the normal 70 degrees at which most velocities are taken. The reason for this is that most of those who are interested are big-game hunters, rather than varmint hunters. Also, most big-game hunting occurs in the fall and early winter when temperatures are likely to be low.

Another reason for the question being directed at lower-than-normal temperature rather than higher, is that most gun-writers often mention that loads worked up to near-maximum, at near the normal 70-degree temperature, are prone to be too hot on a hot day. But, little is said about what happens to a load that develops 3,000 fps at 70 degrees when the thermometer drops to the freezing point, or lower.

A year or so ago, a man who does most of his hunting in the whitetail country of the Northeast (where it gets cold during deer season) had an inquiry. He had missed a deer or two on cold mornings and wondered if it could be caused from the great loss in velocity he thought he was getting at zero temperature. He said a friend told him a certain cartridge was tested with a certain powder, resulting in velocity loss of about 400 fps from the normal 70

Mountain goat hunters at high elevations may encounter extremely cold temperatures. Hunters should practice under these conditions to see if it changes their point of impact.

degrees to freezing. And, worse, the rifle had pointed more than 6 inches low at 100 yards at the lower temperature as compared to sighting at 70 to 75 degrees. I was quite certain that the "friend" was wrong, but I didn't have the experimental data to back it up.

The only information readily available to the shooter, whether he uses factory ammunition or rolls his own, is found in the Speer reloading manual. This information is based on a gradual velocity increase in 10-degree jumps from zero to 100 degrees Fahrenheit. It shows that as velocity increases from 60 degrees, apparently used as normal, the loss or gain above or below that point also increases. The chart is, as any chart of this kind would have to be, based on averages with no allowances made for bore diameter, case capacity or type of powder. The text with the Speer chart mentions that it was not made from actual firing of cartridges, but shows what can be expected from most cartridges as to what the trend will be.

This led me to do a little testing with the cartridge the inquiry referred to. The meager testing indicated there was much more to the velocity vs. temperature bit than most shooters assumed.

Those first tests indicated that there was no "blanket rule" that could be applied for velocity loss as temperatures went down. The first thing I found was that some powders were influenced more by temperature changes than other powders of similar burning rates. It also appeared that rumors suggesting that after a certain temperature was reached, say about freezing, velocity might not drop at all, in fact, could actually gain a little, were true. Of course, this also indicated that velocity gain or loss did not occur in an even curve, but could be subject to sudden dives, depending on the powder and cartridge used.

While the chart in the Speer manual covered a 100-degree range, which would take in 90 percent of the temperature changes encountered in hunting, it was decided that if tests were to be made they should go even further. We would have liked to have tested ammunition down to minus 40 degrees, but not having any freezing unit that would drop the thermometer much below minus 20 degrees, we were forced to use this as the temperature over the 70 degrees used to chronograph ammunition. However, it would be very unusual for anyone to hunt in a temperature of more than 120 degrees, so that was used as the high for testing.

This range of 140 degrees covers about 99 percent of the temperatures during which anyone will be firing. There will be a few shots fired at game in the North at temperatures lower than 20 degrees below zero, but these will be few. Except for polar bear hunting, and a little moose and caribou hunting from people who are native to the country being hunted, extremely little hunting is done with temperatures at minus 10 degrees (let alone minus 20 degrees). Conversely, few hunters will shoot varmints when the temperature soars over 100 degrees. Some African hunting may be done in hotter weather, but probably not at over 120 degrees. Of course, you can leave you ammo in the hot sun where it may reach as much as 150 degrees, but this is not recommended in the best shooting circles.

Testing Ammunition At Various Temperatures

Testing ammunition at temperatures as low as minus 20 degrees, or at 120 degrees at the high end, is not as simple as it might appear. Even with an indoor setup where temperature can be controlled to the normal 70 degrees, you have the problem of keeping ammunition at other temperatures long enough to fire it. A freezer proved capable of holding a low temperature of minus 24 degrees. When leaving the ammunition in the freezer for at least two hours, it was certain that all the powder equaled that temperature. The testing ammo and cartridges were put into a Thermos and placed in the freezer. This was done to hold the cold temperature while taking the ammo and cartridges to the shooting room and firing. Starting at minus 24 degrees, firing temperature was no higher than minus 20 degrees. For the zero reading, the freezer was held at minus 4 degrees. An accuracy-tested thermometer was placed in the freezer to check actual temperature with all settings.

For the 120-degree tests, an electric pot was partially filled with water. A can was submerged with ammunition inside, and a darkroom thermometer included with it. The temperature was held at 122 degrees with the ammunition in place for at least two hours before firing. This arrangement was set up right in the shooting room, so the test cartridges could be fired immediately after removal.

It is possible that the ammunition could have been a couple of degrees under the low-range readings, or a wee bit higher than the 120-degree reading, but certainly not less than the readings indicated on the chart. The normal, 70-degree reading was plus or minus no more than 2 degrees.

It is impossible to conduct complete tests for all popular cartridges with various bullet weights and powders without a specially financed project because of the time and money involved. The next best thing seemed to be selecting a few cartridges that ranged from fairly small caliber, small capacity cases to larger caliber, small to medium capacity cases as well as a sample of small and big bore magnum cases. This would cover at least some of the varmint and big-game hunting, as well as most of the big-game hunting situations. For this reason, we decided on the 6mm Rem., .308 Win., 7mm Rem. Mag. and the .340 Wthby Mag. Because all bullet weights could not be tested, a middle-of-the-range bullet weight for each cartridge was used.

Testing Powders

For powders, we used only those suitable for the best hunting loads. While all powders could not be covered in each case, most were covered that were suitable in one case or another. The list is still quite long, however, because all were tested at four different

Velocity-Temperature Tests: 6mm Remington

Powder	Charge	Primer	Temperature	Velocity	Remarks
N-205	47	CCI 200	-20°	3,072	Velocity quite normal
N-205	47	CCI 200	0°	3,090	at all temperatures, slightly
N-205	47	CCI 200	70°	3,082	higher as temperature goes up.
N-205	47	CCI 200	120°	3,057	Temperature-velocity change, 33 fps*
H-450	47	CCI 250	-20°	2,912	Gradual increase in
H-450	47	CCI 250	0°	2,900	velocity as temperature climbs.
H-450	47	CCI 250	70°	3,033	
H-450	47	CCI 250	120°	3,061	Temperature-velocity change, 161 fps
IMR-4831	46	CCI 200	-20°	2,959	
IMR-4831	46	CCI 250	-20°	2,863	
IMR-4831	46	CCI 200	0°	2,941	Note that magnum primers
IMR-4831	46	CCI 200	70°	2,987	give 96 fps less velocity
IMR-4831	46	CCI 250	70°	3,010	at -20° than standard (No. 200)
IMR-4831	46	CCI 200	120°	3,015	primers!
IMR-4831	46	CCI 250	120°	3.073	Temperature-velocity change, 56 fps
W-W 760	45	CCI 250	-20°	2,978	Velocity jumps drastically
W-W 760	45	CCI 250	0°	2,962	at high temperatures.
W-W 760	45	CCI 250	70°	3,060	
W-W 760	45	CCI 250	120°	3,228	Temperature-velocity change, 266 fps

*Note that N-205 actually gave higher velocity at temperatures below normal 70° than above. Actually this difference could be caused by conditions other than temperature changes.

The results shown in this chart were obtained from using the 6mm Remington Model 700 ADL, 20-inch barrel; Remington cases, weight, 180 grains; and Sierra flat base 85-grain Spitzer.

temperatures. So, we won't list them all here.

I heard, without complete authentication, that both IMR-4350 and H-4831 (the old surplus type) were very susceptible to temperature changes. Limited tests had pointed in that direction also, and the complete tests proved, beyond a doubt, that this was true, at least in the big cases where both powders stand near the top for squeezing velocity from most hunting bullet weights. In the 7mm Rem. Mag., the velocity variation between minus 20 degrees and 120 degrees was 142 fps for H-4831 with the 160-grain BT Sierra bullet, and 159 fps with the Hornady 225-grain in the .340 Wthby. Du Pont's IMR-4350 was worse, giving a variation of 195 fps in the 7mm Mag., and 164 fps in the .340. These variations may have been slightly higher if maximum loads for normal, 70-degree temperatures had been used. Loads for all cartridges with all powders were cut below maximums by at least two grains for the rifles used, so if velocities went up drastically at 120

Velocity-Temperature Tests:
7mm Remington Magnum

Powder	Charge	Primer	Temperature	Velocity	Remarks
H-870	78	CCI 250	-20°	2,917	Great velocity variation
H-870	78	CCI 200	-20°	2,945	between low and high temperatures
H-870	78	CCI 250	0°	2,983	
H-870	78	CCI 250	70°	3,086	
H-870	78	CCI 250	120°	3,149	Temperature-velocity change, 232 fps
H-4831	65	CCI 250	-20°	2,842	Not influenced by high temperatures.
H-4831	65	CCI 200	-20°	2,840	Standard and Magnum primers
H-4831	65	CCI 250	0°	2,878	give nearly the same velocity.
H-4831	65	CCI 250	70°	2,957	
H-4831	65	CCI 200	70°	2,996	
H-4831	65	CCI 250	120°	2,984	Temperature-velocity change, 142 fps
N-205	65	CCI 250	-20°	2,977	Gradual velocity increase
N-205	65	CCI 250	0°	3,045	as temperature goes up.
N-205	65	CCI 250	70°	3,059	
N-205	65	CCI 250	120°	3,094	Temperature-velocity change, 117 fps
IMR-4350	62	CCI 250	-20°	2,819	Considerable velocity increase
IMR-4350	62	CCI 250	0°	2,883	as temperatures climb.
IMR-4350	62	CCI 250	70°	2,977	
IMR-4350	62	CCI 250	120°	3,015	Temperature-velocity change, 195 fps

The results shown in this chart were obtained from using the 7mm Rem. Mag., Remington M-700 BDL, 24-inch barrel; Remington cases, weight 249 grains; and Sierra 160-grain BT.

degrees, pressures would not be too high.

While this seems to be quite a velocity spread, it was no more than expected. The spherical powders used were the ones that may come as a surprise to many reloaders in more ways than one. H-870, the slowest of the Ball powders, has always had the reputation of giving extremely good accuracy coupled with good uniformity from shot to shot. These tests didn't change that angle where firing was done at near normal temperatures. But, if shooting at very low temperatures, or when it is extremely hot, there may be a considerable change of impact. A charge of 78 grains behind the 160-grain bullet in the 7mm Mag. gave a difference of 232 fps between minus 20 degrees and 120 degrees. This velocity change was the greatest between 70 degrees and 120 degrees, and the same situation occurred with H-450 and H-335. It showed up even more with the W-W 760 where velocity jumped 168 fps from 70 degrees to 120 degrees. These tests were

Velocity-Temperature Tests: .308 Winchester

Powder	Charge	Primer	Temperature	Velocity	Remarks
H-4895	45	CCI 200	-20°	2,718	Gradual increase in velocity
H-4895	45	CCI 200	0°	2,738	as temperature goes up.
H-4895	45	CCI 200	70°	2,824	
H-4895	45	CCI 200	120°	2,874	Temperature-velocity change, 156 fps
IMR-4064	44	CCI 200	-20°	2,670	Low velocity variation between
IMR-4064	44	CCI 200	0°	2,643	low and high temperatures.
IMR-4064	44	CCI 200	70°	2,691	
IMR-4064	44	CCI 200	120°	2,727	Temperature-velocity change, 57 fps
H-335	46	CCI 200	-20°	2,643	Only 7 fps velocity spread between
H-335	46	CCI 200	0°	2,676	magnum and standard primers.
H-335	46	CCI 250	0°	2,683	Sharp velocity increase at
H-335	46	CCI 200	70°	2,758	high temperatures.
H-335	46	CCI 200	120°	2,826	Temperature-velocity change, 183 fps

The results shown in this chart were obtained from using the .308 Win. Mark X Cavalier, 24-inch barrel; Remington cases, weight 172 grains; and Speer 150-grain Mag Tip.

conducted a second time to see if some mistake had been made; there was no mistake.

The IMR-4831 used in the 6mm Rem. cartridge showed less variation between low and high temperatures than either H-4831 or IMR-4350. However, this may have varied somewhat if it had been used in other cases. It will also be noted that IMR-4064 was very stable in the .308 Win. In fact, it was affected very little between minus 20 and 70 degrees, with the big jump coming between 70 and 120 degrees.

A study of the charts shows that Norma 205 is by far the most stable powder used through the 140-degree temperature range. It was used in the 6mm Rem., 7mm Rem. Mag. and .340 Wthby, because it gives outstanding results in all three cartridges. There was only 33 fps difference between loads fired at minus 20 degrees and 120 degrees in the 6mm, which is far less variation than the high and low velocities in a string fired at the normal 70 degrees

Velocity-Temperature Tests:
.340 Weatherby Magnum

Powder	Charge	Primer	Temperature	Velocity	Remarks
N-205	83	CCI 250	-20°	2,903	Slight velocity change between
N-205	83	CCI 250	0°	2,902	low and high temperatures.
N-205	83	CCI 250	70°	2,944	
N-205	83	CCI 250	120°	2,969	Temperature-velocity change, 67 fps
H-4831	84	CCI 250	-20°	2,779	Gradual velocity gain as temperature
H-4831	84	CCI 250	0°	2,834	increases, but quite even.
H-4831	84	CCI 250	70°	2,878	
H-4831	84	CCI 250	120°	2,938	Temperature-velocity change, 159 fps
IMR-4350	79	CCI 250	-20°	2,752	Gradual velocity gain as temperature
IMR-4350	79	CCI 250	0°	2,742	increases. Very similar reaction
IMR-4350	79	CCI 250	70°	2,848	to temperature as H-4831.
IMR-4350	79	CCI 250	120°	2,906	Temperature-velocity change, 164 fps

The results shown in this chart were obtained from using the .340 Wthby Mag. custom no free-bore, Model 70 action Hobaugh, 23¹/₂-inch barrel; W-W .375 Winchester cases necked down, weight 240 grains; and 225 Hornady spire point.

with most powders in this cartridge. In the .340 there was only 67 fps velocity difference between low and high temperatures, which is not enough to worry about. The 7mm Rem. Mag. gave the highest velocity variation with N-205 at 117 fps, but also gave higher velocity variation from high to low temperatures with most other powders used than the other cartridges tested. This is a little odd considering that the 7mm Rem. Mag. normally gives more uniform velocity with most good loads than either the 6mm Rem. or the .308 Win. (It may come as a surprise to many handloaders, but magnum cartridges from 7mm up usually give more uniform velocities when loaded full-throttle than do the smaller cartridges, with the standard .22 Long Rifle being one of the poorest.)

One of the strange things to come out of these tests was that with most powders in all of the cartridges tested, velocity dropped little between zero degrees and minus 20 degrees. In fact, most loads showed that velocity was *slightly higher* at minus 20 degrees than at zero! Some scattered tests conducted show that this situation holds true up to around the freezing point, then velocity starts to increase rapidly.

Testing Primers

One of the unexpected things revealed in these tests came from the use of magnum primers in small cases with tubular powders, and standard primers in large cases with spherical powders. We have been led to believe that magnum primers were greatly superior to standard for loading cartridges used in cold weather, because there was less velocity drop as temperatures dropped. We have also been told that magnum primers were a "must" with Ball powders to properly ignite the stuff, especially when temperatures were down. I've been as guilty as most on this line of thinking and writing, because I repeated what I had been told without proving it. A hard look at the charts will show that this is not the case, at least with the brand used.

When the tests were conducted with H-4831 in the 6mm with both CCI 250 Magnum primers and 200 Standard primers, I was convinced a mistake had been made somewhere along the line when I saw that the standard primer gave 96 fps more velocity at minus 20 degrees than did the magnum. The next day, I loaded up a new test batch and ran the tests again. The difference was slightly higher than on the first test; there was no mistake! The original findings proved to be correct.

The charts show that with most loads utilizing either Ball or stick powders, little difference appeared in the velocity delivered by the two types of primers. Some loads went a few fps one way, some the other, at either normal or low temperatures. One interesting point is that with the bulky charge of 78 grains of H-870 in the 7mm Rem. at minus 20 degrees, the standard primer gave 28 fps more velocity than the magnum cap. At the normal 70-degree temperature, the No. 200 primer delivered 39 fps more velocity with a charge of 65 grains of H-4831 than did the 250. This seemed rather peculiar.

There is certainly food for thought in this, not only from the standpoint of velocity, but on the average there was no more velocity variation with the standard primer than with the magnum at any temperature. The only chance of a slip-up here is that the magnum primers were from an older lot than the standard primers, with the possibility that the newer lots of standard primers have been made more potent.

Bullet Impact

Another point that is valuable to the hunter is the change of bullet impact at various temperatures. During velocity testing at various temperatures, one load from each cartridge was checked for bullet impact at 100 yards with the same target used for all temperature tests. There was, of course, a variation in the size of the total group by the various rifles, depending on how well that load did in that rifle. However, no group fired at four different temperatures was over 3 inches with any cartridge; most ran just over 2 inches. Not at all bad when you consider the difference in velocity at the different temperatures, and that they were fired on different days. None showed any tendency to climb or drop more than about an inch over the full, 140-degree temperature range. And, as might be expected with the different barrels, some groups were lower as velocity increased, some higher, while others went right or left. All would have killed a deer cleanly at 300 yards. Only the varmint hunter would have trouble hitting small targets when temperatures changed. Even then, it wouldn't matter too much except when he switched from shooting chucks in August to coyotes in January.

There are two points that must be remembered when contemplating sight changes to compensate for changes in bullet impact due to temperature differences. First, some rifles will shoot higher with loads developing lower velocities, canceling any bullet drop because of the velocity decrease. However, some may go the other direction or to one side or the other, so you'll have to try *your rifle* to find out. Second, if you shoot at, say minus 20 degrees, your rifle will be at that temperature for the first shot, and the barrel will still be fairly cold for the second shot. Some rifles retain the same impact point regardless of temperatures; some throw the first shot several inches from the normal impact point from a barrel at that low temperature. This can be far more important to the hunter than the small amount of impact change that comes from the cartridge's temperature.

Summing Up

It seems that some powders are a better choice for the hunter who will use them over a wide range of temperatures than others. The big difference will be in long-range shooting and in terminal energy. However, the overall difference in velocity shown in the charts between the minus-20-degree and 120-degree temperatures is really not all that bad; the only difference most hunters will

This varmint hunter is hunting at a temperature extreme of 100 degrees. The most significant variation is between the normal temperature for load development (usually around 70 degrees) and temperatures above that point for varmint loads and below that point for big-game loads.

encounter is between the normal 70 degrees and zero degrees. A study of the charts will show that this is mostly no more than 50 fps, or no more than average shot-to-shot variation in a five-shot string.

These tests were by no means as complete as they could be. They could be conducted with the spectrum of cartridges, powders and bullet weights. This would require many months of work and thousands of dollars in time and actual expense. We do feel that these tests shed more light on the temperature-velocity subject than anything we have seen in print up to now, and it should give the reloader something to go by and explode some myths that have persisted through the years.

11

Bullet Performance
And Stopping Power

One point should be made right off the bat, then it's on to the hows and whys. By far the most important factor in making clean kills is bullet performance. Anyone who likes to mess with mathematical formulas can show how well a bullet of a given weight and diameter, and driven at a certain velocity, will kill, in comparison with another bullet of different diameter and weight at the same or different velocity.

Call this energy, momentum, potency or whatever you like, but if it does not include bullet performance it isn't worth anything except for comparison. And, it doesn't make any difference if it comes out in foot-pounds, pounds feet or something else that sounds good. Bullet performance is the deciding factor in determining success or failure.

Take the various methods used in computing the amount of energy a bullet is supposed to impart to the animal or object upon impact. (You can call it something other than energy if it sounds better.) They will give you the same answer in foot-pounds, pounds feet or some other unit of measurement for a solid-jacket bullet as for an expanding bullet. This is ridiculous.

Sure, the solid-jacket, non-expanding bullet is the real thing for clobbering elephants, rhinos and possibly Cape buffalo. It is not necessarily energy that counts here, however; it is the bullet's ability to penetrate deep enough to put the beast down. Use the

When hunting white-tailed deer, a high-velocity, thin-skinned expanding bullet should be used. If put in the ribs, it will hit the vital area, causing the deer to drop in his tracks or only go a few yards before dropping—dead.

Because of severe poaching pressure, elephants and rhinos are endangered species. When elephants were a legal target for sportsmen, however, a solid-jacket, non-expanding bullet was the bullet of choice, as it was the only one with enough punch to penetrate to the animal's vitals.

same bullet on a whitetail buck and he'll go farther before he piles up than the elephant will. He'll go faster, be harder to see and be harder to find at the end, too. Fact is, you may never find him!

Conversely, shoot the whitetail in the ribs with a high velocity, thin-skinned expanding bullet that blows up his boiler room. He may go a few yards or he may drop in his tracks, but he'll be around—dead. Shoot the tusker with an expanding slug, even a big heavy one, and you'll find yourself with a whole lot of trouble.

These cases may be extreme, but they do show the fallacy of trying to compute the killing power of bullets by diameter, weight and velocity. These factors are used as a means of comparing various cartridges, various calibers and various bullet weights fired at various velocities—and they are useful. Add ballistic coefficient by considering the shape, and you can compare remaining energy and velocity at long range. But, all this comparison is rather useless if the bullet fails to do the job on the size of game being hunted.

The expanding bullet is not good elephant medicine because it does not penetrate deep enough, getting to the vital parts to kill or immobilize him. If you could shoot the tusker with an expanding bullet big and heavy enough, and tough enough to hold together after expanding in order to penetrate all, or most of, the way through the animal, then it would kill more quickly than the solid. What this would take I do not know, and, while I'm not particularly susceptible to rifle recoil, I have no desire to experiment along these lines.

The reason the non-expanding, full-jacket bullet is of little value in killing the whitetail (excluding the spine-brain area) is that it leaves a wound channel only the size of the bullet diameter. It does not destroy additional tissue and nerves, nor does it create enough shock to paralyze (unless a heavy bone is struck). The animal scats off into the brush at full throttle, and probably will not die for many hours, even from a center lung shot. You're lucky if you ever find him.

There is a lot of middle ground between these two examples, and it is on that ground that most bullet designs and performances should be considered. Also, the largest number of cartridges and game will fall on this middle ground. Even then, there is a great difference in the bulk, toughness and temperament of animals ranging from pronghorn to moose; there is also a great deal of difference in the conditions under which they will be shot. Accordingly, it takes bullets of different designs, diameters and weights to do the job properly and completely.

Deer Bullets

Game the size of deer—everything from Sitka blacktail to muleys, pronghorn, sheep, goats, black bears and even caribou —will be killed quicker from a high-velocity bullet that expands rapidly than from a slower slug that expands less violently. This applies to all calibers, large or small. However, the caliber need not be large, nor does the bullet have to be heavy with great sectional density. Don't misunderstand me, the heavier, slower, larger caliber bullets of controlled-expansion type will kill these animals, but, on average, they will not kill as quickly.

The reason is that high velocity, quick-expanding bullets hitting in the lung-heart area will expand when entering, and spray pieces of jacket and hunks of core throughout the cavity. With the engine room blown up, the animal dies quickly. The slower, controlled-expansion bullet with its restricted expansion does not tear up as much vital tissue; consequently, it does not kill as fast.

However, I am not referring to the high-velocity .22 caliber cartridges even though the bullets are highly explosive. These tiny bombs will kill game of this size *if* you take the animal broadside in the rib cage, but they will fail miserably if the shot is quartering and a shoulder has to be penetrated. They won't reliably kill game of this size because they explode *before they get inside* if a lot of penetration is required. This also applies to some of the lightest bullets for the 6mm and .25 cartridges and others which are designed for varmint shooting.

Bullets For Elk-Sized Game

When we start hunting elk, moose and the big North American bears, the bullet performance requirements change rapidly. Light, high-velocity bullets with thin jackets are a poor choice. I know some who claim they never shoot except when the animal is turned just right and conditions are ideal. (This may be true.) But, looking at the game they shot and checking the bullet holes, it appears the animal must have swapped ends while the bullet was in flight.

For this size game, and under adverse conditions, you need a bullet that will expand well, yet hold together with enough weight to drive through thick bone, tough muscle or soggy paunch and to penetrate the vitals—from nearly any position. If the animal is in the open, you usually can wait for a better shot unless it keeps moving at the wrong angle. But, game is not always in the open.

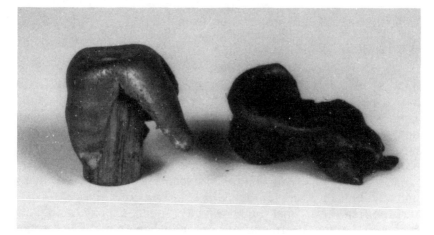

Here is an example of performance difference in premium special-purpose bullets and those of conventional design. Both are 175-grain, 7mm bullets. The premium bullet (left) was taken from a six-point bull elk shot at 50 yards quartering from the rear. It went through 12 inches of paunch and the top of the lungs, and was found under the chest's hide after penetrating 36 inches. Remaining weight was 120 grains. The other bullet (right) was from a cow elk at 50 yards shot through the lungs slightly quartering. It penetrated 24 inches; remaining weight 47.5 grains.

What does it take in a bullet to give this kind of performance? Should it be a larger caliber; should it have to have extreme sectional density, and should it travel at a slower or higher velocity? All these factors enter into bullet performance; yet, none of them is worth anything if the bullet is not properly constructed.

Deep penetration is not required for stopping deer-size animals; yet, they are killed almost as quickly by controlled-expansion bullets as by slower traveling bullets that expand enough to tear a large hole. In the West, you often will find yourself hunting deer, elk or even moose, all on the same day; in the North, it may be sheep or caribou, with moose or grizzly thrown in.

Obviously, the bullet that will do a good job on the larger game will also kill the smaller stuff, within limits. But, use a bullet that works well on small game and you may be in big trouble. And, you'd better plan on finding the animal in something less than an ideal pose. If the position is perfect, fine. If it isn't, however, having a bullet that is capable of digging in deep is better than having to pass up the shot because you are using a deer bullet.

Some hunters firmly believe that if you use a heavy, big-bore bullet that does not travel too fast, you will get near-perfect expansion every time. They also believe that to do this the bullet needs a big, round soft point with a lot of lead exposed. There is a lot of truth in this if ranges are short and *velocity is kept down*. But, if you have to make a long shot you'll probably either miss or wound the animal because of the drop in trajectory with close-up shots in the brush; slow bullets are also usually slow killers. Bullets that travel at low velocity are easier to control for expansion and penetration than those that are fast, but they are not adapted to all-around hunting. Not all animals are killed at close range in the open.

Sectional Density

Sectional density is a factor where bullets of all calibers are used for hunting heavy game. It is absolutely essential that any bullet used in a situation where deep penetration is required have good sectional density. But, sectional density is not enough if the bullet does not hold together. In order to drive an expanded bullet with its large, frontal area through heavy bone and muscle to the vitals, a large portion of the bullet body must remain intact to furnish the mass to push it.

With today's high velocities, it takes a very strong jacket and a good system for holding the core in the jacket to keep the bullet in one piece. Sectional density alone will not do it. If two bullets are identical in caliber, design, construction and core, and jacket material and are fired at similar velocity, but are different weights, then the heavy bullet with the greater sectional density will penetrate deeper. But, if a heavier bullet, with its greater sectional density, breaks up and a lighter one holds together, the lighter bullet will give more penetration.

Some argue that large-caliber bullets, because they are normally quite heavy, penetrate deeper than smaller calibers, even though the smaller bullet has much better sectional density. This is far from true. When the bigger bullet, say, from .35 to .45 caliber, expands to any great extent, there is very little shank left to furnish weight and keep up the momentum required to drive the large frontal area through resisting bone, flesh and fluid.

Also, if velocity is reasonably high as it is with today's magnums, the jacket is more likely to split back so far that the core leaves it, and the whole thing comes apart. Compare the length of a 200-grain, .30 caliber with a 200-grain, .35 bullet, and you'll see what will happen if expansion is equal.

As for big bores giving deeper penetration just because the bullet is big and heavy, a classic example blows a hole in this

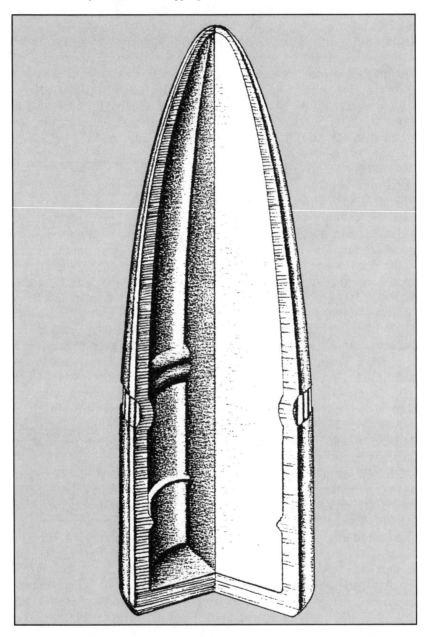

Good bullet construction is extremely important for handling tough, heavy-boned animals. Whenever deep penetration is required, it is essential that the bullet has good sectional density. It should have a strong jacket and a good system for holding the core in the jacket.

theory. I shot a good-sized Shiras bull moose in the ribs with a .375 H&H, handloaded with a 285-grain, Speer bullet that has a rather thin jacket. The bullet, which has been discontinued, barely reached the hide on the far side and only sliced the side of one rib. It came apart with only part of the rear of the jacket remaining. It weighed 41 grains and it hit at 175 yards after leaving the muzzle at a velocity of 2,745 fps.

As a comparison, I once shot an Alaskan moose that was several hundred pounds heavier than the Shiras bull with a 7mm Mashburn Super Magnum loaded with a 175-grain Nosler bullet that left the muzzle at 3,050 fps. At a distance of 300 yards, the bullet sliced through the rear portion of the near shoulder, breaking a rib on the way in, two or more on the way out, smashing the far shoulder blade and almost penetrating the hide on the off-side. The remainder recovered from the bull still weighed 119 grains. The 285-grain, .375 bullet is 110 grains heavier, and has almost as much sectional density—.289 as compared to .310. So, it would appear that bullet construction is much more important for penetration than either caliber or weight.

Penetration

When penetration and expansion are necessary to create shock and destroy nerves and tissue, the big problem is keeping the bullet's core in its jacket for added weight and to control expansion so the jacket ruptures only part way back. You can't drive the flat side of a washer very far into an animal!

For expansion on big game of all sizes at ranges from a few feet up to 400 yards or more, the bullet's jacket must be thin at the point, and the core has to be soft enough to flow outward, expanding the jacket as it goes. The jacket wall must gradually become thicker, so it is strong enough to stop expansion somewhere around the middle. Then, the jacket should be ductile enough so that it does not break off as it's peeled back, but forms a large, frontal area that tears things up as it penetrates the flesh.

This is a rather large order, and it has given manufacturers fits ever since velocities exceeded the 2,000- to 2,500-fps mark. In fact, even today with modern materials and technology, few bullets accomplish this end. Perhaps, the big stumbling block to better big-game bullets is the manufacturing cost. Most big companies, whether they are the big arms-ammo companies or firms making only bullets, produce them competitively for both price and quality. Accurate and well shaped, the bullets do a good job if the game isn't too big or the velocity too high. Most of them are not the ultimate in performance on the big stuff under adverse conditions.

Points are thinned down, and many have some form of splits built into the jacket to ensure quick and "even" expansion. Most bullets that are designed especially for big game are heavier toward the rear which helps to check expansion. Few have any provision for holding the core in the jacket beyond a shallow cannelure or two. While these help somewhat to keep core and jacket together, the jacket usually splits back too far; or, if it doesn't, the core slips out and departs, anyway.

Bullet Testing

Various bullet manufacturers display photos of their bullets fired at various ranges, showing the amount of expansion at these ranges. Often, figures on the retained weight are given, as well, and they are impressive. But water, gelatin, modeling clay or wet lap is good for only one thing: comparison. And, even then, use of these materials will result in a bullet having good expansion and core retention and, consequently, deep penetration, while failing miserably on living game.

These test materials have no thick, tough hides with matted, mud-caked or wet hair, no big bones, no tough muscle and intermittent cavities intermixed with the other ingredients which can tear a bullet into so much metal confetti. The testing materials have a consistency of resistance, form an even side pressure during penetration and cause the bullet to decelerate evenly—which simply doesn't duplicate the situation when live game is hit. Anyone who doesn't find this to be true hasn't dug many bullets out of big, tough critters.

As to the debate about whether high-velocity bullets or low-velocity bullets are best for killing heavy game, killing power is based on two things: destroying a lot of bone tissue and nerves while delivering shock to the nervous system and getting in deep enough under adverse conditions to do it where it counts. If bullets are somewhere near equal weight and other factors are equal, higher-velocity bullets will tear up more flesh and cause more shock. The large-caliber bullet will cause more damage when it expands than the small caliber. But, the more the velocity increases with either one, the more hell it will raise, and the deeper it will penetrate. That is, if you can hold expansion to the same point and retain the same weight percentages. The size of the entrance hole isn't nearly as important as the bullet's performance after it gets inside, or how much of the animal it will penetrate to get there.

I think the above paragraph sums up the small-bore, big-bore argument. For heavy game where a lot of penetration is needed, I prefer a well-designed, 7mm .30 caliber bullet to a poor per-forming bullet of larger caliber. But, if the big-bore bullet is equally well designed and traveling at somewhere near the same velocity, it is more potent—make no mistake about that. No matter how you look at it, or how many formulas you come up with, it is bullet performance that produces killing power. Other factors only contribute.

Brush Bullets

A difference of opinion exists as to what type of cartridge and bullet is best for shooting big game in the brush at close range. But, there isn't nearly the amount of disagreement over this issue as there is regarding most other aspects of big-game shooting. The general consensus is that a large-caliber bullet with a round point, fired at relatively low velocity, is the ideal bullet for bucking brush.

This opinion has a good deal of merit. It is also something that most hunters believe simply because someone made the statement many, many years ago, and it has been repeated ever since. I suspect it all started about the time the big-bore, black-powder rifles with long, lead bullets gave way to smokeless powder cartridges like the .30-30 and .30-40. Perhaps the idea became more firmly entrenched when Charles Newton started the high-velocity trend with his line of small-bore cartridges. Cartridges like the .22 Savage High Power and the .250-3000, with small-caliber, thin-jacketed bullets (at what was then a high velocity of 2,600 to 3,000 fps) were not exactly the answer to a brush hunter's prayers. The big-bore, heavy-bullet, low-velocity cartridges did perform a great deal better when mowing down an acre of brush and trees.

These were at the two extremes. Today, very few hunters use the big-bore, low-velocity cartridges for hunting. At the other extreme, we use cartridges that spit bullets out at a lot higher velocity than either the .22 HP or the .250-3000, but we also have more bullet weights and designs to choose from in most calibers. The main question is not so much which cartridge and bullet are the best combination for shooting big game in the brush, but are any of these combinations capable of mowing down the stuff to

A Model 600 .308 with heavy, round-nose bullets and a low-power, wide-field scope is considered an ideal combination for thick brush areas. But, shooting through a thicket such as this one with any cartridge or bullet will most likely result in a miss or wounded animal.

still get through to the buck or bull?

The answer is simple—*no*. But, before you go down my throat over that flat statement, let's look at some of the fancies and facts.

It is generally assumed that there is less deflection when a round-point bullet strikes a stem of brush or a tree than when a pointed bullet does. In some cases, this may be true. If the bullet just nicks the edge of the material, deflection would be greater for the pointed bullet than for the round point, but even less if the bullet has a perfectly flat, full-diameter point. However, let's not forget one point here: This would be true only if the bullet were a non-expanding bullet. When an expanding bullet strikes a piece of brush or a small tree, it expands. It is hard to say how much of the deflection actually is caused by the shape of the bullet *when* it strikes the stem or by the expanded shape *after* it hits the stem. In fact, it is unlikely that the bullet will even remain in one piece. Of course, the heavier the bullet, the more chance it has of retaining enough weight to continue toward its target. Or, if it breaks up, there may be a piece large and heavy enough to penetrate deep enough into the animal to hit the vitals and kill it—if the piece even hits it.

If the bullet hits the plant or tree stem near the center, the chances that a pointed bullet will be deflected more than a round point are very slight. And, at the ranges likely to be experienced in the brush, the big hunk of exposed lead of most round-point bullets will expand faster and to a greater extent than pointed bullets of the same caliber and weight fired at the same velocity. This being the case, it is more accident than ability if a round-nose bullet reaches the target any better than a pointed one.

We have been speaking mostly in terms of the bullet striking a *single* stem, and not mowing down a thicket of brush and saplings of all sizes and shapes. When a bullet plows into that kind of mess it has about as much chance of getting through to a buck on the far side as the proverbial "snowball in ... "

The most critical point to consider is how far the animal is from the tree or brush that was hit. If it happens to be standing within a few feet of the stem the bullet strikes, the chances are good that the bullet will go on through and kill it. It will be expanded somewhat, depending on the stem's size and the distance the animal is from it. It will cause a large entrance hole, but there will be very little penetration. If the bullet lands off target, the lack of penetration will multiply the possibility that the animal will only be wounded, especially if it is a large animal. If, on the other hand, the animal is several yards, or even feet beyond the object struck by the bullet, the chance of the bullet hitting the animal at all is remote. In most cases, the bullet will have broken into pieces with every hunk going off at a different angle. If it did stay in one piece, the irregular form of expansion is not conducive to true flight. The worst part is that an animal often is hit by a piece or several pieces of the bullet in non-vital spots, and the hunter never knows it.

When an animal is accidentally hit and killed by a bullet or its fragments that have gone through brush or trees, the hunter often takes it for granted that the cartridge and bullet he is using is big medicine for brush shooting, without looking at what actually happened—or what could have happened.

A recent letter from a Canadian friend who lives and hunts moose in Ontario every fall gave an idea of what may be expected of some cartridges that are considered top-drawer, brush-buckers. Using a .350 Rem. Mag. loaded with 250-grain, Bitterroot Bonded

Core bullets to approximately factory-quoted velocity, he had hunted several days without luck when this huge bull behind a screen of birch came along at fairly close range. The bull was well outlined, but birch stems covered nearly every vital spot. Finally, he found a very small hole and touched one off. The bull just walked off as though nothing had happened. In fact, it hadn't—except for a big noise. The big bullet had smashed into a 5-inch birch, traveled several feet and came to rest in another birch. A Canadian bull moose is a big target to miss at short range, but how often have you read or heard what a wonderful brush cartridge the .350 Rem. is?

Various experimenters have conducted many tests to find out how different bullet weights, designs and calibers perform when fired through an obstacle course of wooden dowels simulating brush. Most of these tests show that no bullet is reliable, and that there isn't as much difference between light and heavy bullets, large- and small-caliber bullets, high- and low-velocity bullets, and pointed or round-nose-design bullets as we have been led to believe. But, nearly all of these tests have been made with the target placed within a very short distance of the dowel barrier. This was done so that the bullet would strike somewhere on the target. This could lead to the assumption that the bullet usually did reach the target somewhere near the point it was aimed at. My experience in shooting game in the brush having indicated otherwise, I decided to run a test where various bullets passed through the same object, but with the target a bit farther from the obstruction. This would be more like hunting conditions.

I placed a cardboard box that measured 13x19 inches—which is about the size of the vital, lung-shoulder area of a deer—35 feet beyond a clump of birch on a snow-covered slope. A birch 3 inches in diameter was lined up with the center of the box, 30 feet from the firing position. I could fire several bullets into the birch, one below the other, by simply changing shooting height while still heading them all at the center of the target.

As a starter, the .30-06 was used because it's closest to the average hunting cartridge as one could get. And, to check it against the big-bore, low-velocity numbers of yesteryear, the old .45-70 also was used. One-hundred-eighty-grain Nosler and 220-grain Hornady bullets were used in the .30-06 to give a pointed and round-point form. They were loaded to provide velocities of slightly over 2,800 fps for the 180-grain and 2,585 fps for the 220-grain. Even though the Nosler bullet might be deflected, it

These three loads were fired through a 3-inch birch sapling located about half the distance to a 13x19-inch target located at 22 yards, in a simulation of a typical hunting situation. All three loads are considered good brush-buckers. From left: .30-06 with a 180-grain Nosler at 2,800 fps, .30-06 with 220-grain Hornady at 2,585 fps and Remington factory .45-70 with 405-grain bullet at a little over 1,200 fps. None hit the target.

would still hold together better than anything else except a solid. The .45-70 loads were Remington factory 405-grain ammo that poked along at a bit over 1,200 fps, and should, according to theory, buck a bushel of brush and still smack the buck 50 yards away on the far side.

To make it brief, from several shots fired with each load, not one piece of any bullet even touched the box—at a distance of a little over 20 yards. Twigs and small stems were cut off by core and jacket fragments in a wide arc several feet wide and high beyond the birch. Several bullets had landed in the snow 2 to 4 feet from the box, but the best any would have done was possibly spray the leg, head or rump of a buck. Not a desirable situation!

We make no claim that these limited tests were conclusive, but they do indicate what could be expected under hunting conditions where the game may be even farther from the brush hit by the bullet. Also, these bullets passed through only one 3-inch piece.

This sapling was hit from the three test loads fired at a target. The bullets began expanding, or tearing up, while penetrating the tree. They sprayed fragments in an arc behind it.

Many bullets fired in the brush strike several stems of various sizes en route to the target.

Long experience in actually shooting game in the brush, and the conduct of these limited tests, does prove that no caliber cartridge or bullet is capable of bucking much brush and getting through to the buck on the other side unless the animal is almost tight against the tree or bush. And, even then, the chances of a clean kill are slight. The larger the animal, the more chance there is of only wounding it.

For brush shooting, there is far more merit in using heavy bullets designed for deep penetration than for any ability they may have in chopping down trees. This is because very few animals present a picture-book, broadside shot in the heavy stuff. Even when the animal appears to be at broadside view, it may actually be standing at a considerable angle. He may not only be standing at an angle to the gun, but he may also be partially curved as he tries to see what has spooked him. The bullet may not penetrate his body where you think it would. If you are to get a shot at all, you often have to drive the bullet into a heavy shoulder point so it can angle back into the lungs, or stick it into the flank and drive it through part of the paunch into the broiler room. Or, in the worst cases, you may find the only clear shot you have is to place it at the base of his tail with it penetrating on into the spine. I don't suggest these shots. But, let's face it, they are taken more often than we would like to admit.

In these cases, you'll need a bullet designed to hold together under the severe shock of striking heavy bone and muscle at near-initial muzzle velocity. It will also have to be heavy enough in relation to its diameter (roughly the meaning of sectional density) to retain momentum enough to penetrate deeply. While deep penetration isn't extremely critical on deer, it is of the utmost importance on game the size of elk or moose under these situations. Also, if the game is large and possibly dangerous, like the Alaskan brown bears in the alders, a fairly large caliber is better than a small one. Remember, the larger caliber bullets expand to form larger frontal areas which create larger wound channels that destroy more tissue and give quicker, surer kills. This does not mean that you need a .45 caliber to kill a bull elk in the brush. A poorly designed 400-grain, .45 bullet will not give nearly as much penetration as a well-designed, 200-grain, .30 caliber. However, it does indicate that well-designed, heavy bullets of .30 to .35 caliber are ideal for shooting at heavier game in the brush.

Cartridges, Bullets And Meat Destruction
A friend who is rather new to the outfitting business recently stopped by for a little information regarding cartridges for long-range elk shooting. He had just discovered that a bull hit with a bullet is not necessarily a dead bull. The fall hunts had brought this fact home to him; a number of elk had to be shot several times. One that was shot late in the evening at the edge of a mountain meadow ran off into the timber. Darkness held up finding the bull until the next day, even though it had died within a few minutes. It was, of course, soured and the meat was completely lost.

Because most of his elk shooting is under the same conditions, he wanted to buy a rifle that he could use to put in a finishing shot if it looked as though the elk might reach the timber. During the discussion, I mentioned the 7mm magnums loaded full-throttle with the best 175-grain bullets. "No," my friend said, "I won't use a 7mm magnum, because they ruin too much meat!'' When I asked why he thought that, he told me he had seen an elk shot diagonally through the spine just forward of the hips, ''and the hams were shot full of blood.'' The placement of the hit, the angle of the shot, the kind of bullet used and the fact that the animal had slid down the mountain had nothing to do with it. In my friend's mind, it was the fault of the 7mm magnum cartridge.

There are many hunters like that. They are hunters who have never discovered that a single case does not necessarily prove a point. They are hard to convince, even when you can give them hard, undisputable evidence. But, if there is no concrete proof of exact cause, convincing them that they may be wrong is even more difficult.

There is no disputing the fact that a 7mm magnum is often pretty hard on the chops, but so are dozens of other good big-game cartridges. This fellow was about convinced that a .300 Win. Mag. or .300 Wthby, or a .338 Win. or .340 Wthby would be the answer to his needs. He somehow believed that they would kill like the proverbial lightning bolt, ruining no steaks while doing it. This line of thinking is a little difficult to follow, but it does make you think about just where excessive meat destruction does originate.

Anyone who does much varmint hunting soon becomes aware that high-velocity, explosive bullets tear fearful holes that leave little, if any, edible meat on small game. Exactly the same explosive effect occurs when a fast-expanding bullet hits a big-game animal at high velocity. The bullet that disintegrates inside an animal, or near the surface on angle shots that fail to get inside, not only destroys a great amount of meat in that area, it forces body fluids, including blood, through much tissue surrounding the wound channel. This destructiveness can usually be minimized by the use of controlled-expansion bullets that expand more slowly and retain much of their original weight. This reduces the amount of core and jacket material sprayed through the tissue, making a longer, but smaller, wound channel. The hydraulic action is less severe, with less fluid forced into the surrounding area, so less meat spoilage occurs.

Another way of achieving the same result in high-velocity cartridges is to use heavier bullets that travel slower, thus reducing the explosive effect. But, when you start to believe that this solves the problem, other snags are likely to crop up—snags like the animal's position and the bullet's impact point. If an animal is quartering to the gun and the bullet slams into the heavy shoulder bones on entrance, that shoulder is almost certain to be ruined by the best controlled-expansion bullet. Conversely, if the angle is reversed so that the bullet lands in the forward section of the paunch, then passes through the lungs to either stop or exit in the off-shoulder, both the off-shoulder and ribs may be shot-through with blood and paunch contents. This is caused by bone particles being forced outward from bullet impact, as well as bullet pieces which were torn loose from the same terrific impact force.

No matter how you analyze it, the explosive effect is caused either from high velocity or impact with bone, or other matter of high resistance, forced through the tissue, also creating great hydraulic pressure.

Some very experienced hunters swear by heavy, big-bore bullets fired at low velocity for minimal meat destruction. For the majority of animals killed with those bullets, they are right. However, it's not always true. I used a Model 95 Winchester chambered for the old .35 Winchester cartridge many years ago. Every now and then, the big 250-grain bullet that started at less than 2,200 fps would ruin the whole front end of a deer. Yeah, those bullets had thin jackets that expanded quite well, so maybe that was the problem. And, someone is bound to come up with the idea that the real big bores with lead bullets never ruined any meat. Could be. But, then we find that isn't necessarily so, either.

Hunters who spend a lot of time in mountain country soon discover that the great majority of animals that fall and slide or roll down steep slopes invariably show large areas where blood is forced between hide and meat, as well as between muscle segments of ribs and quarters. This apparently takes place while the heart is still pumping blood through arteries and veins. It is also normally on the side where the bullet has come to rest or has made an exit. It is quite possible that this would occur to some extent even if the animal just fell and bounced down the slope without being shot—they take an awful beating.

I've seen the same thing happen when an animal took off and ran full-throttle for 100 yards or so until it died in midstride. But, just when you decide that post-hit movement is a major factor, something happens to blow holes in that theory.

I once came on a band of elk in a small opening on a heavily timbered ridgetop. A young cow that looked just right for the freezer stood broadside to me, so I put a 160-grain Nosler Partition bullet from a 7mm magnum wildcat into the ribs behind the shoulder. The cow made three or four steps in a half-circle, then

A 160-grain Nosler Partition bullet and a 7mm magnum wildcat should not be considered "too harsh" for use on animals the size of cow elk. It can be extremely frustrating when meat is ruined without a good explanation; but, you can't always blame the ammunition.

collapsed on her side without another kick. The bullet went through and made an exit without touching either shoulder. The wound channel should have been clean, with the surrounding area free of blood, but it wasn't. I don't recall ever seeing a worse mess on the far side. The ribs were useless, and the shoulder muscles were shot full of blood. No, it wasn't the fault of the 7mm magnum or the bullet. I've shot a number of elk, deer, sheep, goats and caribou in the same spot with the same load with very little ruined meat.

If there is a complete answer as to why an excessive amount of meat is ruined sometimes, when another animal is shot in the same place with the same load with little wasted meat, I haven't found it. Nor have other hunters who have honestly tried to analyze the subject. In the meantime, remember that to kill quickly and surely, the bullet must destroy tissue—nerves and vital organs. To do that, it must tear a big hole and deliver a lot of shock. In doing this, it inevitably messes up some good eatin' meat at times. But it is better to lose some good meat caused by a bullet that makes a big, long hole, and kicks up enough hydrostatic shock to kill well and quickly, than to lose the whole animal by having it run off into some dark thicket where it will not be found until long after it is dead—and maybe not found at all.

Is Complete Penetration Necessary?

For as long as I have been interested in guns, loads and hunting, a controversy has grown over whether the bullet that stays inside an animal is more effective than one that penetrates fully and exits. The base of this controversy is the theory that if the bullet penetrates and leaves a hole in the hide where it exited, a great deal of energy is wasted. Conversely, if it expands to the point where it loses enough weight so that it stops inside the animal, thereby expending the last ounce of its energy, shock will be much greater and the kill quicker and more certain.

You'll note I say *theory*—that is all that supports the idea. There is no way of proving how much energy is lost from the bullet that exits as compared to the same bullet with the same striking energy that stays inside.

At first thought, it seems logical that the bullet that stays inside, and expends all of its energy within the animal, kills better than the one that goes through, *theoretically* passing some of its energy off into thin air. Perhaps the theory that the bullet should stay inside to give the surest, fastest kill springs from the fact that the expanding bullet has exactly the same energy in foot-pounds as the non-expanding, full-metal-jacketed bullet when both strike at the same velocity. And, anyone who has killed a lot of big game knows that the bullet that does not expand is a very poor killer on soft-skinned animals. It is also no secret that the bullet that expands very little and goes on to make an exit is a poor and slow killer. But, this has little to do with whether a bullet that expands well and stays inside kills any better than the one that expands equally well but goes through.

To put it another way: take two bullets of equal weight and diameter, traveling at the same velocity, striking with the same energy and landing in the same spot from the same angle; that is, everything is equal, except that one has a thinner jacket that lets it expand a little more so that it stops before it reaches the hide on the off-side or is stopped by the hide. The other bullet has better controlled expansion and makes it through the hide, leaving an exit hole an inch or so in diameter. This second bullet has destroyed about the same amount of tissue and bone as the first one, but had enough momentum left to go through. Actually, if the theory of expended energy is correct, there probably is very little difference between the one that expended 100 percent of its energy within the animal and the other that expended about 95 percent, with the other five percent expended in the atmosphere.

It is a little difficult to see how this small percentage of the striking energy could hasten the animal's demise by very much. In either case, the animal may or may not drop where it stands from a vital hit in the lungs. In the event that it runs a short distance off into the brush, the bullet that made an exit will leave a good blood trail to follow, but there will be little or no blood from the entrance hole of the one that stays inside. I've seen dozens of animals go a considerable distance after being hit broadside through the lungs and others that dropped instantly. It made not the slightest bit of difference whether the bullet stayed inside or made an exit. Some ran; some didn't.

This assumes the bullets are placed in the center of the vital lung area, where internal hemorrhage will prove fatal within a minute or so even if the animal does run. However, the bullet that exits plays a more important role if the hit is not almost instantly fatal. In cases where the animal is hit in such a manner that it lives for several minutes or hours, or might even recover if not found, it will be nearly impossible to follow if the bullet stays inside, because there will be little if any blood trail. The bullet that exits will leave a larger hole, and the profuse bleeding will make tracking the animal much easier. In the case of the novice hunter, it can be the difference between recovery and loss.

But, all of this is by no means the strongest part of the argument against the bullet that will always, or nearly always, stay inside the animal to deliver the last ounce of its energy, even assuming it killed better.

Even animals of the same species vary a great deal in size. (Visualize a spike bull elk and a trophy-class, six-pointer.) And, even if they were the same size, they don't all pose in the classic broadside position. So, the bullet that will stop inside the lungs of a fork-horn muley buck will probably penetrate only one lung of an old mossy horn. And, it might not get through the ribs of a mature bull elk or moose if it hits one. If it lands in the shoulder of the fork horn and has to angle back into the lungs, it won't make it, and there will be no blood trail to follow.

Many animals run some distance after being hit. A bullet that exits an animal will leave a larger hole than one that stays inside. This causes profuse bleeding and will make tracking easier.

Conversely, a bullet that is capable of driving through the heavy shoulder muscle and bone of a big buck deer and continuing on to tear up the lungs—whether it exits or not—will certainly exit on a broadside lung shot of the same deer and make an exit on the little buck from nearly any angle. You also often see both deer and elk the same day in the same places in hunting areas of the West, and there's no way to keep the same bullet inside the deer on a broadside lung shot that will give adequate penetration for a shoulder shot on an elk.

The Best Bullet

If you want to make successful kills on any kind of big game at all practical game ranges (Remember, the bullet striking at close range at near-muzzle velocity will not penetrate as deeply as the same bullet at 300 yards.), the best bullet to use is one that will penetrate to the vitals from nearly any angle on the game being hunted. That same bullet is going to exit on broadside shots on that animal, and all others that are smaller from nearly any angle. You'll find it will kill just as well as the one that stays inside. And, if the animal runs off somewhere, there will most likely be a blood trail to follow. Anyway, it is impossible to pick a bullet that will always stay inside on broadside lung shots and still give adequate penetration for the shots that aren't broadside.

12

Big-Game Bullets

There has always been a great deal of campfire argument over the best design and point shape for a hunting bullet. Most of this settles around bullets made for taking big game. But, when the discussion warms up, it even takes in small-game bullets. As a rule, if the circle around the blaze is moderately well-informed, there is agreement on bullets made strictly for high-velocity cartridges for long-range varmint shooting—that is, so far as shape is concerned, but not always including point design.

Most of this controversy comes from mixing the past with the present. A lot of the best hunters with many, many years of experience, who have killed more game than most of the younger generation will ever have the opportunity to see, are still thinking of the days when 2,500 fps was high velocity, and averages ran around the 2,000-fps level. Most of the cartridges were of .30 caliber or larger, but even smaller caliber cartridges, like the Winchester .25-35 and .25 Remington, pushed light bullets along at very little more than 2,000 fps from 26-inch barrels, and a lot slower from the popular guns with 20-inch tubes.

At that time, the largest number of hunting rifles was lever actions, which, of course, required flat-point bullets, as did other rifles with tubular magazines. These bullets gave reliable expansion and penetration for the velocities at which they were delivered. The fellows who used them learned to like them and, human nature being what it is, they resisted changing to more modern cartridges and new bullet designs and shapes.

Then, too, at the time of the transition from the moderate velocity cartridge to the higher velocity era of the .30-06, .270 Win. and .300 H&H, there were many failures involving the higher velocity rounds because of poor bullet design. The fellows who lost game with them blamed it on everything from the cartridge case, to higher velocity, to the new pointed shapes—usually forgetting that point design, jacket taper, thickness, hardness and toughness, and core hardness make a bullet a success or a failure.

A lot of younger hunters are inclined to believe everything that has been handed down around other campfires, even if it is a product of blackpowder days. Grandpa killed plenty of deer and elk with a flat or round-nosed bullet with a soft point the size of a head of cabbage and as soft as lead can be with a jacket that was barely thick enough to hold it together! Since it worked then, some see no reason why it shouldn't work now! The trouble is, velocities run about 1,000 fps higher today, and average bore diameters are smaller.

Creating further confusion are changes in other equipment such as sights, which also changed hunting methods and ranges. Granddad didn't shoot as far as you do, for at least three simple reasons. His rifle and cartridge were usually not accurate or flat enough to be productive in this kind of shooting. There were far fewer hunters around to keep the game spooked and holed up during shooting hours, so they fed and bedded more where a hunter could get a decent shot at 'em. He also had a longer season in many cases, and he just might have extended it somewhat if the kids were a little hungry. He also devoted more time to hunting and knew a lot more about game (both small and big) and stalking than his grandson ever will.

With today's cartridges shooting bullets that fly almost as flat as a sunbeam, with factory rifles that will shoot into a minute of angle with a little tuning, and with the glass sights we hang on them, it is just as easy to kill a standing deer at 300 yards as it was for grandpa to do it at 150 yards—maybe easier.

Herein lies the reason why the bullet shapes and designs that were so successful in granddad's day are, for most shooting, far from ideal for today's hunting and rifles.

Round Nose Is Out

Every now and then someone breaks into print singing the

These sectioned .30 caliber, Remington Core-Lokt, 180-grain bullets make it readily apparent why the round nose, with its large amount of exposed lead, expands more rapidly than the pointed bullet.

praises of the soft-point bullet with a big hunk of core exposed on its round point. It is claimed that this point design always has been, and still is, the most reliable of all expanding bullet designs. Also, this point shape and design will expand more reliably at all ranges, and have a better killing effect than the pointed variety.

As already pointed out, this was once very true, and it still is under certain conditions when used in some cartridges and bullet weights. But, as an all-around, hunting bullet for average hunting conditions with most modern cartridges, and for most modern hunters with their limited time and hunting knowledge, it is far from ideal.

There are certain areas where the round-nosed, soft-point bullet is ideal, where it performs better than any other point shape. But, these areas and the game hunted there are limited.

If you do your hunting in heavy brush and timber where you know the range will not be long, the soft point with a big hunk of lead exposed on its blunt front end is very reliable. Flat trajectory is of no importance, so you can forget that. If velocity is not too high, it will usually penetrate well in heavy bone and muscle of large animals. However, a lot more of this penetrating ability is not because of the point design, but because such bullets are normally of the heavier weights in the caliber used, as well as being the normal selection for the larger calibers.

When shooting into heavy brush and timber, where ranges are short and trajectory is of no consequence, the round-point bullet is at its best. It is less likely to deflect off a stray, unseen twig.

Therefore, in many of the round-point bullet weights, velocity is down and sectional density is up—a combination that usually produces deep penetration.

The round point is also very reliable for use on big, dangerous game that anyone is stupid to shoot at unless the range is short. This is especially true where the large-caliber, heavy bullets are used in full-jacket form for shooting the heaviest African and Asian species. Here, a pointed bullet is inclined to veer off or "cartwheel," failing to reach the vital spot for which it is intended. Even on the big North American bears, chances are the range will be short so you won't sweat over trajectory. Here, the soft point with a big, blunt nose will work fine if it is designed for the velocity at which it is being fired.

This is a pitfall that may cause you many long hours of tracking, often without recovering the animal because the bullet failed to work as it should have.

The larger area of core exposed on a bullet point and the softer the lead core, the more violent expansion will be. To control this expansion so the bullet does not blow up and strip the jacket from the core, tearing a fearful hole but giving little penetration, the jacket must be thicker around the exposed lead than with the pointed design. These round-point bullets are also much shorter than their pointed counterparts. Thus, when the jacket peels back during expansion, it is inclined to reach a point nearer the heel than the pointed bullet jacket would. The nearer the heel it unfolds, the more chance there is that the core and jacket will part company, with subsequent loss of penetration.

If a jacket is thick, hard and tough enough to stand up under the .300 Win. Mag., it is unlikely that it will expand well with the lower velocity of a .308 Win. Conversely, the bullet that is ideal for the .308 Win. will be blown to steam when impacting under the potent .300 charge. Yet, the same bullet is usually used for all cartridges of that caliber. Because of the point shape and the aforementioned reasons, expansion is harder to control with a round-nose bullet than with a pointed bullet when velocity varies greatly. There is a little more jacket length to work with in tapering the thickness on the pointed bullet than there is on the round-nose. This will often determine whether the bullet stays in one piece while expanding.

There is yet another problem where round-nose bullets are used for all-around hunting. Namely, the range at which game may be shot. Anyone who has ever checked a ballistic sheet for the

These sectioned bullets show jacket designs of several modern bullets. Left to right: Remington Pointed Core-Lokt, Remington Round Nose Core-Lokt, Winchester Silvertip, Nosler Partition Jacket, Swedish Norma, German H-Mantel and British Kynoch.

trajectory of bullets of identical weight—one with a spitzer point and the other with a round point—was immediately impressed with how much easier it would be to hit an animal at long range with the pointed bullet. What is seldom considered is the difference in the velocity of the two shapes at the longer ranges. This not only affects energy, but governs the expansion of the bullet. If a bullet does not expand as it should, it will not kill well. And it will not expand as it should when velocity goes below a certain point. If it does, it will blow up at the closer ranges, and we are right back to the .308 and .300 Win. situation.

Pointed Bullet Design

If the pointed bullet is superior to the round or flat point for all-around hunting use, both as big-game and varmint bullets in modern, high-velocity cartridges, then what is the difference in the mechanical design of the various bullets and how does it affect bullet performance?

If a poll were taken to find out which pointed bullet design is the most reliable for a hunting bullet for all game sizes, considering all game ranges, there is little doubt that those with experience would almost unanimously pick the soft point. This point would have a large amount of lead exposed, similar to the Speer, Sierra, Hornady or Nosler. You'll find little argument that this pointed, soft-point design is very reliable if the jacket is properly thinned and tapered. With some of the older bullets made by private companies like Barnes, the jacket was often not thinned at the point, and as soon as velocity dropped off a few hundred feet per second, the bullets failed to expand unless a large bone was struck. The jacket material was made from soft copper, which tended to expand much as the core does. In fact, the taper of the jacket was reversed and much thicker at the point than farther back, with very little hole left under the soft point.

History Of Big-Game Bullet Design

Back in the days of the muzzleloader, when round balls were the rule, velocities were low and the killing ability of the ball depended almost entirely on its diameter. The bigger the hole it punched in an animal, the sooner the animal expired. Anything under a .40 caliber was certainly a small-bore and not suited to taking large animals.

When the conical bullet came into general use, it was still in large calibers, but bullet weight increased in proportion to the length. Penetration, which is so vital to killing heavy game, increased accordingly. While the round ball remained about the same size and shape during penetration, the conical bullet tended to expand up front, so that the frontal area was bigger than the rest of the bullet. This created greater shock effect, and increased the kill potential.

Velocities, however, were still low. If the range was at all long and the target was a small animal which presented little resistance, such bullets mushroomed very little, if at all. In this case, penetration was better, but destruction of vital organs was little better than that of the round ball.

When metallic cartridges were first introduced, bullets remained similar in shape to the conical style used in the muzzleloader. And, it was during this period of replacing muzzleloader bullets with the first of the lead bullets for metallic cartridges that serious experimentation began to find a better big-game bullet.

The hollow point and the flat point certainly created more shock than did the solid round point, and these points are still with us today, especially low-velocity pistol loads. It is also worth noting that almost all cartridges used during the buffalo-hunter era

Bullets for big game should have a good ballistic coefficient for flat trajectory and retained velocity at long range. This Dall ram was shot with the .300 Win. Mag. with a 180-grain, Nosler bullet ahead of 78 grains of H-4831 powder.

had bullets with flat points. While these cartridges still enjoy a wide reputation for their killing ability, remember that their velocity was quite low. These bullets were usually of good sectional density (especially for the Sharps cartridges), however, and they ranged from .40 to .50 caliber. Bullets of that diameter need not expand too much to deliver great shock.

When smokeless powder appeared on the scene, along with the cartridge cases designed to handle it, the bullet situation became even more complicated. Velocities went up, and bores became smaller. Lead bullets could not withstand these velocities—bores leaded and accuracy was nil—so the lead was wrapped in a metal envelope called a bullet jacket.

In most cases, the core lead was very soft and the jacket thin. A large amount of lead protruding from the front end of the jacket formed the original soft point. This point was either flat for use in the tubular magazines of the very popular lever action or, at best, rounded. Bores were still large and velocities low by today's standards. But, these bullets gave good results on most game, be it large or small. The big soft points expanded rapidly and, at these low velocities, the thin jacket adequately restricted that expansion in time to retain deep penetration. Another point is that these bullets were usually heavy with good sectional density, and the cores normally stayed in the jackets.

Just when everything was going well and bullets were giving good results on big game, the search for higher velocity and flatter trajectory commenced. With new progressive burning powders, bores became even smaller, decreasing from the .35 and .40 calibers to the .30 and .25s. With the lighter bullets, velocity increased and trajectories flattened, making hits surer at longer ranges. To make the most of this increase in velocity, bullet points became sharp to cut through the air more easily to retain the initial velocity longer. This served to upset the excellent results obtained with soft cores and thin jackets. The soft cores sprayed like water, and the thin jackets disintegrated on impact with heavy hide and tough muscle. Penetration went down the drain.

Cores were hardened and jacket material toughened and made thicker, but the pointed bullets left smaller soft points exposed while the jacket became thicker near the point when swaged to shape. These bullets worked quite well at close range while velocity was still high, but failed miserably when velocity dropped off at long range. They failed to expand at all, except when striking heavy bone, and punched bore-sized holes in and out. Many animals escaped only to die slow, lingering deaths.

This leads up to the advent of the modern, controlled-expansion bullet. This bullet is designed to expand well at close range when velocity is still high, yet retain its core and much of its original weight which is vital to deep penetration on heavy animals. These bullets are also designed to expand well at the longest game ranges where velocity is lower. This is a big order which has not always been filled.

Many gimmicks for filling this order and still retaining the spitzer point arose. Some of the best known are the old Winchester Umbrella Point and the Remington Bronze Point. The Winchester point later became known as the Precision Point. These bullets had tough jackets with a sharp insert of hard metal fitted into a cavity in the point and designed for a dual purpose: first, to keep the small point from being battered in the magazine, and, second, to push back and start the jacket expansion. These bullets were top-hole as

The tips of the Winchester Precision (far left) and the Remington Bronze Point (second from left) are designed to drive back inside the jacket to begin expansion. The European capped design (second from right) shows a hollow cap that uses trapped air to begin bullet expansion. The Winchester Western Silvertip (at far right) has a very thin cap over a soft lead point, protecting it from battering, but expansion is about the same as a conventional soft point.

far as good ballistic shape is concerned, and still have many staunch supporters. But, after shooting and seeing many head of game shot with both bullets, I have little enthusiasm for this design.

This design depends on velocity at point of impact to drive the tiny, sharp point back and start expansion of the jacket. If velocity is high, as at close range, they work quite well, but often blow up completely and give little penetration. At long range, they are inclined to penetrate too deeply before expansion takes place. In fact, if they don't hit bone on the way through, they often will not expand at all. At times, they leave an extremely large exit hole; yet, the animal will go a long way before collapsing—they didn't expand until striking bone on the off side. This caused the large exit hole, but little damage was done inside where it counts. They are at their best in high-velocity cartridges with light bullet weights—and on light game.

One of the first true, controlled-expansion bullets was the old Peters 225-grain, .30 caliber, belted bullet. This bullet had a heavy belt (gilding metal, I believe) around the outside of the jacket, and a large cavity point—the object being for the point to expand back to this belt and then stop. The fitting of the belt over the jacket reduced the inside jacket diameter locking the core into place so that most of the original weight remained.

This bullet worked quite well on heavy game giving extremely deep penetration, but it had its drawbacks. It is really too bad that more work was not done along this line since many think that the basic design was on the right track. One of the main disadvantages of this bullet was that the belt was installed too far forward on the jacket. This did not allow enough point expansion, and the frontal area of the expanded bullet was not large enough for quick kills. Another disadvantage was that it had a very long bearing surface that resulted in high pressures and reduced velocity. Also, the point shape was wrong for long-range work, but this was of little consequence for the ranges and work for which it was intended.

This design later led to the Peters Inner-Belted bullet, forerunner of the Remington Core-Lokt. This design was, and still is, very reliable in most weights and calibers for almost all big game at reasonable distances. These bullets came out first in round-nose shape and, while they worked very well as far as expansion and penetration go, they left something to be desired for long-range shooting. With a scalloped jacket around the large soft point, expansion was very uniform, resulting in a classic "mushroom." Later, Remington-Peters brought out the Core-Lokt bullet in pointed form for most calibers and weights. Very little lead is exposed in this bullet, and the jacket is serrated at the point rather than notched.

I have used many, many of these bullets in both forms on animals ranging from small deer to very large elk, with excellent results. They expand well even on thin-skinned game at long range; yet, hold together on heavy game at close range for deep and reliable penetration. It has always seemed that I got deeper penetration with the pointed bullet than with the round nose. This is perhaps because the pointed bullet gives somewhat less expansion. This is a favorite of factory bullets for game of all sizes and with all cartridges.

Winchester came along with its "Silvertip" at about the same time. The Silvertip is a very thin metal cap enclosing a large lead point. Its advantages are that the soft point is protected from battering under recoil in the magazine, and, in most instances, the point shape is good. The jacket is quite thin at the point and grows somewhat thicker toward the base. Instead of the thick portion found near the midsection in the Remington Core-Lokt, it has one or two deep cannelure grooves to help bind the core in the jacket.

While many hunters swear by the Silvertip, I have never liked it in anything except large calibers such as the .375 H&H Mag.—and then in heavy weights. Lighter, high-velocity bullets tend to expand very rapidly; jackets blow up and the core leaves them, resulting in poor penetration.

The Silvertip seems to be at its best on small- to medium-size game where deep penetration is not necessary. My limited observation in testing the Winchester Power Point bullet runs along the same line; some results have been good, some pretty erratic.

Bullets For Handloaders

We have many fine bullets made especially for handloaders —bullets like Speer, Hornady, Sierra and Barnes. These bullets are as good or better than any factory bullet; they are accurate and they are tough, but they are not made with controlled expansion as a base. They are also made to fill the need of the average rifleman for everything from target to big game, with varmints thrown in. Most of these bullets expand well at nearly any reasonable range, and they hold together quite well for good penetration.

As far as big-game shooting is concerned, I have had more experience with bullets made by Barnes and Speer than any of the others. For many years, I used Barnes bullets in the various .333 caliber OKH cartridges with good results. These bullets are made with copper tubing jackets, and this soft copper tends to split and roll back to form a large, jagged frontal area—better than any material I know of.

The biggest problem I have found with these bullets is that the jacket is not thinned at the point. Swaging the point makes this even heavier. This leaves a very small hole filled with lead where the core is extruded to form a pointed soft point. These bullets expand quite well because of the soft copper jacket (if the light .032 jacket is used). With the heavier .049 jacket, I found that the lead point had to be removed and the jacket hollow-pointed to give adequate expansion at long range. They worked well after this was done, giving good expansion and penetration.

Speer bullets always expand well at any range. When using

The ideal elk bullet should have good ballistic shape for long range and a jacket design assuring controlled expansion and deep penetration at close quarters when the shot must be taken at undesirable angles. This pair, a 180-grain Nosler Partition .30 (left) and a 250-grain Bitterroot .338 (right) perform well at reasonable ranges.

them where deep penetration is needed, however, I always pick a long, heavy bullet. While the jackets are tough, sectional density is needed for deep penetration. Results on heavy game have always been good with 275-grain, .338 and 225-grain, 8mm bullets.

When searching for a bullet that gives optimum performance on all sizes of big game, we tried about everything. Bullets that perform well on light, thin-skinned game are sorely lacking on heavy game with tough hide and large bones; bullets that do well on heavy game at close range would not expand at long range on lighter game. But, if any one bullet for all calibers and cartridge-case capacities approaches the ideal, it would be the Nosler Partition.

Years ago, I carried on a lengthy correspondence with the dean of Alaskan brown bear hunters, the late Hosea Sarber, regarding the ideal bullet design for all game at all ranges. He said a bullet should have a solid partition near the center, with a lead core inserted from each end. He thought that such a bullet, with a thin jacket at the point, would give excellent long-range expansion, while the solid partition would ensure enough retained weight for the required deep penetration on brown bear. His dream came true with the development of the Nosler bullet, but he did not live to try it out.

Ever since John Nosler sent me a few of his first cavity-point bullets to test, I have been using them for most of my big-game hunting. I've used them in everything from 6mm to .375; on everything from 30-pound coyotes to a nearly 2,000-pound Alaskan moose; and, from 5 feet off the muzzle on a charging grizzly to a long, 500-yard pronghorn shot. In every case, performance has been outstanding. They have always expanded on any class of big game at any hunting distance if the cartridge created enough velocity for it to be a realistic shot at that range.

I've put Noslers in one side and out the other on such heavyweights as big bull elk and moose, as well as good-sized grizzlies. The few bullets I have recovered usually had lost the core from the front end, but the rear end was intact, retaining an average of two-thirds the bullet's weight. Enough rolled-back jacket material also was retained for a spread of at least twice the diameter of the original bullet. I have heard of instances where the front end of the jacket sheared off at the groove over the partition, leaving only a slug with the original bullet diameter to go on, but I have never had this happen even when I was using the hottest magnum cartridges at close range.

One bullet of true big-game, controlled-expansion design I have used is the Bonded Core cavity-point bullet made by Bill Steigers of the Bitterroot Bullet Co. This is indeed an interesting design, one that may go far with the big-game hunter who wants a bullet that will expand to form an extremely large frontal area (one that is jagged and cuts like a buzz saw), and still retain the weight to punch through the vitals of even the heaviest game.

This bullet has a thick, pure copper jacket (in tests of the 250-grain .338s, it runs .060), a large cavity point and a core that is solidly bonded to the jacket. Examination of wound channels indicates that it expands rapidly, but does not come apart. Retained weight is phenomenal!

This bullet's accuracy is good with the limited number I had for testing. Because of the lightness of the heavy jacket and the cavity-point spitzer design, it is a bit longer than most other bullets of the same weight. For this reason, plus the fact that it has a rather long bearing surface, powder charges need to be cut a couple of grains in most calibers and weights.

It can be summed up this way: If heavy bullets are used at low velocity (under 2,500 fps), most of them will give good results on any game if the range is not too long. For light, thin-skinned game at all ranges, a thin-jacketed, light, high-velocity bullet will do a fast, clean job of putting it down, but it will also ruin a lot of

Nosler bullets work great on the majority of big-game animals. They have been used on 30-pound animals, as well as 2,000-pound animals (such as this moose) with outstanding results.

steaks. And, when the game gets large, with heavy hides, muscles and bones, and the distance to the animal may be anything from a brown bear only feet away in the alders to a caribou 400 to 500 yards across the tundra moss, you'd better have a bullet designed to handle about any situation. This requires a bullet of good sectional density with a core and point that will reliably expand at long range at much lower velocity. Yet, the core must stay in the jacket so that enough weight is retained to drive it into the vitals from nearly any angle.

Here's something to remember: No matter how much you pay for your rifle or who makes it or what cartridge you choose, the success or failure of a $3,000 hunting trip may hang on the way a relatively inexpensive bullet performs!

13

Varmint Bullets

To many hunters, a bullet is simply something that comes out of the end of a rifle barrel and zips toward the target with great speed and reasonable accuracy. If the target is a game animal, the bullet is supposed to bring a sudden end to its earthly wandering. If the cartridge that sends the bullet on its way is considered top-hole for that particular game, there should be no question of its ability to kill quickly and cleanly.

The ideal varmint bullet, on the other hand, is not made to penetrate. In fact, it should be designed to expand rapidly and violently on the skin of the smallest animals within the cartridge's range limitations. The faster and more complete the expansion of a varmint bullet; the quicker and surer the kill. The truth is a good varmint bullet should blow up completely on contact with feathers, fur or even a husky blade of grass.

There are other reasons for complete disintegration of a varmint bullet besides the quick and humane demise of the target. The majority of varmint hunting is perhaps done in and around farms—land where farm buildings may be (and usually are) close by, and there are people and livestock. The ideal varmint bullet should blow up completely on contact with the ground, brush or even weeds, so that it will not ricochet.

Even in the so-called "wide open" Western range country, cattle, horses, sheep or riders may be in the next draw or over the

Complete disintegration of varmint bullets is necessary especially when hunting near buildings where ricochets could endanger humans and livestock. An ideal varmint bullet should blow up on contact.

next hill. A bullet that does not blow up into small, harmless fragments may whine off into the blue, coming to rest in an object other than the one you fired at.

Several other areas exist where the standards and requirements for big-game and varmint bullets differ. First, there is the level of accuracy. Sure, we all like an accurate rifle, cartridge and bullet for any kind of hunting, but there is a lot of difference between the accuracy necessary for big-game hunting and serious varmint shooting.

If the big-game hunter has a rifle that will consistently shoot into two minutes of angle, he is not too bad off for even long-range, big-game shooting, providing the bullet continues that degree of accuracy out to 300 or 400 yards. Actually, most big-game animals are taken at a range of 100 yards or so, and any rifle that will group all its bullets within a 3- to 4-inch circle at that range is not lacking for big-game hunting.

The varmint hunter sights in on a ground squirrel measuring little more than 2 inches in width, sitting on his dirt mound 200 yards away. Anything less than a minute of angle accuracy will result in a complete miss. Even at 100 yards, there is little room for any type of error.

Because this squirrel is much smaller than a big-game animal, a hunter must sight his rifle in more carefully. Accuracy is extremely important and there is little room for error when shooting at small game.

The varmint rifle, then, must be capable of placing all of its bullets within an inch at 100 yards. If you can cut that down by half, that's even better. Not all varmint rifles are capable of that kind of accuracy, but if the bullet doesn't have that accuracy level, the most accurate rifle will not help much.

Not all varmint bullets meeting this standard of accuracy at 100 yards will sustain it at longer ranges—200, 300 and 400 yards—for as far as the velocity generated by the cartridge will hold up enough to expand the bullet sufficiently for effective varmint shooting. Most bullets designed especially for varmint cartridges, like the hotshot .22s and the 6mm, retain accuracy to any reasonable range, but not all varmint hunting is done with this type of cartridge.

Many hunters like to use their big-game rifles for shooting varmints during the off-season, with light, high-velocity bullets for flatter trajectory and easier hits. These lighter, larger caliber bullets within thin jackets are usually designed especially for varmint shooting. They have very poor sectional density and are extremely short for the caliber. Losing velocity rapidly, these bullets' trajectories are often not as flat at the longer ranges as the muzzle velocity would indicate. Many of them also lose accuracy rapidly with the increase in range.

Another fault in larger caliber bullets used for varmint hunting is that they usually do not entirely disintegrate upon impact with either flesh or other small objects. While the cores of these larger bullets tend to break up to the extent that little is left to continue flight beyond impact, the mass of jacket around the bullet base often remains intact. This hunk of jacket material will continue to travel for long distances. At ranges where velocity is greatly reduced, there may be a sizable chunk of both core and jacket left after impact to go whining into the next pasture. If you shoot the larger bores at varmints, you had better make sure that there is a hill behind them.

There are plenty of good varmint bullets on the market. Nearly all of the independent manufacturers who produce for the handloading fraternity make topflight varmint bullets. So do most of the commercial ammunition manufacturers. Some of the factory ammunition delivers deadly accuracy, as well.

When Remington-Peters hit the market with the new Power-Lokt hollow-point varmint bullet in both .22 and 6mm calibers, I tested factory ammunition in both cartridge sizes in Remington Model 700 rifles. Using factory bullets in a .22-250 Rem., I found the accuracy was not outstanding (at least in the test rifle used), averaging around 1¼ MOA. Handloads for this particular rifle, using 36 grains of 4,320 to power the 55-grain, Power-Lokt bullet for a muzzle velocity of 3,720 fps, produced ⅝-inch groups.

Peters' factory ammunition loaded with the Power-Lokt, 80-grain, hollow-point varmint bullet shot as well in an extremely accurate Model 700 6mm Rem. as any handload I could ever cook up. This included handloads using the same bullet.

This Power-Lokt bullet is one of the finest varmint bullets available today, but it has one bad feature. The core and jacket are solidly bonded together. Although the core almost completely disintegrates on impact, a small amount of it adheres to the jacket base. Also, the base and a small portion of the body jacket seem inclined to remain intact. This leaves enough remaining weight for a ricochet if conditions are right. This particle is too small and light to be especially dangerous, but could cause trouble. However, this bullet is excellent as far as accuracy and explosive effect on varmints are concerned.

Bullet-making firms such as Speer, Sierra and Hornady have long made high-quality varmint bullets in many calibers. Perhaps more varmint bullets are sold in .22 caliber than all of the others combined, so let's take a look at this popular size varmint bullet first.

.22 Caliber

While most of the .22 caliber varmint cartridges are factory-loaded with 55-grain bullets—the .222 Rem. Mag., .223 Rem., .22-250 Rem. and the .225 Win. being originally loaded with only that bullet weight—I have, strangely enough, never obtained top-hole accuracy with any 55-grain bullet except those put out by the factory.

I have not had especially good accuracy from the 60-grain Hornady in most rifles, although the .225 Win. did shoot quite well with rather mild charges. Hornady's 50-grain and even the little 45-grain bullet shoot very well in most rifles, and they always give excellent blow-up on the smallest varmints.

One of the consistently accurate bullets, especially for long-range shooting in .22 caliber rifles, is the 52-grain Speer hollow point. I have yet to see an accurate barrel that would not shoot this bullet well. It holds up wonderfully for those long shots, and has a terrific explosive effect.

Perhaps the most accurate varmint bullet I ever tried in any of

Modern varmint bullets designed for high-velocity cartridges deliver flat trajectory, long-range accuracy and have explosive expansion on impact. Left to right: Sierra, 50-grain, soft point; Speer, 52-grain, hollow point; Remington Power-Lokt, 55-grain, hollow point; Nosler Zipedo, 55-grain, hollow point; Hornady, 60-grain, soft-point .22; Hornady, 75-grain, hollow point; and, Remington, 80-grain, hollow-point, Power-Lokt in 6mm.

the hot, .22 varmint cartridges is the 50-grain, Sierra soft point. In the .225 Win. varmint rifle, this bullet has always shot into ¼ inch and down to ³⁄₁₆ inch on a still day on the 100-yard target, with a charge of 33 grains of 4064 and CCI No. 200 primers. In the .22-250 with a Sporter weight barrel, a load of 36.5 grains of 4320 has shot groups of under 1 inch repeatedly. This bullet is also highly explosive.

For some strange reason, I have never had particularly good results with the 53-grain, Sierra Bench Rest bullets. They have never shot badly, nor been outstanding in any rifle I've tried.

6mm Varmint Bullets

In bores larger than .22, there are more true varmint bullets made for the .243—6mm if you will—caliber than any other. Almost every manufacturer puts out excellent bullets for this popular caliber. Let us not become confused, however, for not all 6mm bullets are made for varmint shooting. Those above 80 grains are usually made for big-game shooting, being designed to penetrate deeply. Sure, they will blow up a jackrabbit if the range isn't too long, but they also will whistle off into the next county after they do.

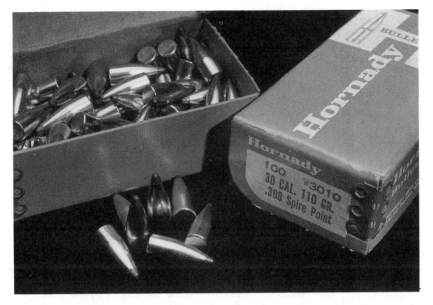

When using high caliber cartridges, you will need heavier bullets. For varmint shooting, you should use bullets no heavier than .30 caliber, 110-grain bullets.

Many good bullets in this caliber are made especially for varmint shooting, in addition to the 80-grain, Power-Lokt mentioned earlier. One of the finest I have ever used is the 75-grain, hollow-point Hornady. This bullet combines good shape and the ability to explode on contact with the most fragile objects. It also retains its original accuracy level out to at least 400 yards.

The 75-grain, Speer hollow point is also a good varmint bullet that will blow up on the smallest varmints, but there are some rifles that will not handle it with any great degree of accuracy. These bullets shot poorly in my Model 700 6mm Rem., but bullets from the same box made excellent groups in a custom rifle chambered for the .243 Win. This may be due to the 9-inch twist of the Remington 700 barrel, as compared to the 10-inch twist of the custom .243 Win. barrel.

"Big Bore" Varmint Bullets
When you go up in caliber to the 6.5-, .270-, 7mm- and .30-caliber cartridges, heavier bullets are needed. These bullets will weigh from 87 to 130 grains, depending on caliber. For straight varmint shooting, however, I wonder if such calibers are really suitable.

When Speer brought out a 100-grain, hollow-point bullet for the 6.5-magnum cartridges, Dave Andrews, ballistician at Speer, told me that they are very accurate in the 6.5 magnums. With the accuracy required for varmints, this bullet will work well in 6.5-caliber cartridges of the magnum class.

The 100-grain, varmint bullets for the .270 have always been good if the barrel will shoot them accurately, but some barrels refuse to digest them. The 130-grain, .270 bullet will give varmint accuracy in many good rifles. It shoots plenty flat and blows up any varmint at long range, but it will also travel far after striking either the ground or small, feathered or furred game.

Bullets in 7mm made for varmint shooting and weighing 100 to 130 grains are fine if they blow up sufficiently, but this caliber bullet is not as far advanced for strictly varmint work as some bullets of other calibers.

If you want to go big, then the 110-grain, .30 caliber bullet may be the top of the heap for varmint hunting. Again, some barrels give lousy accuracy with this short bullet. They also have a poor ballistic coefficient and lose velocity and, sometimes, accuracy quickly. The 150-grain, .30 caliber bullet will blow varmints sky-high, but there had better be a mountain behind them.

14

The Best Shots

Perhaps you have heard some hunter say that if he couldn't get a shot at some big-game animal's head or neck he wouldn't shoot. His reasoning for this is he would either kill the animal cleanly in its tracks or miss it completely. It sounds like a humane way to hunt, but is it?

I've hunted with a few of these neck-head shot advocates. And, I've seen them shoot at animals that went down as if the ground had disappeared, but then came to life and hightailed it into the next county. The answer was always the same: "He was only creased, but it won't hurt him any. If the bullet had really hit him solid, he'd never have moved an ear." Again, it sounds plausible, but it isn't always true.

Let's take a long, hard look at neck and head shots and see what's wrong with them. First, we'll look at the positive side. *If* the bullet breaks the spinal cord or penetrates the brain, that animal will make no more tracks. But, if the bullet does not hit the brain on a head shot or break the neck bone completely, the story may have a different ending.

The spinal column is a mighty small area compared to the rest of any big-game animal's neck, and some animals have a lot more neck and a lot less bone than others. Also, the shape of the animal's neck does not always parallel the bone's curve on the inside. And, the way the hair grows often makes the shape of the

In some big-game animals, like this whitetail deer, the spinal column is a small area compared to the rest of the neck. If your bullet misses the bone in a neck shot, there is more than a 50 percent chance the animal will run off.

neck a lot different. As an example, elk and caribou have a mane that hangs down to the bottom of the neck, which means the bone is in the top one-fourth of the neck profile. Conversely, a Rocky Mountain goat has a mane on top of his neck which places the spinal column somewhere in the center of the broadside profile, with the exact location depending on which end of the neck you are aiming at. Behind the skull, the neck bone is close to the top; back near the shoulder, it is slightly below center.

If your bullet misses the bone, there is more than a 50-50 chance that the animal will run off, unless you can get in another shot. He is almost certain to hit the deck when shot, but if you don't stay put and watch him for several minutes, he will most likely run off. And, when he does, he will leave little or no blood, unless you cut the jugular vein; in that case, he will bleed profusely and will die within a short distance from where he was hit. A jugular shot is mostly accidental and not considered good shooting or bullet placement.

If the bullet lands in the fleshy part of the neck, the animal *may* recover. But, the swelling may make it impossible for the animal to swallow, inhibit blood circulation or hinder proper breathing. A slow, agonizing death is not a pleasant thought!

Even worse, either the esophagus or windpipe may be cut. If the esophagus is hit, the animal will slowly starve to death; if it's the windpipe, it may drown in its own blood after a short time. Either way, the chances of your finding it are very small. It will run, leave no visible blood trail, and may not lie down to die for many hours.

Some hunters say that if you're using a small caliber cartridge with a light, fast-expanding bullet, the neck is the place to hit. This isn't always true. Many big-game animals—moose, elk, caribou and buck mule deer during the rut—have large, heavily muscled necks. I've seen several animals that were shot in the neck with light bullets that blew up before reaching the neck bone. I once opened a big muley buck's neck and removed a 117-grain, .25-35 bullet that had expanded perfectly and lodged against the bone. It caused no damage whatsoever except to flatten the buck temporarily. While running away, he was finished off with a lung shot with one of the same bullets. During the rut, his neck had swollen to twice its normal size.

For animals the size of a big bull elk or a bull moose (especially the Alaskan variety), it takes a bullet specifically designed for deep penetration to drive in deep enough to break the bone. Often, when one of these big fellows goes down from being hit in the neck, only to get up and take off, the hunter assumes that the bullet only creased him when, in fact, the bullet actually was placed right. It just didn't go deep enough to break the bone.

The head shot is even worse because the brain is quite small compared with the size of the head. A bull elk or moose, for instance, has a head that is 2 feet long by over a foot deep under the antlers, but the brain is about the size of a small grapefruit. Miss it, and he may not even go down. You could shoot out an eye, break the jaw or blow the bull's nose away, and he'll go for many miles and live for days. You'll just go home with a guilty conscience.

I've encountered several deer that had been shot in the head but were running around with hanging jaws several days after they were hit. A couple of years ago, I was hunting elk and flushed a big cow out of her bed in a timbered draw-bottom. She moved onto an open hillside, stopping where I could get a clear view of her body through treetop branches. I thought something was swinging under her head, but couldn't be sure so I shot her through the lungs. She had been shot before in the head and her lower jaw was hanging only by the hide. Her tongue had been severed near the tip—a sad sight. Naturally, she was of no use for meat, but I was thankful I had found her and put her out of her misery.

If you miss while aiming for the lung-shoulder area by the same amount that you might miss on a shot at the brain or neck bone, you will still kill the animal quickly. He may go a few yards, but he'll be somewhere close and very dead.

Bullet Trailing

When asking how a certain brand make and design performed in a given cartridge on a certain species of game, you may have received the answer: "It killed him didn't it? And, that's all I'm interested in."

This simple answer seems to settle the issue. The hunter is happy because he has sidestepped the problem of bullet performance and he feels better because he doesn't need to find out why it killed. But, there are many cases in which the bullet fails to give a quick, clean kill when it seems to be placed exactly right. What then?

Hunters often condemn one bullet because an animal seemingly hit in a vital area ran off and had to be tracked down. But, they sing the praises of another that landed in about the same place and

When a hunter is field dressing an animal, he should trace the bullet's path carefully. This allows him to learn why the bullet succeeded or failed at its specific mission.

the animal died almost instantly. Yet, they never bother to trace the path the bullet took to find out why it failed or succeeded.

I'll grant you it's a messy, time-consuming job. But, highly revealing! A bullet that kills like lightning when it lands in the lungs of a small, big-game animal that is standing broadside, may not perform when you put it into the shoulder of a larger animal. Whether it kills or not, you'll never know why unless you do some digging.

I've been a bullet digger almost since the day I killed my first big-game animal. I guess it all started with my first big-game rifle. I killed a lot of game with that rifle, but I soon realized that a deer shot in the lungs didn't die as soon as it should. The bullets always went through a deer standing broadside—usually went through lengthwise, too—and often left a fairly large exit hole in the hide on the off-side. But, when I started removing the lungs and examining them carefully, I could find a small wound channel from point of entrance through the lungs, normally increasing in size about the time the bullet exited. Those bullets were not expanding very much until they had nearly penetrated the entire lung area. The deer didn't die instantly because little tissue was destroyed and internal hemorrhaging was slow.

These same bullets worked well on quartering shots into the shoulder, and performed nicely on elk—tearing a good-sized hole in the far lung on broadside shots and penetrating shoulders with ease on a quartering shot to blow even larger holes in the lungs. Careful tracing of the bullet's path showed *what* it had done. Digging out bullets that didn't exit revealed *why* they had done it.

This convinced me that more velocity and thinner jacket points for reliable expansion on deer-sized game was needed, so I started using 180- and 172-grain bullets. They blew a terrific hole in a buck's lungs, if the range wasn't too long, and he died fast. They killed elk on broadside lung shots, but lacked penetration on quartering shots from either end. When you followed the bullet path, you found a wound channel that blossomed out just under the hide, with hunks of lead and pieces of copper sprayed through the meat in every direction. This created a terrific wound that soon ended when the jacket completely ruptured and parted company with the core. Consequently, penetration wasn't great enough to reach the vitals of an elk shot from the wrong angle.

After having done this research, I got along well with the Krag using both bullet weights because, knowing how each performed and why, I could place them to get a quick, sure kill on the game I was hunting.

I use the .30-40 cartridge as an example because there were no reliable, special-purpose bullets in those days (the 1930s). Hunting bullets were all pretty much alike. Velocity and sectional density were used to control expansion and penetration because there was no other choice.

When digging bullets, it is not normally possible to slice the animal from end to end or side to side along the bullet's path to find out what action it took, especially on big animals like bull elk or moose. Open the animal up in the normal manner used to clean it, but avoid cutting up the innards any more than necessary. If a bullet which entered the shoulder or lungs has passed on into the paunch or intestines, carefully sort them out, following the bullet's path until you find it. At times, this is impossible because it may drop out into the grass or snow and be lost. Or, it may be lost in the mass of grass and water in the paunch. At least you'll know about how deep it penetrated and what it did along the way.

If the bullet passed through the lungs and heart area, lay them out after removal so that you can see when expansion started, what form the wound channel took, and how far the bullet traveled before losing its tearing energy. At times, you'll note that a bullet tears a much larger hole in the lungs of one animal than an identical bullet from the same rifle does in another animal of similar size. If you trace the bullet from the time it punctured the hide, you'll usually find out why. The bullet that passes between the ribs on entrance may not expand rapidly enough to tear up the lungs to any great extent, but if it hits a rib on the way out, it may leave a large exit hole in the hide. Expansion was delayed because the thin hide and soft lung tissue did not provide sufficient resistance. If it smashes one or more ribs on the way in, lung damage will be terrific, but if it exits the body, the hole may be small. This is because it expanded violently on the ribs as it entered, shedding velocity and much of its weight in the first few inches of penetration.

Bullets that are fired into animals quartering away from the gun, entering the lungs and angling into the off-shoulder, are easy to trace in the shoulder's heavy meat. The wound channel is easy to see and analyze, and the bullet is usually recoverable. If the bullet enters the shoulder and penetrates into the lungs, you'll be able to check the wound channel easily in the shoulder and lungs. If it goes on into the paunch, however, the chance of recovery is small. But, that kind of penetration, especially if the wound channel is large with plenty of tissue destroyed, tells you performance was good and the bullet retained a lot of its original weight. If it smashed the large shoulder bones of an elk or moose, and still penetrated and tore up the lungs for a quick kill, it is a top-drawer performer. This kind of performance requires a bullet of high sectional density designed to hold together and retain most of its original weight.

The point is, you will never know why the bullet killed quickly or did a sloppy job unless you do some digging. And, while you're digging, don't take anything for granted. Make sure you know what it did, and why.

What Is Overkill?

Occasionally, someone comes up with a phrase or term that catches on and is often repeated. Apparently, no one ever stops to think that it doesn't really make sense. Often, it is misleading and

In order to increase your hunting success, you need to know what you did right each time you kill an animal. The best way to learn is to get in there and "dig."

has little or no foundation in facts. Some of these are simply amusing, but others can give the wrong impression entirely.

On the amusing side, how often have you heard or read about someone shooting an animal "in the front shoulder," or "behind the front shoulder?" Actually, the term is technically correct but it's redundant because no animal has a rear shoulder. They have only forequarters or hindquarters, shoulders (front) and hams. So where else can you shoot it except in the front shoulder, if it is hit in the shoulder.

"Front shoulder" has been around longer than I can remember, but a more recent word used by some gun writers is "overkill." Now, I ask you, what is overkill? This word is, of course, applied to situations where the hunter used a cartridge more powerful than was needed to shoot the animal. But, it still doesn't make sense in my dim mind. It seems that if you kill an animal instantly with a bullet from any cartridge, he is about as dead as he

This Texas hog was taken with a T/C Contender chambered for the .30-30 Win. Would this hog have been any "less" or "more" dead if a magnum rifle was used? No. But, if a longer or more difficult shot had been required, there would have been fewer worries with a more powerful cartridge.

can get. It matters little if the bullet is a 50-grain peewee from a .222 or a 500-grain blockbuster from a .458.

To put it another way, shoot a deer through the lungs with a .243, a .270 or a .30-06. He runs 50 yards or so and piles up in a heap, very dead. Now, shoot the same deer in the same place with a 7mm Mag., a .300 Mag. or a .338 Mag.—he goes the same distance and piles up just as dead, but no deader. But, somehow, when the deer is shot with the big cartridge, it's "overkill."

Why, I ask?

True, the hunter may be "over-gunned" because the cartridge is more powerful than necessary for the size of the animal shot, but it seems doubtful that it was overkilled.

It's not so much that there is anything wrong with the word, but there are implications that give some food for thought. Strangely enough, some hunters, especially those just starting out, seem to think that if a more powerful cartridge "overkills" game, there is nothing but tail and horns to pack home. They also think there is something wrong in using a cartridge that carries a bit more punch than is needed for the animal being shot.

First, let's take a look at the assumption that the more powerful cartridges suited to heavier game will turn any smaller animal inside out and render it unfit for the table. This is not necessarily so, and often not true at all. While there are exceptions to every rule, two causes of large amounts of bloodshot or torn-up meat are high velocity and bullets that expand violently, qualities which are usually coupled together. Sure, the big cartridges deliver higher velocities with heavy bullets than the small ones, but usually not with the bullet weights normally used in the respective cartridges.

If you want spectacular "drop-'em-in-their-tracks" kills with the animals the size of deer, the bullet that blows to confetti is the one to use, but don't expect to eat much of the shoulders if that's where you hit them. And, it doesn't matter whether the cartridge is standard or magnum. Quick, spectacular kills and little loss of meat do not go together except on brain, neck and some spine spots.

If I'm hunting where only antelope or deer will be found, I may choose a 6mm for the job. But, in most of the West and North, for example, there is usually larger game, such as elk, moose or grizzly, to be found on the same trip or day. If you have only a .243 Win. and you come onto a big animal under anything except extremely favorable conditions, you will either have to pass up the shot or you'll have a major trailing job on your hands—possibly losing a wounded animal. A bigger bore and heavier bullet (not necessarily a magnum) can save the day and the price of an unsuccessful trip. If deer, sheep or goat are all you see, the more potent cartridge will work just as well as the small one.

One of my favorite mule deer and antelope cartridges is a 7mm magnum in one form or another, and I've killed a lot of deer, sheep and goats with one of the big .30s, as well as some with bullets from a .338. Maybe they killed them a little too dead, and I just didn't know what to look for. Still, I wonder, what is overkill?

So He Didn't Drop Instantly

It seems that in nearly everything we hear and read, the criterion for determining any cartridge's killing power is whether the animal "dropped in his tracks." Most of this is done to emphasize how good the storyteller's pet cartridge or load is, with maybe a touch of dramatization thrown in to make a good story better. If someone admits that the buck or bull ran a few yards before it expired, the immediate assumption is that the cartridge or load was completely inadequate, or that the bullet was poorly placed.

Most of us have been guilty of creating this impression at one time or another. While hunters who have killed a lot of game know these instant kills are the exception rather than the rule, inexperienced hunters often get the wrong impression—an impression that causes unnecessary loss of a number of game animals each year.

If the brain is struck, or the forward part of the spinal cord severed, death comes with bullet impact and the animal will drop where it stands. But, unfortunately, not all bullets landing in the head find the brain, and not all neck and spine shots sever the spinal cord. So, rather than dwelling on the relatively unusual brain or spinal cord hits, let's discuss the more common rib shots where the bullet penetrates the heart or lung area.

True, some animals shot in the lungs and/or heart drop instantly and die almost as instantly, but these cases are rare. Even if they do drop, they may jump up almost as quickly and dash off for some distance before they drop for good.

Too much emphasis has been put on the heart shot as an instant killer of any, and all, game. The majority of deer shot through the heart will take off as though they had a bee under their tails, often making a great, high jump as they start, and going anywhere from a few feet to well over 100 yards. A heart-shot deer is dead. Just because it doesn't drop in its tracks doesn't mean its heart was not hit. Other species, as well as individual animals of the same species, react differently; elk and moose often show little or no indication of having been hit. They may stand still until they die, or casually walk away as if nothing had happened.

Whether it belongs to the black or grizzly clans, a bear usually reacts violently when hit, regardless of where the bullet lands. A hit in the heart or lung area will usually flatten the bear, but its normal reaction is to bounce back on its feet and go like heck for some distance.

It doesn't seem to make much difference whether the game animal is standing still, walking or running all out, or whether it is aware of the hunter's presence. A standing deer, for instance, whether he sees the hunter or not, is more likely to run with a solid lung or heart hit than to drop in its tracks. If it is running when hit, it will most likely keep running instead of piling up when hit. Even a deer that is solidly hit while lying in its bed often springs up and

Bears are usually violent after they've been hit. This black bear's normal reaction was to run before dropping. A hunter should be prepared to shoot again when approaching a bear—for safety's sake.

dashes some distance before falling to earth.

Recently, I shot a big mule deer buck in his bed as he lay quartering away. The buck was completely unaware of any danger until the 95-grain, 6mm Nosler slammed into his ribs just below the spine and ranged down and forward, tearing through the lungs and through the off-shoulder to the hide at its point. He came out of his bed and leaped away as if the bullet had landed low and peppered him with shale. He made the first 30 yards in great bounds around the mountain, then turned downhill and two jumps later tumbled down the mountainside.

The cartridge's caliber matters little, providing it is potent enough to tear up a lot of lung tissue or punch a big hole in the heart. Someone may assume that the 6mm Rem. lacked punch enough to anchor the buck in his bed, but this isn't necessarily so.

I remember shooting a similar-sized buck with a .30 magnum and a highly explosive, 172-grain bullet that started at over 3,000 fps. The buck was hit broadside in the ribs. The bullet tore a hole so big through both lungs that you could stick your head in. With an exit hole over 4 inches in diameter, pieces of lung were scattered over a 10-foot area on the snowy hillside. That buck ran around the mountain for over 100 yards, then turned downhill and, after another 30 yards or so, smashed into a big fir so hard that one antler was broken off near the skull.

The answer in both these cases was that these bucks were dead and didn't know it. One buck was running completely blind, dead on his feet; the other had enough life left in him to bound up from his bed and run until the last spark was gone.

This doesn't mean that heart or lung shots are not fatal if the bullets expand correctly; normally, there is no surer shot. It simply means that in the majority of cases, game solidly hit in the vital chest area do not drop instantly. And, if any hunter who has killed or has seen much game killed thinks back over those kills, he will find that most animals died after traveling a few feet up to as much as 200 yards after impact. In fact, if he averaged those figures, he'll find that the average distance traveled by deer will run close to 50 yards. He would probably find that more deer traveled over 50 yards after being shot than dropped instantly and stayed down.

Those instances when an animal drops upon being shot, as though the earth had been jerked from under him, seem to always take precedence in our memories over the many times when the animal ran off into the brush before it died. Those quick kills are "braggin'" shots!

The worst part is that thousands of first-time hunters and some with limited experience get the notion that every animal they shoot will drop in its tracks when hit. If it runs off out of sight, they assume a miss and make no attempt to follow the animal. Thousands of game animals are lost each fall because of this misconception. This is especially true in heavy cover, where only a few jumps will put an animal out of sight. It often happens in open country where a ridge, draw or hollow can conceal the animal. In many cases, if the hunter followed the animal for only a few yards or even scouted the area beyond where it disappeared, he would probably find it lying dead in plain sight.

Remember, a very small percentage of the animals shot will fall in their tracks. And, when someone tells you that his pet rifle always "drops 'em where they stand," hand him a salt tablet.

15

No Magic Involved

Some people's nature is to believe that anything they happen to own is just a little superior to a similar item owned by someone else. You know how it is, if they happen to be driving a Ford this year, no other car is quite as good. But, if they buy a Chevy next year, the fellow who drives a Ford is herding a pile of junk. And, this line of thinking is probably more prevalent among hunters than anyone else.

It shows itself in the brand of rifle or shotgun used, the scope mount on it and the brand of ammunition used in it. It seems completely impossible to them that anyone else could use another brand without risking complete failure. These things can be at least partially understood because of the individual's likes and dislikes, but the attitude some people have toward calibers and cartridges is downright ridiculous.

When I was growing up and starting to hunt big game, there were still many lever-action rifles in use all over the West. Many of these were M94 Winchesters chambered for the .25-35, .30-30 and .32 Winchester Special cartridges. I can still hear some of the hot arguments between owners of .30-30s and .32 Specials. The .30-30 fans swore they couldn't see how anyone killed anything with a .32 Special, and the fellows who owned the .32s thought the .30-30 boys had sawdust in their heads instead of brains. It is amazing how much more wallop one packed than the other, or how much farther away one would shoot as flat as a beam of light, while the other hit down the hill so far below the buck that he didn't know he'd been shot at. The most amazing part is, of course, that there isn't a dime's worth of difference between the two. They both use 170-grain, flat-point bullets in cases of the same capacity. And, while the .32 is slightly larger in diameter and pushes the bullet a wee bit faster, the .30 makes up for the slight difference with better sectional density and ballistic coefficient. Put them in a bag, shake them up, and they'll fall out of the same hole!

At that time, the bolt guns were just starting to catch on, and the most popular cartridges were the .30-40 and the .30-06. Here again, the battle lines formed with some claiming the .30-40 killed a whole lot better than the newer cartridge, while the ought-six fans felt so superior that they hated to pack their new rifles in company with the old Krag. Most .30-40 owners did admit that the larger cartridge had a bit more range, but contended that the old Krag cartridge had some hidden killing power the '06 lacked!

Not long ago, a friend of mine was singing the praises of the .243 Win. When I showed little enthusiasm for his claims of his rifle's phenomenal killing power, he looked at me critically and asked if I had ever killed any big game with the cartridge. I told him I had shot many varmints with one, but no big game. But, I said that I had killed many deer with the 6mm Rem. and the .240 Wthby and had failed to notice the spectacular kills he had experienced. His answer was, "You should try the .243 Win. sometime. It always drops a deer in his tracks!" He also added that for some reason he couldn't actually define, the .243 Win. killed much better than any other 6mm cartridges.

Not long ago, a big outdoor magazine ran an article by a well-known outdoor writer on the famous old Holland & Holland cartridges, the .300 and .375. I don't think there is any argument among hunters who have ever used either cartridge that they were and still are good killers.

But, the part that gave me acute gas pains was this fellow's claim that there was something supernatural in the way these two cartridges killed everything from ground squirrels to elephants. He couldn't explain exactly what it was, but apparently some witch's brew was poured into the case along with the bullet and powder.

Just why the .300 H&H should kill any better than the .308 Norma, the .300 Win. or the .300 Wthby (all of which have more of the same thing); or, why the .375 H&H is more potent than the .375 Wthby or the blockbusting .378, escapes my feeble mind. All these cartridges in respective calibers fire the same bullets, as do many wildcats of the same calibers. The only difference is that some squirt bullets of the same weight out a bit faster than others. According to all rules of mathematics and ballistics, the cartridge that starts a bullet the fastest of the same weight, caliber and shape, not only packs more punch but shoots flatter. Any advantage in killing power lies with the cartridge delivering the highest velocity. And, while both H&H cartridges are extremely reliable killers, they are at the back of the line in velocity behind any of the commercial magnums of the same calibers.

The believers often claim that a particular combination of bore diameter, bullet weight and velocity give the cartridge just the right touch—a touch that a cartridge of either more or less velocity does not have. Now, stop and give this a long, hard look. Using factory ballistics, the .300 H&H starts a 180-grain bullet at 2,920 fps with 3,400 foot-pounds of energy. Using an average-pointed bullet, the velocity drops to just over 2,000 fps at 400 yards, and the energy to a bit over 1,600 fp. How can it have that "mystical something" at all ranges that no other cartridge has when the .30-30 has nearly as much velocity and energy at its normal 100-yard range as the .300 does at 400 yards where it is often asked to kill? On the other hand, the .300 Win., 180-grain is still steaming along at exactly the same speed at 300 yards as the .300 H&H is at 200. Now, it appears that somewhere within that range of distances all of the .30-caliber cartridges have the same velocity and energy.

The point is that if there were some bullet-diameter/bullet-weight/velocity/energy combination that provided a magic touch of killing power, any given cartridge would have it at only one range, give or take a few yards. And, any other cartridge in the same caliber would also probably have it at some range.

Also, it seems rather odd that there would be one cartridge within a given caliber that would always lay the game flat without a quiver, when other cartridges shooting bullets of the same diameter, weight and make, and at nearly the same velocity, usually kill them only after they have made a few jumps.

The truth is that if there is any difference in killing power between two cartridges of the same caliber, the advantage lies with the one that has the highest velocity, if the bullet performs correctly at that velocity. The secret is that if one cartridge outperforms a more powerful number of the same caliber, the bullet used performed better for the kind of game being shot.

The cold fact is that no cartridge holds mystical killing power;

a cartridge packs only the killing power that velocity, energy and bullet action can deliver at the range at which the game is hit. There is no magic involved!

How Big Are They?

Probably more confusion, misconception and plain corral dust appear in tales told and written about the size of big-game animals than in any other aspect of hunting. Like fishermen, hunters are prone to overestimate the size of animals they take, as well as the ones they missed or just saw as they disappeared over the hill.

Few hunters actually measure or weigh the animals they talk about so if the big one that Uncle Snuffy killed was so big, this one must be a little larger. This is human nature, and it also applies to a lot of things not even connected with hunting or fishing. But, an unusual aspect of these tales is that a few of them actually run counter to the natural instinct to enlarge, and the animals are portrayed as being smaller than they actually are. This material often comes from sources that should be completely reliable. In this case, it is not that the material is incorrect, but it's the manner in which it is presented.

Take the weight of an elk, for example. Most of us have read the reports on the weight of elk killed in Yellowstone Park by park personnel when the herd had to be thinned because it outgrew its range. According to these reports, few mature bulls ran over 700 pounds on the hoof. I have no quarrel with the figures—they are undoubtedly correct—but remember that the bulls were killed in the middle of the winter when many were close to starvation. These reports lead some people to believe that this *is* the normal weight level of mature bull elk. They do not know that the same bulls weighed several hundred pounds more when the rut started the previous September.

I've seen reports on studies made of Rocky Mountain goats that gave the weights of old billies at 200 pounds or less. Again, most were trapped during late winter or early spring after losing at least a third of their weight the previous fall.

I've never been able to weigh a really big trophy-class goat because you don't pack a scale around in goat country or pack the goat out whole. But, I do know from weighing other game that I've skinned that several were at least one-third heavier than their winter weight.

I have never weighed a bull elk on the hoof, but I have weighed the skinned quarters ready to be cut and wrapped, totaling

The average adult male black bear (above) has an overall length of 4½ to 6½ feet; a height at shoulder of 3 feet; and weighs 250 to 400 pounds. The average adult male grizzly bear (below) has an overall length of 6 to 7 feet; a height at shoulder of 3½ feet; and weighs 450 to 800 pounds.

The average adult male Alaskan brown bear (above) has an overall length of 8 to 9 feet; a height at shoulder of 4½ feet; and weighs 800 to 1,200 pounds. The average mature bull elk (below) has an overall length of 7½ to 10 feet; a height at shoulder of 4½ to 5 feet; and weighs 700 to 1,000 pounds.

The average mature buck mule deer (above) has an overall length of 6 to 6½ feet; a height at shoulder of 3½ feet; and weighs 150 to 200 pounds. The average mature buck blacktail deer (below) has an overall length of 5½ to 6 feet; a height at shoulder of 3½ feet; and weighs 150 to 175 pounds.

The average mature buck whitetail deer (above) has an overall length of 5 to 6 feet; a height at shoulder of 3 to 3½ feet; and weighs 125 to 160 pounds. The average mature bull moose (below) has an overall length of 8 to 10 feet; a height at shoulder of 5½ to 7½ feet; and weighs 900 to 1,800 pounds.

The average mature bull caribou (above) has an overall length of 6¹/₂ to 7¹/₂ feet; a height at shoulder of 3¹/₂ to 5 feet; and weighs 300 to 400 pounds. The average mature buck pronghorn antelope (below) has an overall length of 4 to 5 feet; a height at shoulder of 3 feet; and weighs 100 to 120 pounds.

The average mature billy mountain goat (above) has an overall length of 5 to 6 feet; a height at shoulder of 3 to 3½ feet; and weighs 150 to 300 pounds. The average adult ram Bighorn sheep (below) has an overall length of 5 to 6 feet; a height at shoulder of 3 to 3½ feet; and weighs 150 to 200 pounds.

The cottontail rabbit (above) has an overall length of 15 to 18 inches and weighs 2 to 4 pounds. The snowshoe hare (below) has an overall length of 15 to 20½ inches and weighs 2 to 4½ pounds.

The adult male coyote (above) has an overall length of 44 to 54 inches; a height at shoulder of 23 to 26 inches; and weighs 30 pounds. The adult male wolverine (below) has an overall length of 38 to 40 inches; a height at shoulder of 16 to 17 inches; and weighs 16 to 35 pounds.

500 pounds of clear meat. This would project to about half-a-ton on the hoof, live weight, and that was near the end of the rutting season when the bull had lost a lot of weight.

There is one other point at which size is underestimated, and it causes confusion along with missed shots at long range. Some scope manufacturers provide a body depth scale, from back to belly line, to use in judging distance for rangefinder stadia wires and reticles. The figures I've seen are much too conservative when you consider that body depth is from *hairline to hairline*. Take deer bodies listed at 18 inches. This supposedly includes all deer, but there's a lot of difference in body depth between the several whitetail subspecies and a mature muley buck. Most big mule deer bucks will go 20 to 22 inches.

Elk are listed at only 2 feet from top to bottom, and I've taped several bulls that spanned 34 to 36 inches hairline to hairline. Any decent bull will measure 30 inches or more.

Goats and sheep also are underestimated. I've measured a number of rams, including Dall, that were 22 inches from back to brisket. Any big billy goat with a decent fall coat of hair measures at least 2 feet of what you see from broadside. We could go on through the full list of North American, big-game animals, but these examples illustrate the point. Remember that meat or the vitals are not the point here. It's what the hunter sees through the scope.

An animal's height at the shoulder is another statistic that is usually badly miscalculated in the minds of most hunters. How often have you heard some hunter talk about a buck mule deer that stood 4 feet at the shoulder? The truth is that very few will stand 3½ feet, and 40 inches will catch most of them. Big Dall, Stone and Bighorn rams also stand 40 to 42 inches from hoof to shoulder.

Little is ever said about the height of caribou. There is a difference between the size of the various subspecies, but for whatever it's worth, I've measured some trophy-class bulls from various parts of Alaska that averaged about 52 inches. Some barren ground caribou may average shorter; the mountain caribou slightly taller.

Mature bull elk will average around 62 inches at the shoulder, with the real old-timers going as much as 65 inches. That is taller than many saddle horses.

But, when we hear about the shoulder height of moose, the tales often are a lot taller than the moose. I've taped Shiras, Canadian and Alaska-Yukon bulls, and all are big, but not as high at the hump as some would have us believe. Shiras bulls run from 6 feet to 6 feet, 8 inches, with few, if any, larger. Canadian bulls vary a lot, but 6 feet, 8 inches or so will catch most of them. The largest Alaskan bull I taped went an even 7 feet from the heel of his hoof to the top of the shoulder hump. You could have measured that bull to at least 7½ feet if the tape went to the end of his toes, but a moose doesn't prance around ballet-style.

When considering the size of bears, things really get fouled up. Black bears aren't so bad, but most are estimated at double their actual weight. Listen to grizzly stories and you'll find that most of them weigh 800 to 1,000 pounds, with brown bear half-again as heavy. It's just not fashionable to kill anything smaller. Few hunters or guides have the faintest idea what a bear weighs by looking at it. And, about the only ones that are actually weighed are those caught and tranquilized during studies made on Alaskan brown bears from Admiralty Island to the Alaska Peninsula. There are records of several hundred bears that were captured, measured and many of them weighed in the spring, summer and fall. And, it is possible that some of the spring and summer bears would have weighed a half-ton if fat, but the fact remains that none did.

Hide size is often just as misleading. You are supposed to lay the hide on a flat surface and spread it out, then measure from claw point to claw point across the front legs, and from tip of tail to end of nose *without* touching the hide. Unfortunately, it's not always done that way. Slippery guides and hunters can make a 10-footer out of any honest 8-footer if they pull a little in the right places at the right time.

The truth is that very little authentic data is available to the average hunter on the size and weight of American, big-game animals, and much of what is told and printed only serve to confuse the issue. You can measure your own kills, but you're not likely to weigh many of the big ones.

16

Selecting The Right Ammunition

After all the time and effort put into setting up a hunting trip, you should never settle for just "any" ammunition. Selecting rifle ammunition can be very confusing and time consuming. There are many manufacturers who make several types of cartridges and bullets. However, the final decision is always yours and should be made carefully.

First, you will need to comply with the rifle manufacturer's specifications. A firearm's chamber is designed to shoot one specific cartridge safely and accurately. Don't ever try to use a cartridge for which your firearm was not designed. The result could be disastrous!

Second, when choosing a bullet you will need to know the size of game you will be hunting. Also, you should know the type of terrain and situation the game will most likely be in. This information is pertinent in making the right selection.

The following pages contain ballistic charts from the United States' top three ammunition manufacturers: Federal Cartridge Company, Winchester and Remington. These ballistic charts contain rimfire cartridges and centerfire rifle cartridges, as well as various bullet definitions. Even though critics question the applicability of factory ballistic results, they are certainly a helpful starting point in selecting and testing hunting ammunition for your particular set of hunting conditions.

PREMIUM® HIGH ENERGY RIFLE

Usage Key: □ = Varmints, predators, small

USAGE	FEDERAL LOAD NO.	CALIBER	BULLET WGT. IN GRAINS	GRAMS	BULLET STYLE	FACTORY PRIMER NO.	VELOCITY IN FEET PER SECOND (TO NEAREST 10 FPS)						ENERGY IN FOOT-POUNDS (TO NEAREST 5 FOOT-POUNDS)					
							MUZZLE	100 YDS.	200 YDS.	300 YDS.	400 YDS.	500 YDS.	MUZZLE	100 YDS.	200 YDS.	300 YDS.	400 YDS.	500 Y
NEW	P308T2	308 Win. (7.62x51mm)	165	10.69	Trophy Bonded Bear Claw	210	2870	2600	2350	2120	1890	1690	3020	2485	2030	1640	1310	10-
NEW	P308G	308 Win. (7.62x51mm)	180	11.66	Nosler Partition	210	2740	2550	2370	2200	2030	1870	3000	2600	2245	1925	1645	139
NEW	P3006T3	30-06 Spring (7.62x63mm)	180	11.66	Trophy Bonded Bear Claw	210	2880	2630	2380	2160	1940	1740	3315	2755	2270	1855	1505	12
NEW	P3006R	30-06 Spring (7.62x63mm)	180	11.66	Nosler Partition	210	2880	2690	2500	2320	2150	1980	3315	2880	2495	2150	1845	15
NEW	P300WT3	300 Win. Mag.	180	11.66	Trophy Bonded Bear Claw	215	3100	2830	2580	2340	2110	1900	3840	3205	2660	2190	1790	144
NEW	P300WE	300 Win. Mag.	200	12.96	Nosler Partition	215	2930	2740	2550	2370	2200	2030	3810	3325	2885	2495	2145	184
NEW	P338T2	338 Win. Mag.	225	14.58	Trophy Bonded Bear Claw	215	2940	2690	2450	2230	2010	1810	4320	3610	3000	2475	2025	16-
NEW	P338D	338 Win. Mag.	250	16.20	Nosler Partition	215	2800	2610	2420	2250	2080	1920	4350	3775	3260	2805	2395	20.

PREMIUM® HUNTING RIFLE

Usage Key: □ = Varmints, predators, small

USAGE	FEDERAL LOAD NO.	CALIBER	BULLET WGT. IN GRAINS	GRAMS	BULLET STYLE*	FACTORY PRIMER NO.	VELOCITY IN FEET PER SECOND (TO NEAREST 10 FPS)						ENERGY IN FOOT-POUNDS (TO NEAREST 5 FOOT-POUNDS)					
							MUZZLE	100 YDS.	200 YDS.	300 YDS.	400 YDS.	500 YDS.	MUZZLE	100 YDS.	200 YDS.	300 YDS.	400 YDS.	500 Y
	P223E	223 Rem. (5.56x45mm)	55	3.56	Sierra GameKing BTHP	205	3240	2770	2340	1950	1610	1330	1280	935	670	465	315	2
	P22250B	22-250 Rem.	55	3.56	Sierra GameKing BTHP	210	3680	3280	2920	2590	2280	1990	1655	1315	1040	815	630	48
	P243C	243 Win. (6x6mm)	100	6.48	Sierra GameKing BTSP	210	2960	2760	2570	2380	2210	2040	1950	1690	1460	1260	1080	92
	P243D	243 Win. (6x6mm)	85	5.50	Sierra GameKing BTHP	210	3320	3070	2830	2600	2380	2180	2080	1770	1510	1280	1070	89
	P243F	243 Win. (6x6mm)	70	4.54	Nosler Ballistic Tip	210	3400	3070	2760	2470	2200	1950	1795	1465	1185	950	755	59
	P6C	6mm Rem.	100	6.48	Nosler Partition	210	3100	2860	2640	2420	2220	2020	2135	1820	1545	1300	1090	90
	P257B	257 Roberts (High-Velocity + P)	120	7.77	Nosler Partition	210	2780	2560	2360	2160	1970	1790	2060	1750	1480	1240	1030	85
NEW	P257WBA	257 Weatherby Magnum	115	7.45	Nosler Partition	210	3150	2900	2660	2440	2220	2020	2535	2145	1810	1515	1260	104
NEW	P257WBT1	257 Weatherby Magnum	115	7.45	Trophy Bonded Bear Claw	210	3150	2890	2640	2400	2180	1970	2535	2125	1775	1470	1210	99
	P2506C	25-06 Rem.	117	7.58	Sierra GameKing BTSP	210	2990	2770	2570	2370	2190	2000	2320	2000	1715	1465	1240	104
	P2506D	25-06 Rem.	100	6.48	Nosler Ballistic Tip	210	3210	2960	2720	2490	2280	2070	2290	1940	1640	1380	1150	95
NEW	P2506E	25-06 Rem.	115	7.45	Nosler Partition	210	2990	2750	2520	2300	2100	1900	2285	1930	1620	1350	1120	91
NEW	P2506T1	25-06 Rem.	115	7.45	Trophy Bonded Bear Claw	210	2990	2740	2500	2270	2050	1850	2285	1910	1590	1310	1075	87
	P270C	270 Win.	150	9.72	Sierra GameKing BTSP	210	2850	2660	2480	2300	2130	1970	2705	2355	2040	1760	1510	129
	P270D	270 Win.	130	8.42	Sierra GameKing BTSP	210	3060	2830	2620	2410	2220	2030	2700	2320	1980	1680	1420	119
	P270E	270 Win.	150	9.72	Nosler Partition	210	2850	2590	2340	2100	1880	1670	2705	2225	1815	1470	1175	93
	P270F	270 Win.	130	8.42	Nosler Ballistic Tip	210	3060	2840	2630	2430	2230	2050	2700	2325	1990	1700	1440	121
	P270T1	270 Win.	140	9.07	Trophy Bonded Bear Claw	210	2940	2700	2480	2260	2060	1860	2685	2270	1905	1590	1315	108
NEW	P270T2	270 Win.	130	8.42	Trophy Bonded Bear Claw	210	3060	2810	2570	2340	2130	1930	2705	2275	1905	1585	1310	107
	P270WBA	270 Weatherby Magnum	130	8.42	Nosler Partition	210	3200	2960	2740	2520	2320	2120	2955	2530	2160	1835	1550	130
	P270WBT1	270 Weatherby Magnum	140	9.07	Trophy Bonded Bear Claw	210	3100	2840	2600	2370	2150	1950	2990	2510	2100	1745	1440	117
	P730A	7-30 Waters	120	7.77	BTSP	210	2700	2300	1930	1600	1330	1140	1940	1405	990	685	470	34
	P7C	7mm Mauser (7x57mm Mauser)	140	9.07	Nosler Partition	210	2660	2450	2260	2070	1890	1730	2200	1865	1585	1330	1110	93
	P764A	7x64 Brenneke	160	10.37	Nosler Partition	210	2650	2480	2310	2150	2000	1850	2495	2180	1895	1640	1415	121
	P280A	280 Rem.	150	9.72	Nosler Partition	210	2890	2620	2370	2140	1910	1710	2780	2295	1875	1520	1215	97
	P280T1	280 Rem.	140	9.07	Trophy Bonded Bear Claw	210	2990	2630	2310	2040	1730	1480	2770	2155	1655	1250	925	68
	P708A	7mm-08 Rem.	140	9.07	Nosler Partition	210	2800	2590	2390	2200	2020	1840	2435	2085	1775	1500	1265	106
NEW	P708B	7mm-08 Rem.	140	9.07	Nosler Ballistic Tip	210	2800	2610	2430	2260	2100	1940	2440	2135	1840	1590	1360	116
	P7RD	7mm Rem. Magnum	150	9.72	Sierra GameKing BTSP	215	3110	2920	2750	2580	2410	2250	3220	2850	2510	2210	1930	169
	P7RE	7mm Rem. Magnum	165	10.69	Sierra GameKing BTSP	215	2950	2800	2650	2510	2370	2230	3190	2865	2570	2300	2050	182
	P7RF	7mm Rem. Magnum	160	10.37	Nosler Partition	215	2950	2770	2590	2420	2250	2090	3090	2715	2375	2075	1800	155
	P7RG	7mm Rem. Magnum	140	9.07	Nosler Partition	215	3150	2930	2710	2510	2320	2130	3085	2660	2290	1960	1670	141
NEW	P7RH	7mm Rem. Magnum	150	9.72	Nosler Ballistic Tip	215	3110	2910	2720	2540	2370	2200	3220	2825	2470	2150	1865	161
	P7RT1	7mm Rem. Magnum	175	11.34	Trophy Bonded Bear Claw	215	2860	2660	2470	2290	2120	1950	3180	2750	2375	2040	1740	147
	P7RT2	7mm Rem. Magnum	160	10.37	Trophy Bonded Bear Claw	215	2940	2630	2350	2080	1830	1600	3070	2460	1950	1530	1185	90
	P7WBA	7mm Weatherby Magnum	160	10.37	Nosler Partition	215	3050	2850	2650	2470	2290	2120	3305	2880	2505	2165	1865	160
	P7WBT1	7mm Weatherby Magnum	160	10.37	Trophy Bonded Bear Claw	215	3050	2730	2420	2140	1880	1640	3305	2640	2085	1630	1255	95
	P3030D	30-30 Win.	170	11.01	Nosler Partition	210	2200	1900	1620	1380	1190	1060	1830	1355	990	720	535	42
	P308C	308 Win. (7.62x51mm)	165	10.69	Sierra GameKing BTSP	210	2700	2520	2330	2160	1990	1830	2670	2310	1990	1700	1450	123
	P308E	308 Win. (7.62x51mm)	180	11.66	Nosler Partition	210	2620	2430	2240	2060	1890	1730	2745	2355	2005	1700	1430	120
	P308F	308 Win. (7.62x51mm)	150	9.72	Nosler Ballistic Tip	210	2820	2610	2410	2220	2040	1860	2650	2270	1935	1640	1380	115
	P308T1	308 Win. (7.62x51mm)	165	10.69	Trophy Bonded Bear Claw	210	2700	2440	2200	1970	1760	1570	2670	2185	1775	1425	1135	90
	P3006B	30-06 Spring (7.62x63mm)	165	10.69	Sierra GameKing BTSP	210	2800	2610	2420	2240	2070	1910	2870	2490	2150	1840	1580	134
	P3006F	30-06 Spring (7.62x63mm)	180	11.66	Nosler Partition	210	2700	2500	2320	2140	1970	1810	2915	2510	2150	1830	1550	135
	P3006G	30-06 Spring (7.62x63mm)	150	9.72	Sierra GameKing BTSP	210	2910	2690	2480	2270	2070	1880	2820	2420	2040	1710	1430	118
	P3006L	30-06 Spring (7.62x63mm)	180	11.66	Nosler Partition	210	2700	2540	2380	2220	2080	1930	2915	2570	2260	1975	1720	149
	P3006P	30-06 Spring (7.62x63mm)	150	9.72	Nosler Ballistic Tip	210	2910	2700	2490	2300	2110	1940	2820	2420	2070	1760	1485	124
	P3006Q	30-06 Spring (7.62x63mm)	165	10.69	Nosler Ballistic Tip	210	2800	2610	2430	2250	2080	1920	2870	2495	2155	1855	1585	135
	P3006T1	30-06 Spring (7.62x63mm)	165	10.69	Trophy Bonded Bear Claw	210	2800	2540	2290	2050	1830	1630	2870	2360	1915	1545	1230	97
	P3006T2	30-06 Spring (7.62x63mm)	180	11.66	Trophy Bonded Bear Claw	210	2700	2460	2220	2000	1800	1610	2915	2410	1975	1600	1290	103
	P300MC	300 Win. Magnum	200	12.96	Sierra GameKing BTSP	215	2830	2680	2530	2380	2240	2110	3560	3180	2830	2520	2230	1970
NEW	P300WT4	300 Win. Magnum	150	9.72	Trophy Bonded Bear Claw	215	3280	2980	2700	2430	2190	1950	3570	2450	2420	1970	1590	1270
NEW	P35WT1	35 Whelen	225	14.58	Trophy Bonded Bear Claw	210	2500	2300	2110	1930	1770	1610	3120	2650	2235	1870	1560	1290

+P ammunition is loaded to a higher pressure. Use only in firearms so recommended by the gun manufacturer.
*BTHP = Boat-Tail Hollow Point   BTSP = Boat-Tail Soft Point

☐ = Medium game   ☐ = Large, heavy game   ☐ = Dangerous game   ☐ = Target shooting, training, practice

| | | WIND DRIFT IN INCHES @ 10 MPH CROSSWIND | | | | | HEIGHT OF BULLET TRAJECTORY IN INCHES ABOVE OR BELOW LINE OF SIGHT IF ZEROED AT @ YARDS. SIGHTS 1.5 INCHES ABOVE BORE LINE. | | | | | | | | | TEST BARREL LENGTH | FEDERAL LOAD |
| | | | | | | | AVERAGE RANGE | | | LONG RANGE | | | | | | | |
100 YDS.	200 YDS.	300 YDS.	400 YDS.	500 YDS.	50 YDS.	100 YDS.	200 YDS.	300 YDS.	50 YDS.	100 YDS.	200 YDS.	300 YDS.	400 YDS.	500 YDS.	INCHES	NO.
1.0	3.8	9.2	17.0	28.4	-0.2	⊕	-3.6	-13.6	+0.7	+1.8	⊕	-8.2	-24.0	-49.9	24	P308T2
0.7	2.9	6.8	12.6	20.2	-0.1	⊕	-3.8	-13.9	+0.8	+1.9	⊕	-8.2	-23.5	-47.1	24	P308G
0.9	3.6	8.7	16.1	26.6	-0.2	⊕	-3.5	-13.3	+0.7	+1.8	⊕	-8.0	-23.3	-48.2	24	P3006T3
0.7	2.8	6.3	11.7	19.0	-0.2	⊕	-3.3	-12.2	+0.7	+1.7	⊕	-7.2	-21.0	-42.2	24	P3006R
0.8	3.3	7.7	14.5	23.6	-0.3	⊕	-2.9	-10.9	+0.5	+1.4	⊕	-6.6	-19.7	-40.4	24	P300WT3
0.7	2.6	6.0	11.2	18.2	-0.2	⊕	-3.2	-11.6	+0.6	+1.6	⊕	-6.9	-20.1	-40.4	24	P300WE
0.9	3.4	8.1	15.1	24.7	-0.2	⊕	-3.3	-12.4	+0.6	+1.7	⊕	-7.5	-22.0	-45.0	24	P338T2
0.7	2.8	6.6	12.3	19.7	-0.2	⊕	-3.6	-13.1	+0.7	+1.8	⊕	-7.8	-22.5	-44.9	24	P338D

☐ = Medium game   ☐ = Large, heavy game   ☐ = Dangerous game   ☐ = Target shooting, training, practice

| | | WIND DRIFT IN INCHES @ 10 MPH CROSSWIND | | | | | HEIGHT OF BULLET TRAJECTORY IN INCHES ABOVE OR BELOW LINE OF SIGHT IF ZEROED AT @ YARDS. SIGHTS 1.5 INCHES ABOVE BORE LINE. | | | | | | | | | TEST BARREL LENGTH | FEDERAL LOAD |
| | | | | | | | AVERAGE RANGE | | | LONG RANGE | | | | | | | |
100 YDS.	200 YDS.	300 YDS.	400 YDS.	500 YDS.	50 YDS.	100 YDS.	200 YDS.	300 YDS.	50 YDS.	100 YDS.	200 YDS.	300 YDS.	400 YDS.	500 YDS.	INCHES	NO.
1.3	5.8	14.2	27.7	47.6	-0.3	⊕	-2.7	-10.8	+0.4	+1.4	⊕	-6.7	-20.5	-43.4	24	P223E
0.8	3.6	8.4	15.8	26.3	-0.4	⊕	-1.7	-7.6	0	+0.9	⊕	-5.0	-15.1	-32.0	24	P22250B
0.6	2.6	6.1	11.3	18.4	-0.2	⊕	-3.1	-11.4	+0.6	+1.5	⊕	-6.8	-19.8	-39.9	24	P243C
0.7	2.7	6.3	11.6	18.8	-0.3	⊕	-2.2	-8.8	+0.2	+1.1	⊕	-5.5	-16.1	-32.8	24	P243D
0.8	3.4	8.1	15.2	25.1	-0.3	⊕	-2.2	-9.0	+0.2	+1.1	⊕	-5.7	-17.1	-35.7	24	P243F
0.7	2.9	6.7	12.5	20.4	-0.3	⊕	-2.8	-10.5	+0.4	+1.4	⊕	-6.3	-18.7	-38.1	24	P6C
0.8	3.3	7.7	14.3	23.5	-0.1	⊕	-3.8	-14.0	+0.8	+1.9	⊕	-8.2	-24.0	-48.9	24	P257B
0.7	3.0	6.9	12.9	21.1	-0.3	⊕	-2.7	-10.2	+0.4	+1.3	⊕	-6.2	-18.4	-37.5	24	P257WBA
0.7	3.1	7.3	13.7	22.4	-0.3	⊕	-2.7	-10.4	+0.4	+1.4	⊕	-6.3	-18.8	-38.5	24	P257WBT1
0.7	2.8	6.5	12.0	19.6	-0.2	⊕	-3.0	-11.4	+0.5	+1.5	⊕	-6.8	-19.9	-40.4	24	P2506C
0.7	2.9	6.7	12.4	20.2	-0.3	⊕	-2.5	-9.7	+0.3	+1.2	⊕	-6.0	-17.5	-35.8	24	P2506D
0.8	3.2	7.4	13.9	22.6	-0.2	⊕	-3.1	-11.7	+0.6	+1.6	⊕	-7.0	-20.8	-42.2	24	P2506E
0.8	3.4	7.9	14.8	21.4	-0.2	⊕	-3.2	-11.9	+0.6	+1.6	⊕	-7.2	-21.1	-43.2	24	P2506T1
0.7	2.7	6.3	11.6	18.9	-0.2	⊕	-3.4	-12.5	+0.7	+1.7	⊕	-7.4	-21.4	-43.0	24	P270C
0.7	2.8	6.6	12.1	19.7	-0.2	⊕	-2.8	-10.7	+0.5	+1.4	⊕	-6.5	-19.0	-38.5	24	P270D
0.9	3.9	9.2	17.3	28.5	-0.2	⊕	-3.7	-13.8	+0.8	+1.9	⊕	-8.3	-24.4	-50.5	24	P270E
0.7	2.7	6.4	11.9	19.3	-0.2	⊕	-2.8	-10.7	+0.5	+1.4	⊕	-6.5	-18.8	-38.2	24	P270F
0.8	3.2	7.6	14.2	23.0	-0.2	⊕	-3.3	-12.2	+0.6	+1.6	⊕	-7.3	-21.5	-43.7	24	P270T1
0.7	3.2	7.4	13.9	22.5	-0.2	⊕	-2.9	-11.1	+0.5	+1.5	⊕	-6.7	-19.8	-40.5	24	P270T2
0.7	2.7	6.3	11.7	19.0	-0.3	⊕	-2.5	-9.6	+0.3	+1.2	⊕	-5.9	-17.3	-35.1	24	P270WBA
0.8	3.1	7.4	13.7	22.5	-0.3	⊕	-2.8	-10.8	+0.4	+1.4	⊕	-6.6	-19.3	-39.6	24	P270WBT1
1.6	7.2	17.7	34.5	58.1	0	⊕	-5.2	-19.8	+1.2	+2.6	⊕	-12.0	-37.6	-81.7	24	P730A
1.3	3.2	8.2	15.4	23.4	-0.1	⊕	-4.3	-15.4	+1.0	+2.1	⊕	-9.0	-26.1	-52.9	24	P7C
0.7	2.8	6.6	12.3	19.5	-0.1	⊕	-4.2	-14.9	+0.9	+2.1	⊕	-8.7	-24.9	-49.4	24	P764A
0.9	3.8	9.0	16.8	27.8	-0.2	⊕	-3.6	-13.4	+0.7	+1.8	⊕	-8.0	-23.8	-49.2	24	P280A
1.2	4.9	11.8	22.5	37.8	-0.2	⊕	-3.5	-13.7	+0.7	+1.6	⊕	-8.4	-25.4	-54.3	24	P280T1
0.8	3.1	7.3	13.5	21.8	-0.2	⊕	-3.7	-13.5	+0.8	+1.8	⊕	-8.0	-23.1	-46.6	24	P708A
0.7	2.7	6.4	11.9	19.1	-0.2	⊕	-3.6	-13.1	+0.7	+1.8	⊕	-7.7	-14.1	-44.5	24	P708B
0.5	2.2	5.1	9.3	15.0	-0.3	⊕	-2.6	-9.8	+0.4	+1.3	⊕	-5.9	-17.0	-34.2	24	P7RD
0.5	2.0	4.6	8.4	13.5	-0.2	⊕	-3.0	-10.9	+0.5	+1.5	⊕	-6.4	-18.4	-36.6	24	P7RE
0.6	2.5	5.6	10.4	16.9	-0.2	⊕	-3.1	-11.3	+0.6	+1.5	⊕	-6.7	-19.4	-39.0	24	P7RF
0.6	2.6	6.0	11.1	18.2	-0.3	⊕	-2.6	-9.9	+0.4	+1.3	⊕	-6.0	-17.5	-35.6	24	P7RG
0.5	2.3	5.4	9.9	16.2	-0.3	⊕	-2.6	-9.9	+0.4	+1.3	⊕	-6.0	-10.9	-35.0	24	P7RH
0.7	2.8	6.5	12.1	19.6	-0.2	⊕	-3.4	-12.5	+0.7	+1.7	⊕	-7.4	-21.5	-43.3	24	P7RT1
1.0	4.3	10.3	19.5	32.4	-0.2	⊕	-3.5	-13.4	+0.7	+1.8	⊕	-8.1	-24.4	-51.1	24	P7RT2
0.6	2.5	5.8	10.7	17.3	-0.2	⊕	-2.8	-10.5	+0.4	+1.4	⊕	-6.3	-18.4	-37.1	24	P7WBA
1.0	4.2	10.1	19.1	31.9	-0.2	⊕	-3.2	-12.4	+0.6	+1.6	⊕	-7.6	-22.7	-47.8	24	P7WBT1
0.9	8.0	19.4	36.7	59.8	-0.3	⊕	-8.3	-29.8	+2.4	+4.1	⊕	-17.4	-52.4	-109.4	24	P30300
0.7	3.0	7.0	13.0	21.1	-0.1	⊕	-4.0	-14.4	+0.9	+2.0	⊕	-8.4	-24.3	-49.0	24	P308C
0.8	3.3	7.7	14.3	23.3	-0.1	⊕	-4.4	-15.8	+1.0	+2.2	⊕	-9.2	-26.5	-53.6	24	P308E
0.7	3.1	7.2	13.3	21.7	-0.2	⊕	-3.6	-13.2	+0.7	+1.8	⊕	-7.8	-22.7	-46.0	24	P308F
1.0	4.2	10.0	18.7	31.1	-0.1	⊕	-4.4	-15.9	+1.0	+2.2	⊕	-9.4	-27.7	-57.5	24	P308T1
0.7	2.8	6.6	12.3	19.9	-0.2	⊕	-3.6	-13.2	+0.8	+1.8	⊕	-7.8	-22.4	-45.2	24	P3006D
0.7	3.0	7.3	13.4	27.7	-0.1	⊕	-4.0	-14.6	+0.9	+2.0	⊕	-8.6	-24.6	-49.6	24	P3006F
0.7	3.0	7.1	13.4	22.0	-0.2	⊕	-3.3	-12.4	+0.6	+1.7	⊕	-7.4	-21.5	-43.7	24	P3006G
0.5	2.6	6.0	11.0	18.0	-0.1	⊕	-3.9	-13.9	+0.9	+1.9	⊕	-8.1	-23.1	-46.1	24	P3006L
0.7	2.9	6.8	12.7	20.7	-0.2	⊕	-3.3	-12.2	+0.6	+1.6	⊕	-7.3	-21.1	-42.8	24	P3006P
0.7	2.8	6.6	12.1	19.7	-0.2	⊕	-3.6	-13.2	+0.7	+1.8	⊕	-7.7	-22.3	-45.0	24	P3006O
1.0	4.0	9.6	17.8	29.7	-0.1	⊕	-3.9	-14.5	+0.8	+2.0	⊕	-8.7	-25.4	-53.1	24	P3006T1
0.9	4.0	9.4	17.7	29.4	-0.1	⊕	-4.3	-15.6	+1.0	+2.2	⊕	-9.2	-27.0	-56.1	24	P3006T2
0.5	2.2	5.0	9.2	14.9	-0.2	⊕	-3.4	-12.2	+0.7	+1.7	⊕	-7.1	-20.4	-40.5	24	P300WC
0.8	3.3	7.8	14.6	24.0	-0.3	⊕	-2.4	-9.6	+0.3	+1.2	⊕	-6.0	-17.9	-37.1	24	P300WT4
0.9	3.8	8.6	16.1	26.6	0.0	⊕	-5.1	-17.9	+1.3	+2.6	⊕	-10.2	-29.9	-61.0	24	P35WT1

These trajectory tables were calculated by computer using the best available data for each load. Trajectories are representative of the nominal behavior of each load at standard conditions (59°F temperature; barometric pressure of 29.53 inches; altitude at sea level). Shooters are cautioned that actual trajectories may differ due to variations in altitude, atmospheric conditions, guns, sights, and ammunition.

CLASSIC® HUNTING RIFLE

Usage Key: ☐ = Varmints, predators, small g...

USAGE	FEDERAL LOAD NO.	CALIBER	BULLET WGT. IN GRAINS	GRAMS	BULLET STYLE**	FACTORY PRIMER NO.	VELOCITY IN FEET PER SECOND (TO NEAREST 10 FPS)						ENERGY IN FOOT-POUNDS (TO NEAREST 5 FOOT-POUNDS)				
							MUZZLE	100 YDS.	200 YDS.	300 YDS.	400 YDS.	500 YDS.	MUZZLE	100 YDS.	200 YDS.	300 YDS.	400 YDS.
☐	222A	222 Rem. (5.56x43mm)	50	3.24	Hi-Shok Soft Point	205	3140	2600	2120	1700	1350	1110	1095	750	500	320	200
☐	222B	222 Rem. (5.56x43mm)	55	3.56	Hi-Shok FMJ Boat-tail	205	3020	2740	2480	2230	1990	1780	1115	915	750	610	485
☐	223A	223 Rem. (5.56x45mm)	55	3.56	Hi-Shok Soft Point	205	3240	2750	2300	1910	1550	1270	1280	920	650	445	295
☐	223B	223 Rem. (5.56x45mm)	55	3.56	Hi-Shok FMJ Boat-tail	205	3240	2950	2670	2410	2170	1940	1280	1060	875	710	575
☐	22250A	22-250 Rem.	55	3.56	Hi-Shok Soft Point	210	3680	3140	2660	2220	1830	1490	1655	1200	860	605	410
☐ NEW	243AS	243 Win. (6.16x51mm)	80	5.18	Sierra Pro-Hunter SP	210	3350	2960	2590	2260	1950	1670	1995	1550	1195	905	675
☐	243B	243 Win. (6.16x51mm)	100	6.48	Hi-Shok Soft Point	210	2960	2700	2450	2220	1990	1790	1945	1615	1330	1090	880
☐ NEW	6AS	6mm Rem.	80	5.18	Sierra Pro-Hunter SP	210	3470	3060	2690	2350	2040	1750	2140	1665	1290	980	735
☐	6B	6mm Rem.	100	6.48	Hi-Shok Soft Point	210	3100	2830	2570	2330	2100	1890	2135	1775	1470	1205	985
☐ NEW	2506BS	25-06 Rem.	117	7.58	Sierra Pro-Hunter SP	210	2990	2730	2480	2250	2030	1830	2320	1985	1645	1350	1100
☐	6555B	6.5x55 Swedish	140	9.07	Hi-Shok Soft Point	210	2600	2400	2220	2040	1860	1700	2100	1795	1525	1285	1080
☐	270A	270 Win.	130	8.42	Hi-Shok Soft Point	210	3060	2800	2560	2330	2110	1900	2700	2265	1890	1565	1295
☐	270B	270 Win.	150	9.72	Hi-Shok Soft Point RN	210	2850	2500	2180	1890	1620	1390	2705	2085	1585	1185	870
☐	7A	7mm Mauser (7x57mm Mauser)	175	11.34	Hi-Shok Soft Point RN	210	2440	2140	1860	1600	1380	1200	2315	1775	1340	1000	740
☐	7B	7mm Mauser (7x57mm Mauser)	140	9.07	Hi-Shok Soft Point	210	2660	2450	2260	2070	1890	1730	2200	1865	1585	1330	1110
☐	280B	280 Rem.	150	9.72	Hi-Shok Soft Point	210	2890	2670	2460	2260	2060	1880	2780	2370	2015	1695	1420
☐	7RA	7mm Rem. Magnum	150	9.72	Hi-Shok Soft Point	215	3110	2830	2570	2320	2090	1870	3220	2670	2200	1790	1450
☐	7RB	7mm Rem. Magnum	175	11.34	Hi-Shok Soft Point	215	2860	2650	2440	2240	2060	1880	3180	2720	2310	1960	1640
☐	30CA	30 Carbine (7.62x33mm)	110	7.13	Hi-Shok Soft Point RN	205	1990	1570	1240	1040	920	840	965	600	375	260	210
☐	76239B	7.62x39mm Soviet	123	7.97	Hi-Shok Soft Point	210	2300	2030	1780	1550	1350	1200	1445	1125	860	655	500
☐	3030A	30-30 Win.	150	9.72	Hi-Shok Soft Point FN	210	2390	2020	1680	1400	1180	1040	1900	1355	945	650	460
☐	3030B	30-30 Win.	170	11.01	Hi-Shok Soft Point RN	210	2200	1900	1620	1380	1190	1060	1830	1355	990	720	535
☐	3030C	30-30 Win.	125	8.10	Hi-Shok Hollow Point	210	2570	2090	1660	1320	1080	960	1830	1210	770	480	320
☐	300A	300 Savage	150	9.72	Hi-Shok Soft Point	210	2630	2350	2100	1850	1630	1430	2305	1845	1460	1145	885
☐	300B	300 Savage	180	11.66	Hi-Shok Soft Point	210	2350	2140	1940	1750	1570	1410	2205	1825	1495	1215	985
☐	308A	308 Win. (7.62x51mm)	150	9.72	Hi-Shok Soft Point	210	2820	2530	2260	2010	1770	1560	2650	2140	1705	1345	1050
☐	308B	308 Win. (7.62x51mm)	180	11.66	Hi-Shok Soft Point	210	2620	2390	2180	1970	1760	1600	2745	2290	1895	1555	1270
☐	3006A	30-06 Springfield (7.62x63mm)	150	9.72	Hi-Shok Soft Point	210	2910	2620	2340	2080	1840	1620	2820	2280	1825	1445	1130
☐	3006B	30-06 Springfield (7.62x63mm)	180	11.66	Hi-Shok Soft Point	210	2700	2470	2250	2040	1850	1660	2915	2435	2025	1665	1360
☐ NEW	3006CS	30-06 Springfield (7.62x63mm)	125	8.10	Sierra Pro-Hunter SP	210	3140	2780	2450	2140	1850	1600	2735	2145	1660	1270	955
☐ NEW	3006HS	30-06 Springfield (7.62x63mm)	220	14.25	Sierra Pro-Hunter SP RN	210	2410	2130	1870	1630	1420	1250	2835	2215	1705	1300	985
☐ NEW	3006JS	30-06 Springfield (7.62x63mm)	180	11.66	Sierra Pro-Hunter SP RN	210	2700	2350	2020	1730	1470	1250	2915	2200	1630	1190	860
☐ NEW	300WBS	300 Win. Magnum	180	11.66	Sierra Pro-Hunter SP	215	2960	2750	2540	2340	2160	1980	3500	3010	2580	2195	1860
☐ NEW	300WGS	300 Win. Magnum	150	9.72	Sierra Pro-Hunter SP	215	3280	3030	2800	2570	2360	2160	3570	3055	2600	2205	1860
☐ NEW	303AS	303 British	180	11.66	Sierra Pro-Hunter SP	210	2460	2230	2020	1820	1630	1460	2420	1995	1625	1315	1060
☐	303B	303 British	150	9.72	Hi-Shok Soft Point	210	2690	2440	2210	1980	1780	1590	2400	1980	1620	1310	1055
☐	32A	32 Win. Special	170	11.01	Hi-Shok Soft Point	210	2250	1920	1630	1370	1180	1040	1910	1395	1000	710	520
☐	*8A	8mm Mauser (8x57mm JS Mauser)	170	11.01	Hi-Shok Soft Point	210	2360	1970	1620	1330	1120	1000	2100	1465	995	670	475
☐	338C	338 Win. Magnum	225	14.58	Hi-Shok Soft Point	210	2780	2570	2370	2180	2000	1830	3860	3305	2815	2380	2000
☐	357G	357 Magnum	180	11.66	Hi-Shok Hollow Point	100	1550	1160	980	860	770	680	960	535	385	295	235
☐	35A	35 Rem.	200	12.96	Hi-Shok Soft Point	210	2080	1700	1380	1140	1000	910	1920	1280	840	575	445
☐	375A	375 H&H Magnum	270	17.50	Hi-Shok Soft Point	215	2690	2420	2170	1920	1700	1500	4340	3510	2810	2220	1740
☐	375B	375 H&H Magnum	300	19.44	Hi-Shok Soft Point	215	2530	2270	2020	1790	1580	1400	4265	3425	2720	2135	1665
☐	44A	44 Rem. Magnum	240	15.55	Hi-Shok Hollow Point	150	1760	1380	1090	950	860	790	1650	1015	640	485	395
☐ NEW	4570AS	45-70 Government	300	19.44	Sierra Hollow Point FN	210	1880	1650	1430	1240	1110	1010	2355	1815	1355	1015	810

*Only for use in barrels intended for .323 inch diameter bullets. Do not use in 8x57mm J Commission Rifles (M1888) or in sporting or other military arms of .318 inch bore diameter.
**RN = Round Nose SP = Soft Point FN = Flat Nose FMJ = Full Metal Jacket

GOLD MEDAL® MATCH RIFLE

Usage Key: ☐ = Varmints, predators, small game

USAGE	FEDERAL LOAD NO.	CALIBER	BULLET WGT. IN GRAINS	GRAMS	BULLET STYLE	FACTORY PRIMER NO.	VELOCITY IN FEET PER SECOND (TO NEAREST 10 FPS)									
							MUZZLE	100 YDS.	200 YDS.	300 YDS.	400 YDS.	500 YDS.	600 YDS.	700 YDS.	800 YDS.	900 YDS.
☐	GM223M	223 Rem. (5.56x45mm)	69	4.47	Sierra MatchKing BTHP	GM205M	3000	2720	2460	2210	1980	1760	1560	1390	1240	1130
☐	GM308M	308 Win. (7.62x51mm)	168	10.88	Sierra MatchKing BTHP	GM210M	2600	2420	2240	2070	1910	1760	1610	1480	1360	1260
☐	GM3006M	30-06 Springfield (7.62x63mm)	168	10.88	Sierra MatchKing BTHP	GM210M	2700	2510	2330	2150	1990	1830	1680	1540	1410	1300

☐ = Medium game   ☐ = Large, heavy game   ☐ = Dangerous game   ☐ = Target shooting, training, practice

WIND DRIFT IN INCHES — 10 MPH CROSSWIND					HEIGHT OF BULLET TRAJECTORY IN INCHES ABOVE OR BELOW LINE OF SIGHT IF ZEROED AT ⊕ YARDS. SIGHTS 1.5 INCHES ABOVE BORE LINE.										TEST BARREL LENGTH INCHES	FEDERAL LOAD NO.
					AVERAGE RANGE				LONG RANGE							
100 YDS	200 YDS	300 YDS	400 YDS	500 YDS	50 YDS	100 YDS	200 YDS	300 YDS	50 YDS	100 YDS	200 YDS	300 YDS	400 YDS	500 YDS		
7	7.3	18.3	36.4	63.1	-0.2	⊕	-3.7	-15.3	+0.7	+1.9	⊕	-9.7	-31.6	-71.3	24	222A
9	3.4	8.5	16.8	26.3	-0.2	⊕	-3.1	-12.0	+0.6	+1.6	⊕	-7.3	-21.5	-44.6	24	222B
4	6.1	15.0	29.4	50.8	-0.3	⊕	-3.2	-12.9	+0.5	+1.6	⊕	-8.2	-26.1	-58.3	24	223A
8	3.3	7.8	14.5	24.0	-0.3	⊕	-2.5	-9.9	+0.3	+1.3	⊕	-6.1	-18.3	-37.8	24	223B
2	5.2	12.5	24.4	42.0	-0.4	⊕	-2.1	-9.1	+0.1	+1.0	⊕	-6.0	-19.1	-42.6	24	22250A
)	4.3	10.4	19.8	33.3	-0.3	⊕	-2.5	-10.2	+0.3	+1.3	⊕	-6.4	-19.7	-42.2	24	243AS
9	3.6	8.4	15.7	25.8	-0.2	⊕	-3.3	-12.4	+0.6	+1.6	⊕	-7.5	-22.0	-45.4	24	243B
)	4.1	9.9	18.8	31.6	-0.3	⊕	-2.2	-9.3	+0.2	+1.1	⊕	-5.9	-18.2	-39.0	24	6AS
8	3.3	7.9	14.7	24.1	-0.3	⊕	-2.9	-11.0	+0.5	+1.4	⊕	-6.7	-19.8	-40.6	24	6B
8	3.4	8.1	15.1	24.9	-0.2	⊕	-3.2	-12.0	+0.6	+1.6	⊕	-7.2	-21.4	-44.0	24	2506BS
6	3.4	8.0	14.8	24.1	-0.1	⊕	-4.5	-16.2	+1.1	+2.3	⊕	-9.4	-27.2	-55.0	24	6555B
8	3.2	7.6	14.2	23.3	-0.2	⊕	-2.9	-11.2	+0.5	+1.5	⊕	-6.8	-20.0	-41.1	24	270A
2	5.3	12.8	24.5	413	-0.1	⊕	-4.1	-15.5	+0.9	+2.0	⊕	-9.4	-28.6	-61.0	24	270B
5	6.2	15.0	28.7	47.8	-0.1	⊕	-6.2	-22.6	+1.6	+3.1	⊕	-13.3	-40.1	-84.6	24	7A
3	3.2	8.2	15.4	23.4	-0.1	⊕	-4.3	-15.4	+1.0	+2.1	⊕	-9.0	-26.1	-52.9	24	7B
7	3.1	7.2	13.4	219	-0.2	⊕	-3.4	-12.6	+0.7	+1.7	⊕	-7.5	-21.8	-44.3	24	280B
8	3.4	8.1	15.1	24.9	-0.3	⊕	-2.9	-11.0	+0.5	+1.4	⊕	-6.7	-19.9	-41.0	24	7RA
7	3.1	7.2	13.3	21.7	-0.2	⊕	-3.5	-12.8	+0.7	+1.7	⊕	-7.6	-22.1	-44.9	24	7RB
4	15.0	35.5	63.2	96.7	+0.6	⊕	-12.8	-46.9	+3.9	+6.4	⊕	-27.7	-81.8	-167.8	18	30CA
5	6.4	15.2	28.7	47.3	+0.2	⊕	-7.0	-25.1	+1.9	+3.5	⊕	-14.5	-43.4	-90.6	20	76239B
0	8.5	20.9	40.1	66.1	+0.2	⊕	-7.2	-26.7	+1.9	+3.6	⊕	-15.9	-49.1	-104.5	24	3030A
9	8.0	19.4	36.7	59.8	+0.3	⊕	-8.3	-29.8	+2.4	+4.1	⊕	-17.4	-52.4	-109.4	24	3030B
2	10.1	25.4	49.4	816	+0.1	⊕	-6.6	-26.0	+1.7	+3.3	⊕	-16.0	-50.9	-109.5	24	3030C
1	4.8	11.6	219	36.3	0	⊕	-4.8	-17.6	+1.2	+2.4	⊕	-10.4	-30.9	-64.4	24	300A
1	4.6	10.9	20.3	33.3	+0.1	⊕	-6.1	-21.6	+1.7	+3.1	⊕	-12.4	-36.1	-73.8	24	300B
0	4.4	10.4	19.7	32.7	-0.1	⊕	-3.9	-14.7	+0.8	+2.0	⊕	-8.8	-26.3	-54.8	24	308A
9	3.9	9.2	17.2	28.3	-0.1	⊕	-4.6	-16.5	+1.1	+2.3	⊕	-9.7	-28.3	-57.8	24	308B
)	4.2	9.9	18.7	312	-0.2	⊕	-3.6	-13.6	+0.7	+1.8	⊕	-8.2	-24.4	-50.9	24	3006A
9	3.7	8.8	16.5	271	-0.1	⊕	-4.2	-15.3	+1.0	+2.1	⊕	-9.0	-26.4	-54.0	24	3006B
8	4.3	10.8	20.5	34.4	-0.3	⊕	-3.0	-11.9	+0.5	+1.5	⊕	-7.3	-22.3	-47.5	24	3006CS
4	6.0	14.3	27.2	45.0	-0.1	⊕	-6.2	-22.4	+1.7	+3.1	⊕	-13.1	-39.3	-82.2	24	3006HS
5	6.4	15.7	30.4	51.2	-0.1	⊕	-4.9	-18.3	+1.1	+2.4	⊕	-11.0	-33.6	-71.9	24	3006JS
7	2.8	6.6	12.3	20.0	-0.2	⊕	-3.1	-11.7	+0.6	+1.6	⊕	-7.0	-20.3	-41.1	24	300WBS
7	2.7	6.3	115	18.8	-0.3	⊕	-2.3	-9.1	+0.3	+1.1	⊕	-5.6	-16.4	-33.6	24	300WGS
	4.5	10.6	19.9	32.7	0	⊕	-5.5	-19.6	+1.4	+2.8	⊕	-11.3	-33.2	-68.1	24	303AS
	4.1	9.8	18.1	29.9	-0.1	⊕	-4.4	-15.9	+1.0	+2.2	⊕	-9.4	-27.6	-56.8	24	303B
3	8.4	20.3	38.6	63.0	+0.3	⊕	-8.0	-29.2	+2.3	+4.0	⊕	-17.2	-52.3	-109.8	24	32A
1	9.3	22.9	43.9	71.7	+0.2	⊕	-7.6	-28.5	+2.1	+3.8	⊕	-17.1	-52.9	-111.9	24	8A
8	3.1	7.3	13.6	22.2	-0.1	⊕	-3.8	-13.7	+0.8	+1.9	⊕	-8.1	-23.5	-47.5	24	338C
8	21.7	45.2	76.1	NA	⊕	-3.4	-29.7	-88.2	+1.7	⊕	-22.8	-77.9	-173.8	-321.4	18	357G
7	12.0	29.0	53.3	83.3	+0.5	⊕	-10.7	-39.3	+3.2	+5.4	⊕	-23.3	-70.0	-144.0	24	35A
	4.5	10.8	20.3	33.7	-0.4	⊕	-5.5	-18.4	+1.0	+2.4	⊕	-10.9	-33.3	-71.2	24	375A
2	5.0	119	22.4	371	+0.5	⊕	-6.3	-21.2	+1.3	+2.6	⊕	-11.2	-33.3	-69.1	24	375B
2	17.8	39.8	68.3	102.5	⊕	-2.2	-21.7	-67.2	+1.1	⊕	-17.4	-60.7	-136.0	-250.2	20	44A
7	7.6		35.7	NA	⊕	-1.3	-14.1	-43.7	+0.7	⊕	-11.5	-39.7	-89.1	-163.1	24	4570AS

These trajectory tables were calculated by computer using the best available data for each load. Trajectories are representative of the nominal behavior of each load at standard conditions (59°F temperature, barometric pressure of 29.53 inches; altitude at sea level). Shooters are cautioned that actual trajectories may differ due to variations in altitude, atmospheric conditions, guns, sights, and ammunition.

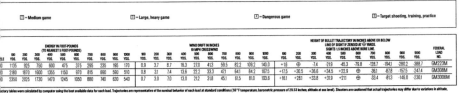

☐ = Medium game   ☐ = Large, heavy game   ☐ = Dangerous game   ☐ = Target shooting, training, practice

ENERGY IN FOOT-POUNDS (TO NEAREST 5 FOOT-POUNDS)										WIND DRIFT IN INCHES — 10 MPH CROSSWIND										HEIGHT OF BULLET TRAJECTORY IN INCHES ABOVE OR BELOW LINE OF SIGHT IF ZEROED AT ⊕ YARDS. SIGHTS 1.5 INCHES ABOVE BORE LINE.										FEDERAL LOAD NO.
100 YDS	200 YDS	300 YDS	400 YDS	500 YDS	600 YDS	700 YDS	800 YDS	900 YDS	1000 YDS	100 YDS	200 YDS	300 YDS	400 YDS	500 YDS	600 YDS	700 YDS	800 YDS	900 YDS	1000 YDS	100 YDS	200 YDS	300 YDS	400 YDS	500 YDS	600 YDS	700 YDS	800 YDS	900 YDS	1000 YDS	
1135	925	750	600	475	375	295	235	195	170	0.9	3.7	8.7	16.3	27.0	41.3	59.5	82.2	109.2	140.0	+1.6	⊕	-7.4	-21.9	-45.3	-79.8	-128.7	-194.1	-280.2	-388.7	GM223M
2180	1870	1600	1355	1150	970	815	690	590	510	0.8	3.1	7.4	13.6	22.2	33.3	47.1	64.1	84.2	107.5	+17.5	+30.5	+36.6	+34.5	+22.9	⊕	-36.1	-87.8	-157.5	-247.4	GM308M
2350	2025	1730	1470	1245	1050	880	740	630	540	0.7	3.0	7.0	13.0	21.2	31.8	45.1	61.5	81.0	103.6	+16.1	+28.1	+33.8	+31.9	+21.0	⊕	-33.4	-81.3	-146.0	-230.1	GM3006M

These trajectory tables were calculated by computer using the best available data for each load. Trajectories are representative of the nominal behavior of each load at standard conditions (59°F temperature, barometric pressure of 29.53 inches; altitude at sea level). Shooters are cautioned that actual trajectories may differ due to variations in altitude, atmospheric conditions, guns, sights, and ammunition.

These tables were calculated by computer. A standard scientific technique was used to predict trajectories from the best available data for each round. Trajectories shown typify the ammunition's performance at sea level, but note that they may vary due to atmospheric conditions, and the equipment.

All velocity and energy figures in these charts have been derived by using test barrels of indicated lengths.

Ballistics shown are for 24" barrels, except those for 30 carbine, .350 Remington magnum and .44 Remington magnum, which are for 20" barrels, and the 6mm BR Remington and 7mm BR Remington which have a 15" barrel. These barrel lengths were chosen as representative, as it's impractical to show performance figures for all barrel lengths.

The muzzle velocities, muzzle energies and trajectory data in these tables represent the approximate performance expected of each specified loading. Differences in barrel lengths, internal firearm dimensions, temperature and test procedure can produce actual velocities that vary from those given here.

Centerfire Rifle Velocity vs. Barrel Length

Muzzle Velocity   Approx. Change in Muzzle Velocity
Range (ft./sec.)   per 1" Change in Barrel Length (ft./sec.)

2000-2500	10
2500-3000	20
3000-3500	30
3500-4000	40

1. Determine how much shorter, or longer, your barrel is than the test barrel.
2. In the left column of the above table, select the muzzle-velocity class of your cartridge.
3. To the right of that class, read the approximate change in velocity per inch of barrel length.
4. Multiply this number by the difference in the length of your barrel from that of the test barrel.
5. If your barrel is shorter than the test barrel, subtract this figure from the muzzle velocity shown for your cartridge.
6. If your barrel is longer, add this figure to the muzzle velocity shown.

The trajectory figures shown in these ballistic tables are the rise or drop, in inches, of the bullet from a direct line of sight at selected yardage. Sighting-in distances have been set at 100 to 250 yards.

The line of sight used is 0.9" above the axis of the bore. This height is common to iron sights and low-mounted scopes.

The trajectory tables can also be used for rifles with high-mounted scopes, that is, 1½" above the axis of the bore. The difference in drops at even the extreme 500-yard range is not significant enough to negate the figures shown.

Since the rise or drop figures shown at the stated yardage are points of impact, you must hold low for positive figures, high for negative figures.

Many shooters who use the same cartridge often find it helpful to commit the rise and drop figures for that cartridge to memory, or tape them to their rifle stock. That way, they know instantly the right "hold" as soon as they estimate the target's range.

Specifications are nominal. Ballistics figures established in test barrels. Individual rifles may vary from test-barrel specifications.

* Inches above or below line of sight. Hold low for positive numbers, high for negative numbers.
† 280 Rem. and 7mm Express* Rem. are interchangeable.
‡ Interchangeable in 244 Rem.
§ Subject to stock on hand.
¹ Bullet does not rise more than one inch above line of sight from muzzle to sighting-in range.
² Bullet does not rise more than three inches above line of sight from muzzle to sighting-in range.
NOTE: 0.0 indicates yardage at which rifle was sighted in.

Remington. 1996 Centerfire Rifle

Caliber	Order No.	Wt. (grs.)	Bullet Style	Primer No.	Muzzle	100 yds.	200 yds.	300 yds.	400 yds.	500 yds.
.17 Remington	R17REM	25	Hollow Point Power-Lokt*	7 ½	4040	3284	2644	2086	1606	1235
.22 Hornet	R22HN1	45	Pointed Soft Point	6 ½	2690	2042	1502	1128	948	840
	R22HN2	45	Hollow Point	6 ½	2690	2042	1502	1128	948	840
.220 Swift	R220S1	50	Pointed Soft Point	9 ½	3780	3158	2617	2135	1710	1357
.222 Remington	R222R1	50	Pointed Soft Point	7 ½	3140	2602	2123	1700	1350	1107
	R222R3	50	Hollow Point Power-Lokt*	7 ½	3140	2635	2182	1777	1432	1172
.222 Remington Mag.	R222M1	55	Pointed Soft Point	7 ½	3240	2748	2305	1906	1556	1272
.223 Remington	R223R1	55	Pointed Soft Point	7 ½	3240	2747	2304	1905	1554	1270
	R223R2	55	Hollow Point Power-Lokt*	7 ½	3240	2773	2352	1969	1627	1341
	R223R3	55	Metal Case	7 ½	3240	2759	2326	1933	1587	1301
	R223R4	60	Hollow Point Match	7 ½	3100	2712	2355	2026	1726	1463
.22-250 Remington	R22501	55	Pointed Soft Point	9 ½	3680	3137	2656	2222	1832	1493
	R22502	55	Pointed Soft Point Core-Lokt*	9 ½	3680	3209	2785	2400	2046	1725
.243 Win.	R243W1	80	Pointed Soft Point	9 ½	3350	2955	2593	2259	1951	1670
	R243W2	80	Hollow Point Power-Lokt*	9 ½	3350	2955	2593	2259	1951	1670
	R243W3	100	Pointed Soft Point Core-Lokt*	9 ½	2960	2697	2449	2215	1993	1786
	ER243WA	105	Extended Range	9 ½	2920	2689	2470	2261	2062	1874
6MM Remington	R6MM1	80	Pointed Soft Point	9 ½	3470	3064	2694	2352	2036	1747
	R6MM4	100	Pointed Soft Point Core-Lokt*	9 ½	3100	2829	2573	2332	2104	1889
	ER6MMRA§	105	Extended Range	9 ½	3060	2822	2596	2381	2177	1982
6MM BR Remington	R6MMBR§	100	Pointed Soft Point	7 ½	2550	2310	2083	1870	1671	1491
.25-20 Win.	R25202	86	Soft Point	6 ½	1460	1194	1030	931	858	797
.250 Savage	R250SV	100	Pointed Soft Point	9 ½	2820	2504	2210	1936	1684	1461
.257 Roberts	R257	117	Soft Point Core-Lokt*	9 ½	2650	2291	1961	1663	1404	1199
	ER257A§	122	Extended Range	9 ½	2600	2331	2078	1842	1625	1431
.25-06 Remington	R25062	100	Pointed Soft Point Core-Lokt*	9 ½	3230	2893	2580	2287	2014	1762
	R25063	120	Pointed Soft Point Core-Lokt*	9 ½	2990	2730	2484	2252	2032	1825
	ER2506A	122	Extended Range	9 ½	2930	2706	2492	2289	2095	1911
6.5x55 Swedish	R65SWE1	140	Pointed Soft Point Core-Lokt*	9 ½	2550	2353	2164	1984	1814	1654
.264 Win. Mag.	R264W2	140	Pointed Soft Point Core-Lokt*	9 ½M	3030	2782	2548	2326	2114	1914
.270 Win.	R270W1	100	Pointed Soft Point	9 ½	3320	2924	2561	2225	1916	1636
	R270W2	130	Pointed Soft Point Core-Lokt*	9 ½	3060	2776	2510	2259	2022	1801
	R270W3	130	Bronze Point	9 ½	3060	2802	2559	2329	2110	1904
	R270W4	150	Soft Point Core-Lokt*	9 ½	2850	2504	2183	1886	1618	1385
	RS270WA	140	Swift A-Frame™ PSP	9 ½	2925	2652	2394	2152	1923	1711
	ER270WB§	135	Extended Range	9 ½	3000	2780	2570	2369	2178	1995
	ER270WA	140	Extended Range Boat Tail	9 ½	2960	2749	2548	2355	2171	1995
7MM BR Remington	R7MMBR§	140	Pointed Soft Point	7 ½	2215	2012	1821	1643	1481	1336
7MM Mauser (7 x 57)	R7MSR1 ★	140	Pointed Soft Point Core-Lokt*	9 ½	2660	2435	2221	2018	1827	1648
7 x 64	R7X641	140	Pointed Soft Point Core-Lokt*	9 ½	2950	2714	2489	2276	2073	1881
	R7X642	175	Pointed Soft Point Core-Lokt*	9 ½	2650	2445	2248	2061	1883	1716
7MM-08 Remington	R7M081 ★	140	Pointed Soft Point Core-Lokt*	9 ½	2860	2625	2402	2189	1988	1798
	R7M083	120	Hollow Point	9 ½	3000	2725	2467	2223	1992	1778
	ER7M08A	154	Extended Range	9 ½	2715	2510	2315	2128	1950	1781
.280 Remington	R280R3 ★	140	Pointed Soft Point Core-Lokt*	9 ½	3000	2758	2528	2309	2102	1905
	R280R1	150	Pointed Soft Point Core-Lokt*	9 ½	2890	2624	2373	2135	1912	1705
	R280R2	165	Soft Point Core-Lokt*	9 ½	2820	2510	2220	1950	1701	1479
	ER280RA	165	Extended Range	9 ½	2820	2623	2434	2253	2080	1915
7MM Remington Mag.	R7MM2	150	Pointed Soft Point Core-Lokt*	9 ½M	3110	2830	2568	2320	2085	1866
	R7MM3	175	Pointed Soft Point Core-Lokt*	9 ½M	2860	2645	2440	2244	2057	1879
	R7MM4 ★	140	Pointed Soft Point Core-Lokt*	9 ½M	3175	2923	2684	2458	2243	2039
	RS7MMA	160	Swift A-Frame™ PSP	9 ½M	2900	2659	2430	2212	2006	1812
	ER7MMA	165	Extended Range	9 ½M	2900	2699	2507	2324	2147	1979
7MM Wby. Mag.	R7MWB15	140	Pointed Soft Point	9 ½M	3225	2970	2729	2501	2283	2077
	R7MWB2	175	Pointed Soft Point Core-Lokt*	9 ½M	2910	2693	2486	2288	2098	1918
	ER7MWBA§	165	Extended Range	9 ½M	2950	2747	2553	2367	2189	2019
.30 Carbine	R30CAR	110	Soft Point	6 ½	1990	1567	1236	1035	923	842
.30 Remington	R30REM	170	Soft Point Core-Lokt*	9 ½	2120	1822	1555	1328	1153	1036
.30-30 Win. Accelerator*	R3030A	55	Soft Point	9 ½	3400	2693	2085	1570	1187	986
.30-30 Win.	R30301	150	Soft Point Core-Lokt*	9 ½	2390	1973	1605	1303	1095	974
	R30302	170	Soft Point Core-Lokt*	9 ½	2200	1895	1619	1381	1191	1061
	R30303	170	Hollow Point Core-Lokt*	9 ½	2200	1895	1619	1381	1191	1061
	ER3030A	160	Extended Range	9 ½	2300	1997	1719	1473	1268	1116
.300 Savage	R30SV3	180	Soft Point Core-Lokt*	9 ½	2350	2025	1728	1467	1252	1098
	R30SV2	150	Pointed Soft Point Core-Lokt*	9 ½	2630	2354	2095	1853	1631	1432

★ New For 1996

allistics Tables

	Energy (ft.-lbs.)					Short-range Trajectory*						Long-range Trajectory*							Barrel
e	100 yds.	200 yds.	300 yds.	400 yds.	500 yds.	50 yds.	100 yds.	150 yds.	200 yds.	250 yds.	300 yds.	100 yds.	150 yds.	200 yds.	250 yds.	300 yds.	400 yds.	500 yds.	Length
	599	388	242	143	85	0.1	0.5	0.0	-1.5	-4.2	-8.5	2.1	2.5	1.9	0.0	-3.4	-17.0	-44.3	24"
	417	225	127	90	70	0.3	0.0	-2.4	-7.7	-16.9	-31.3	1.6	0.0	-4.5	-12.8	-26.4	-75.6	-163.4	24"
	417	225	127	90	70	0.3	0.0	-2.4	-7.7	-16.9	-31.3	1.6	0.0	-4.5	-12.8	-26.4	-75.6	-163.4	
	1107	760	506	325	204	0.2	0.5	0.0	-1.6	-4.4	-8.8	1.3	1.2	0.0	-2.5	-6.5	-20.7	-47.0	24"
	752	500	321	202	136	0.5	0.9	0.0	-2.5	-6.9	-13.7	2.2	1.9	0.0	-3.8	-10.0	-32.3	-73.8	24"
	771	529	351	228	152	0.5	0.9	0.0	-2.4	-6.6	-13.1	2.1	1.8	0.0	-3.6	-9.5	-30.2	-68.1	
	922	649	444	296	198	0.4	0.8	0.0	-2.2	-6.0	-11.8	1.9	1.6	0.0	-3.3	-8.5	-26.7	-59.5	24"
	921	648	443	295	197	0.4	0.8	0.0	-2.2	-6.0	-11.8	1.9	1.6	0.0	-3.3	-8.5	-26.7	-59.6	
	939	675	473	323	220	0.4	0.8	0.0	-2.1	-5.8	-11.4	1.8	1.6	0.0	-3.2	-8.2	-25.5	-56.0	24"
	929	660	456	307	207	0.4	0.8	0.0	-2.1	-5.9	-11.6	1.9	1.6	0.0	-3.2	-8.4	-26.2	-57.9	
	979	739	547	397	285	0.5	0.8	0.0	-2.2	-6.0	-11.5	1.9	1.6	0.0	-3.2	-8.3	-25.1	-53.6	
	1201	861	603	410	272	0.2	0.5	0.0	-1.6	-4.4	-8.7	2.3	2.6	1.9	0.0	-3.4	-15.9	-38.9	24"
	1257	947	703	511	363	0.2	0.5	0.0	-1.5	-4.1	-8.0	2.1	2.5	1.8	0.0	-3.1	-14.1	-33.4	
	1551	1194	906	676	495	0.3	0.7	0.0	-1.8	-4.9	-9.4	2.6	2.9	2.1	0.0	-3.6	-16.2	-37.9	
	1551	1194	906	676	495	0.3	0.7	0.0	-1.8	-4.9	-9.4	2.6	2.9	2.1	0.0	-3.6	-16.2	-37.9	24"
	1615	1332	1089	882	708	0.5	0.9	0.0	-2.2	-5.8	-11.0	1.9	1.6	0.0	-3.1	-7.8	-22.6	-46.3	
	1686	1422	1192	992	819	0.5	0.9	0.0	-2.2	-5.8	-11.0	2.0	1.6	0.0	-3.1	-7.7	-22.2	-44.8	
	1667	1289	982	736	542	0.3	0.6	0.0	-1.6	-4.5	-8.7	2.4	2.7	1.9	0.0	-3.3	-14.9	-35.0	24"
	1777	1470	1207	983	792	0.4	0.8	0.0	-1.9	-5.2	-9.9	1.7	1.5	0.0	-2.8	-7.0	-20.4	-41.7	
	1856	1571	1322	1105	916	0.4	0.8	0.0	-2.0	-5.2	-9.8	1.7	1.5	0.0	-2.7	-6.9	-20.0	-40.4	
	1185	963	776	620	494	0.3	0.0	-1.9	-5.6	-11.4	-19.3	2.8	2.3	0.0	-4.3	-10.9	-31.7	-65.1	15"
	272	203	165	141	121	0.0	-4.1	-14.4	-31.8	-57.3	-92.0	0.0	-8.2	-23.5	-47.0	-79.6	-175.9	-319.4	24"
	1392	1084	832	630	474	0.2	0.0	-1.6	-4.7	-9.6	-16.5	2.3	2.0	0.0	-3.7	-9.5	-28.3	-59.5	24"
	1363	999	718	512	373	0.3	0.0	-1.9	-5.8	-11.9	-20.7	2.9	2.4	0.0	-4.7	-12.0	-36.7	-79.2	24"
	1472	1170	919	715	555	0.3	0.0	-1.9	-5.5	-11.2	-19.1	2.8	2.3	0.0	-4.3	-10.9	-32.0	-66.4	
	1858	1478	1161	901	689	0.4	0.7	0.0	-1.9	-5.0	-9.7	1.6	1.4	0.0	-2.7	-6.9	-20.5	-42.7	
	1985	1644	1351	1100	887	0.5	0.8	0.0	-2.1	-5.6	-10.7	1.9	1.6	0.0	-3.0	-7.5	-22.0	-44.8	24"
	1983	1683	1419	1189	989	0.5	0.9	0.0	-2.2	-5.7	-10.8	1.9	1.6	0.0	-3.0	-7.5	-21.7	-43.9	
	1720	1456	1224	1023	850	0.3	0.0	-1.8	-5.4	-10.8	-18.2	2.7	2.2	0.0	-4.1	-10.1	-29.1	-58.7	24"
	2406	2018	1682	1389	1139	0.5	0.8	0.0	-2.0	-5.4	-10.2	1.8	1.5	0.0	-2.9	-7.2	-20.8	-42.2	24"
	1898	1456	1099	815	594	0.3	0.7	0.0	-1.8	-5.0	-9.7	2.7	3.0	2.2	0.0	-3.7	-16.6	-39.1	
	2225	1818	1472	1180	936	0.5	0.8	0.0	-2.0	-5.5	-10.4	1.8	1.5	0.0	-2.9	-7.4	-21.6	-44.3	
	2267	1890	1565	1285	1046	0.4	0.8	0.0	-2.0	-5.3	-10.1	1.8	1.5	0.0	-2.8	-7.1	-20.6	-42.0	24"
	2087	1587	1185	872	639	0.7	1.0	0.0	-2.6	-7.1	-13.6	2.3	2.0	0.0	-3.8	-9.7	-29.2	-62.2	
	2186	1782	1439	1150	910	0.6	0.9	0.0	-2.3	-6.0	-11.5	2.0	1.7	0.0	-3.2	-8.1	-23.8	-48.9	
	2315	1979	1682	1421	1193	0.5	0.8	0.0	-2.0	-5.5	-10.1	1.8	1.5	0.0	-2.8	-7.1	-20.4	-41.0	
	2349	2018	1724	1465	1237	0.5	0.8	0.0	-2.1	-5.5	-10.3	1.9	1.5	0.0	-2.9	-7.2	-20.7	-41.6	
	1259	1031	839	681	555	0.5	0.0	-2.7	-7.9	-15.4	-25.9	1.8	0.0	-4.1	-10.9	-20.6	-50.0	-95.2	15"
	1843	1533	1266	1037	844	0.2	0.0	-1.7	-5.0	-10.0	-17.0	2.5	2.0	0.0	-3.8	-9.6	-27.7	-56.3	24"
	2289	1926	1610	1336	1100	0.5	0.9	0.0	-2.1	-5.7	-10.7	1.9	1.6	0.0	-3.0	-7.6	-21.8	-44.2	24"
	2322	1964	1650	1378	1144	0.2	0.0	-1.7	-4.9	-9.9	-16.8	2.5	2.0	0.0	-3.9	-9.4	-26.9	-54.3	
	2142	1793	1490	1228	1005	0.6	0.9	0.0	-2.3	-6.1	-11.6	2.1	1.7	0.0	-3.2	-8.1	-23.5	-47.7	
	1979	1621	1316	1058	842	0.5	0.8	0.0	-2.1	-5.7	-10.8	1.9	1.6	0.0	-3.0	-7.6	-22.3	-45.8	24"
	2155	1832	1548	1300	1085	0.7	1.0	0.0	-2.5	-6.7	-12.6	2.3	1.9	0.0	-3.5	-8.8	-25.3	-51.0	
	2363	1986	1657	1373	1128	0.5	0.8	0.0	-2.1	-5.5	-10.4	1.8	1.5	0.0	-2.9	-7.3	-21.1	-42.9	
	2293	1875	1518	1217	968	0.6	0.9	0.0	-2.3	-6.2	-11.8	2.1	1.7	0.0	-3.3	-8.3	-24.2	-49.7	
	2308	1805	1393	1060	801	0.2	0.0	-1.5	-4.6	-9.5	-16.4	2.3	1.9	0.0	-3.7	-9.4	-28.1	-58.8	24"
	2520	2171	1860	1585	1343	0.6	0.9	0.0	-2.3	-6.1	-11.4	2.1	1.7	0.0	-3.2	-8.0	-22.8	-45.6	
	2667	2196	1792	1448	1160	0.4	0.8	0.0	-1.9	-5.2	-9.9	1.7	1.5	0.0	-2.8	-7.0	-20.5	-42.1	
	2718	2313	1956	1644	1372	0.6	0.9	0.0	-2.3	-6.0	-11.3	2.0	1.7	0.0	-3.2	-7.9	-22.7	-45.8	24"
	2655	2240	1878	1564	1292	0.4	0.7	0.0	-1.8	-4.8	-9.1	2.6	2.9	2.0	0.0	-3.4	-14.5	-32.6	
	2511	2097	1739	1430	1166	0.6	0.9	0.0	-2.2	-5.9	-11.3	2.0	1.7	0.0	-3.2	-7.9	-23.0	-46.7	
	2669	2303	1978	1689	1434	0.5	0.9	0.0	-2.1	-5.7	-10.7	1.9	1.6	0.0	-3.0	-7.5	-21.4	-42.9	
	2741	2315	1943	1621	1341	0.3	0.7	0.0	-1.7	-4.6	-8.8	2.5	2.8	2.0	0.0	-3.2	-14.0	-31.5	
	2818	2401	2033	1711	1430	0.5	0.9	0.0	-2.2	-5.7	-10.8	1.9	1.6	0.0	-3.0	-7.6	-21.8	-44.0	24"
	2765	2388	2053	1756	1493	0.5	0.8	0.0	-2.1	-5.5	-10.3	1.9	1.6	0.0	-2.9	-7.2	-20.6	-41.3	
7	600	373	262	208	173	0.9	0.0	-4.5	-13.5	-28.3	-49.9	0.0	-4.5	-13.5	-28.3	-49.9	-118.6	-228.2	20"
96	1253	913	666	502	405	0.7	0.0	-3.3	-9.7	-19.6	-33.8	2.2	0.0	-5.3	-14.1	-27.2	-69.0	-136.9	24"
12	886	521	301	172	119	0.4	0.8	0.0	-2.4	-6.7	-13.8	2.0	1.8	0.0	-3.8	-10.2	-35.0	-84.4	24"
02	1296	858	545	399	316	0.5	0.0	-2.7	-8.2	-17.0	-30.0	1.8	0.0	-4.6	-12.5	-24.6	-65.3	-134.9	
27	1355	989	720	535	425	0.6	0.0	-3.0	-8.9	-18.0	-31.1	2.0	0.0	-4.8	-13.0	-25.1	-63.6	-126.7	24"
27	1355	989	720	535	425	0.6	0.0	-3.0	-8.9	-18.0	-31.1	2.0	0.0	-4.8	-13.0	-25.1	-63.6	-126.7	
79	1416	1050	771	571	442	0.5	0.0	-2.7	-7.9	-16.1	-27.6	1.8	0.0	-4.3	-11.6	-22.3	-56.3	-111.9	
07	1639	1193	860	626	482	0.5	0.0	-2.6	-7.7	-15.6	-27.1	1.7	0.0	-4.2	-11.3	-21.9	-55.8	-112.0	24"
03	1845	1462	1143	806	685	0.3	0.0	-1.8	-5.4	11.0	18.8	2.7	2.2	0.0	-4.2	-10.7	-31.5	-65.6	

VENTED TEST-BARREL BALLISTICS
This Remington* patented, industry-accepted method provides data that more precisely reflect actual use of revolver ammunition. It considers cylinder gap, barrel length, powder position, and production tolerances. Although our final values differ from conventional figures, the ammunition is unchanged. Key elements of our patented procedure include: (a) horizontal powder orientation; (b) cylinder gap: .008"; (c) barrel length: 4".

INTERCHANGEABILITY CHART
Cartridges within groups shown are interchangeable. Other substitutions should not be made without specific recommendation of the firearms manufacturer since improper combinations could result in firearm damage or personal injury.

RIMFIRE
22 W.R.F.
22 Remington Special
22 Win. Model 1890 in a 22 Win. Mag. Rimfire but not conversely

CENTERFIRE
25-20 Remington
25-20 W.C.F.
25-20 Win.
25-20 Win. High Speed
25-20 Marlin
25 W.C.F.
6mm Rem. (80 & 90 grain)
244 Remington
25 Automatic
25 Auto. Colt Pistol (ACP)
25 (6.35mm) Automatic Pistol
6.35mm Browning
7mm Express™ Remington
280 Remington
30-30 Sav.
30-30 Win.
30-30 Win. Accelerator*
30-30 Marlin
30-30 Win. High Speed
30 W.C.F.
32 Colt Automatic
32 Auto. Colt Pistol (ACP)
32 (7.65mm) Automatic Pistol
7.65mm Automatic Pistol
7.65mm Browning (not interchangeable with 7.65mm Luger)
32 Short Colt in 32 Long Colt but not conversely SEE NOTE C
32 S.& W. in 32 S.& W. Long but not conversely
32 S.& W. Long
32 Colt New Police
32 Colt Police Positive
32 W.C.F.*
32 Win.*   SEE NOTE A
32-20 Win. High Speed*
32-20 Colt L.M.R
32-20 W.C.F   SEE NOTE G
32-20 Win. and Marlin
38 S.&W.
38 Colt New Police
380 Webley
38 Colt Special
38 S. & W. Special
38 Targetmaster*
38 S. & W. Special Mid-Range   SEE NOTE B & D
38 Special (+P)
38-44 Special (+P)
38 Special
38 Special Flat Point
38 Short Colt in 38 Long Colt but not conversely.
  Both can be used in 38 Special
38 Marlin   SEE NOTE A
38 Win.*
38 Remington*
38-40 Win.   SEE NOTE A
38 W.C.F.*
38 Automatic in 38 Super (+P)
  but not conversely
380 Automatic
9mm Browning Short (Corto Kurz)
9mm Luger   SEE NOTE E
9mm Parabellum
44 S. & W. Special   SEE NOTE F
44 Marlin
44 Win.
44 Remington
44-40 Win.
44 W.C.F.
45-70 Government
45-70 Marlin, Win.
45-70-405

Remington. 1996 Centerfire Rifle

Caliber	Order No.	Wt. (grs.)	Bullet Style	Primer No.	Muzzle	100 yds.	200 yds.	300 yds.	400 yds.
.30-40 Krag	R30402	180*	Pointed Soft Point Core-Lokt*	9 ½	2430	2213	2007	1813	1632
.308 Win.	R308W1	150	Pointed Soft Point Core-Lokt*	9 ½	2820	2533	2263	2009	1774
	R308W2	180	Soft Point Core-Lokt*	9 ½	2620	2274	1955	1666	1414
	R308W3	180	Pointed Soft Point Core-Lokt*	9 ½	2620	2393	2178	1974	1782
	R308W7	168	Boat Tail H.P. Match	9 ½	2680	2493	2314	2143	1979
	ER308WA	165	Extended Range Boat Tail	9 ½	2700	2497	2303	2117	1941
	ER308WB§	178	Extended Range	9 ½	2620	2415	2220	2034	1857
.30-06 Springfield	R30061	125	Pointed Soft Point	9 ½	3140	2780	2447	2138	1853
	R30062	150	Pointed Soft Point Core-Lokt*	9 ½	2910	2617	2342	2083	1843
	R30063	150	Bronze Point	9 ½	2910	2656	2416	2189	1974
	R3006B	165	Pointed Soft Point Core-Lokt*	9 ½	2800	2534	2283	2047	1825
	R30064	180	Soft Point Core-Lokt*	9 ½	2700	2348	2023	1727	1466
	R30065	180	Pointed Soft Point Core-Lokt*	9 ½	2700	2469	2250	2042	1846
	R30066	180	Bronze Point	9 ½	2700	2485	2280	2084	1899
	R30067	220	Soft Point Core-Lokt*	9 ½	2410	2130	1870	1632	1422
	RS3006A	180	Swift A-Frame™ PSP	9 ½	2700	2465	2243	2032	1833
	ER3006A	152	Extended Range	9 ½	2910	2654	2413	2184	1968
	ER3006B	165	Extended Range Boat Tail	9 ½	2800	2592	2394	2204	2023
.300 H&H Mag.	R300HH	180	Pointed Soft Point Core-Lokt*	9 ½ M	2880	2640	2412	2196	1990
.300 Win. Mag.	R300W1	150	Pointed Soft Point Core-Lokt*	9 ½ M	3290	2951	2636	2342	2068
	R300W2	180	Pointed Soft Point Core-Lokt*	9 ½ M	2960	2745	2540	2344	2157
	RS300WA	200	Swift A-Frame™ PSP	9 ½ M	2825	2595	2376	2167	1970
	ER300WB	190	Extended Range Boat Tail	9 ½ M	2885	2691	2506	2327	2156
.300 Wby. Mag.	R300WB1	180	Pointed Soft Point Core-Lokt*	9 ½ M	3120	2866	2627	2400	2184
	ER30WBA§	178	Extended Range	9 ½ M	3120	2902	2695	2497	2308
	ER30WBB	190	Extended Range Boat Tail	9 ½ M	3030	2830	2638	2455	2279
	RS300WBB ★ 200	200	Swift A-Frame™ PSP	9 ½ M	2925	2690	2467	2254	2052
.303 British	R303B1	180	Soft Point Core-Lokt*	9 ½	2460	2124	1817	1542	1311
7.62 x 39MM	R762391	125	Pointed Soft Point	7 ½	2365	2062	1783	1533	1320
.32-20 Win.	R32201	100	Lead	6 ½	1210	1021	913	834	769
	R32202	100	Soft Point	6 ½	1210	1021	913	834	769
.32 Win. Special	R32WS2	170	Soft Point Core-Lokt*	9 ½	2250	1921	1626	1372	1175
8MM Mauser	R8MSR	170	Soft Point Core-Lokt*	9 ½	2360	1969	1622	1333	1123
.338 Win. Mag.	R338W1 ★	225	Pointed Soft Point Core-Lokt*	9 ½ M	2780	2572	2374	2184	2003
	R338W2 ★	250	Pointed Soft Point Core-Lokt*	9 ½ M	2660	2456	2261	2075	1898
	RS338WA	225	Swift A-Frame™ PSP	9 ½ M	2785	2517	2266	2029	1808
.35 Remington	R35R1	150	Pointed Soft Point Core-Lokt*	9 ½	2300	1874	1506	1218	1039
	R35R2	200	Soft Point Core-Lokt*	9 ½	2080	1698	1376	1140	1001
.350 Remington Mag.	R350M1§	200	Pointed Soft Point Core-Lokt*	9 ½ M	2710	2410	2130	1870	1631
.35 Whelen	R35WH1	200	Pointed Soft Point	9 ½ M	2675	2378	2100	1842	1606
	R35WH3	250	Pointed Soft Point	9 ½ M	2400	2197	2005	1823	1652
.375 H&H Mag.	R375M1	270	Soft Point	9 ½ M	2690	2420	2166	1928	1707
	RS375MA	300	Swift A-Frame™ PSP	9 ½ M	2530	2245	1979	1733	1512
.416 Remington Mag.	R416R1§	400	Soft Point	9 ½ M	2400	2042	1718	1436	1212
	R416R2	400	Swift A-Frame™ PSP	9 ½ M	2400	2175	1962	1763	1579
	R416R3§	350	Swift A-Frame™ PSP	9 ½ M	2520	2270	2034	1814	1611
.44-40 Win.	R4440W	200	Soft Point	2 ½	1190	1006	900	822	756
.44 Remington Mag.	R44MG2	240	Soft Point	2 ½	1760	1380	1114	970	878
	R44MG3	240	Semi-Jacketed Hollow Point	2 ½	1760	1380	1114	970	878
	R44MG6	210	Semi-Jacketed Hollow Point	2 ½	1920	1477	1155	982	880
	RH44MGA	275	JHP Core-Lokt*	2 ½	1580	1293	1093	976	896
.444 Mar.	R444M	240	Soft Point	9 ½	2350	1815	1377	1087	941
.45-70 Government	R4570G	405	Soft Point	9 ½	1330	1168	1055	977	918
	R4570L	300	Jacketed Hollow Point	9 ½	1810	1497	1244	1073	969
.458 Win. Mag.	RS458WA ★	450	Swift A-Frame™ PSP	9 ½ M	2150	1901	1671	1465	1289
	R458W1§	500	Metal Case	9 ½ M	2040	1823	1623	1442	1237

NOTE A: *High-speed cartridges must not be used in revolvers. They should be used only in rifles made especially for the
NOTE B: Ammunition with (+P) on the case headstamp is loaded to higher pressure. Use only in firearms designated for t
cartridge and so recommended by the gun manufacturer.
NOTE C: Not for use in revolvers chambered for 32 S. & W. or 32 S. & W. Long.
NOTE D: All 38 Special cartridges can be used in 357 Magnum revolvers but not conversely.
NOTE E: 9mm sub-machine gun cartridges should not be used in handguns.
NOTE F: 44 Russian and 44 S. & W. Special can be used in 44 Remington Magnum revolvers but not conversely.
NOTE G: Not to be used in Win. M-66 and M-73.

★ NEW FOR 1996

Ballistics Tables (continued)

zle yds.	Energy (ft.-lbs.) 100 yds.	200 yds.	300 yds.	400 yds.	500 yds.	Short-range¹ Trajectory* 50 yds.	100 yds.	150 yds.	200 yds.	250 yds.	300 yds.	Long-range² Trajectory* 100 yds.	150 yds.	200 yds.	250 yds.	300 yds.	400 yds.	500 yds.	Barrel Length
60	1957	1610	1314	1064	861	0.4	0.0	-2.1	-6.2	-12.5	-21.1	1.4	0.0	-3.4	-8.9	-16.8	-40.9	-78.1	24"
48	2137	1705	1344	1048	810	0.2	0.0	-1.5	-4.5	-9.3	-15.9	2.3	1.9	0.0	-3.6	-9.1	-26.9	-55.7	
43	2066	1527	1109	799	587	0.3	0.0	-2.0	-5.9	-12.1	-20.9	2.9	2.4	0.0	-4.7	-12.1	-36.9	-79.1	
43	2288	1896	1557	1269	1028	0.2	0.0	-1.8	-5.2	-10.4	-17.7	2.6	2.1	0.0	-4.0	-9.9	-28.9	-58.8	24"
?8	2318	1998	1713	1460	1239	0.2	0.0	-1.6	-4.7	-9.4	-15.9	2.4	1.9	0.0	-3.5	-8.9	-25.3	-50.6	
?0	2284	1942	1642	1379	1152	0.2	0.0	-1.6	-4.7	-9.4	-16.0	2.3	1.9	0.0	-3.5	-8.9	-25.6	-51.5	
43	2306	1948	1635	1363	1130	0.2	0.0	-1.7	-5.1	-10.2	-17.2	2.5	2.1	0.0	-3.8	-9.6	-27.6	-55.8	
36	2145	1662	1269	953	706	0.4	0.8	0.0	-2.1	-5.6	-10.7	1.8	1.5	0.0	-3.0	-7.7	-23.0	-48.5	
20	2281	1827	1445	1131	876	0.6	0.9	0.0	-2.3	-6.3	-12.0	2.1	1.8	0.0	-3.3	-8.5	-25.0	-51.8	
20	2349	1944	1596	1298	1047	0.6	0.9	0.0	-2.2	-6.0	-11.4	2.0	1.7	0.0	-3.2	-8.0	-23.3	-47.5	
?2	2352	1909	1534	1220	963	0.7	1.0	0.0	-2.5	-6.7	-12.7	2.3	1.9	0.0	-3.6	-9.0	-26.3	-54.1	
43	2203	1635	1192	859	625	0.2	0.0	-1.8	-5.5	-11.2	-19.5	2.7	2.3	0.0	-4.4	-11.3	-34.4	-73.7	
43	2436	2023	1666	1362	1105	0.2	0.0	-1.6	-4.8	-9.7	-16.5	2.4	2.0	0.0	-3.7	-9.3	-27.0	-54.9	24"
43	2468	2077	1736	1441	1189	0.2	0.0	-1.6	-4.7	-9.6	-16.2	2.4	2.0	0.0	-3.6	-9.1	-26.2	-53.0	
37	2216	1708	1301	988	758	0.4	0.0	-2.3	-6.8	-13.8	-23.6	1.5	0.0	-3.7	-9.9	-19.0	-47.4	-93.1	
13	2429	2010	1650	1343	1085	0.2	0.0	-1.6	-4.8	-9.8	-16.6	2.4	2.0	0.0	-3.7	-9.4	-27.2	-55.3	
58	2378	1965	1610	1307	1052	0.6	0.9	0.0	-2.3	-6.0	-11.4	2.0	1.7	0.0	-3.2	-8.0	-23.3	-47.7	
72	2462	2100	1780	1500	1256	0.6	1.0	0.0	-2.4	-6.2	-11.8	2.1	1.8	0.0	-3.3	-8.2	-23.6	-47.5	
15	2785	2325	1927	1583	1292	0.6	0.9	0.0	-2.3	-6.0	-11.5	2.1	1.7	0.0	-3.2	-8.0	-23.3	-47.4	24"
405	2900	2314	1827	1424	1095	0.3	0.7	0.0	-1.8	-4.8	-9.3	2.6	2.9	2.1	0.0	-3.5	-15.4	-35.5	
601	3011	2578	2196	1859	1565	0.5	0.8	0.0	-2.1	-5.5	-10.4	1.9	1.6	0.0	-2.9	-7.3	-20.9	-41.9	24"
544	2989	2506	2086	1722	1412	0.6	1.0	0.0	-2.4	-6.3	-11.9	2.1	1.8	0.0	-3.3	-8.3	-24.0	-48.8	
511	3055	2648	2285	1961	1675	0.5	0.9	0.0	-2.2	-5.7	-10.7	1.9	1.6	0.0	-3.0	-7.5	-21.4	-42.9	
890	3284	2758	2301	1905	1565	0.4	0.7	0.0	-1.9	-5.0	-9.5	2.7	3.0	2.1	0.0	-3.5	-15.2	-34.2	
347	3329	2870	2464	2104	1787	0.4	0.7	0.0	-1.8	-4.8	-9.1	2.6	2.9	2.0	0.0	-3.3	-14.3	-31.8	24"
873	3378	2936	2542	2190	1878	0.4	0.8	0.0	-1.9	-5.1	-9.6	1.7	1.4	0.0	-2.7	-6.7	-19.2	-38.4	
799	3213	2701	2256	1870	1538	0.5	0.9	0.0	-2.2	-5.8	-11.0	3.2	3.5	2.4	0.0	-4.0	-17.4	-39.0	
418	1803	1319	950	687	517	0.4	0.0	-2.3	-6.9	-14.1	-24.4	1.5	0.0	-3.8	-10.2	-19.8	-50.5	-101.5	24"
552	1180	882	652	483	370	0.4	0.0	-2.5	-7.3	-14.3	-25.7	1.7	0.0	-4.8	-10.8	-20.7	-52.3	-104.0	24"
825	231	185	154	131	113	0.0	-6.3	-20.9	-44.9	-79.3	-125.1	0.0	-11.5	-32.3	-63.8	-106.3	-230.3	-413.3	24"
825	231	185	154	131	113	0.0	-6.3	-20.9	-44.9	-79.3	-125.1	0.0	-11.5	-32.3	-63.6	-106.3	-230.3	-413.3	
911	1393	998	710	521	411	0.6	0.0	-2.9	-8.6	-17.6	-30.5	1.9	0.0	-4.7	-12.7	-24.7	-63.2	-126.9	24"
102	1463	993	671	476	375	0.5	0.0	-2.7	-8.2	-17.0	-29.8	1.8	0.0	-4.5	-12.4	-24.3	-63.8	-130.7	24"
860	3305	2815	2383	2004	1676	0.6	1.0	0.0	-2.4	-6.3	-12.0	2.2	1.8	0.0	-3.3	-8.4	-24.0	-48.4	
927	3348	2837	2389	1999	1663	0.2	0.0	-1.7	-4.9	-9.8	-16.6	2.4	2.0	0.0	-3.7	-9.3	-26.6	-53.6	24"
871	3165	2565	2057	1633	1286	0.2	0.0	-1.5	-4.6	-9.4	-16.0	2.3	1.9	0.0	-3.6	-9.1	-26.7	-54.9	
762	1169	755	494	359	291	0.6	0.0	-3.0	-9.2	-19.1	-33.9	2.0	0.0	-5.1	-14.1	-27.8	-74.0	-152.3	24"
921	1200	841	577	445	369	0.8	0.0	-3.8	-11.3	-23.5	-41.2	2.5	0.0	-6.3	-17.1	-33.6	-87.7	-176.4	
261	2579	2014	1553	1181	897	0.2	0.0	-1.7	-5.1	-10.4	-17.9	2.6	2.1	0.0	-4.0	-10.3	-30.5	-64.0	20"
177	2510	1958	1506	1145	869	0.2	0.0	-1.8	-5.3	-10.8	-18.5	2.6	2.2	0.0	-4.2	-10.6	-31.5	-65.9	
197	2680	2230	1844	1515	1242	0.4	0.0	-2.2	-6.3	-12.6	-21.3	1.4	0.0	-3.4	-9.0	-17.0	-41.0	-77.8	
337	3510	2812	2228	1747	1361	0.2	0.0	-1.7	-5.1	-10.3	-17.6	2.5	2.1	0.0	-3.9	-10.0	-29.4	-60.7	24"
262	3357	2608	2001	1523	1163	0.3	0.0	-2.0	-6.0	-12.3	-21.0	3.0	2.5	0.0	-4.7	-12.0	-35.6	-74.5	
115	3702	2620	1832	1305	1001	0.4	0.0	-2.5	-7.5	-15.5	-27.0	1.7	0.0	-4.2	-11.3	-21.9	-56.7	-115.1	
115	4201	3419	2760	2214	1775	0.4	0.0	-2.2	-6.5	-13.0	-22.0	1.5	0.0	-3.5	-9.3	-17.6	-42.9	-82.2	24"
935	4004	3216	2557	2017	1587	0.3	0.0	-2.0	-5.9	-11.9	-20.2	2.9	2.4	0.0	-4.5	-11.4	-33.4	-68.7	
629	449	360	300	254	217	0.0	-6.5	-21.6	-46.3	-81.8	-129.1	0.0	-11.8	-33.3	-65.5	-109.5	-237.4	-426.2	24"
1650	1015	661	501	411	346	0.0	-2.7	-10.0	-23.0	-43.0	-71.2	0.0	-5.9	-17.6	-36.3	-63.1	-145.5	-273.0	
1650	1015	661	501	411	346	0.0	-2.7	-10.0	-23.0	-43.0	-71.2	0.0	-5.9	-17.6	-36.3	-63.1	-145.5	-273.0	20"
1719	1017	622	450	361	300	0.0	-2.2	-8.3	-19.7	-37.6	-63.2	0.0	-5.1	-15.4	-32.1	-56.7	-134.0	-256.2	
1524	1020	730	582	490	422	1.7	0.0	-6.9	-20.0	-40.1	-68.7	0.0	-6.9	-20.0	-40.1	-68.7	-153.8	-283.0	
2942	1755	1010	630	472	381	0.6	0.0	-3.2	-9.9	-21.3	-38.5	2.1	0.0	-5.6	-15.9	-32.1	-87.8	-182.7	24"
1590	1227	1001	858	758	679	0.0	-4.7	-15.8	-34.0	-60.0	-94.5	0.0	-8.7	-24.6	-48.2	-80.3	-172.4	-305.9	24"
2182	1492	1031	767	625	533	0.0	-2.3	-8.5	-19.4	-35.9	-59.0	0.0	-5.0	-14.8	-30.1	-52.1	-119.5	—	
4618	3609	2789	2144	1659	1321	0.6	0.0	-3.0	-8.8	-17.6	-30.1	2.0	0.0	-4.8	-12.6	-24.0	-59.5	-115.7	24"
4620	3689	2924	2308	1839	1469	0.7	0.0	-3.3	-9.6	-19.2	-32.5	2.2	0.0	-5.2	-13.6	-25.8	-63.2	-121.7	

Specifications are nominal. Ballistics figures established in test barrels.
Individual rifles may vary from test-barrel specifications.
*Inches above or below line of sight. Hold low for positive numbers, high for negative numbers.
† 280 Remington and 7mm Express® Remington are interchangeable.
‡ Interchangeable in 244 Remington
§ Subject to stock on hand.
¹ Bullet does not rise more than one inch above line of sight from muzzle to sighting-in range.
² Bullet does not rise more than three inches above line of sight from muzzle to sighting-in range.
NOTE: 0.0 indicates yardage at which rifle was sighted in.

CENTERFIRE RIFLE BALLISTICS

Game Selector		CXP Class	Examples
V-Varmint		1	Prairie dog, coyote, woodchuck
D-Deer		2	Antelope, deer, black bear
O/P-Open or Plains		3	Elk, moose
M-Medium Game		30	All game in category 3 plus large dangerous game (i.e. Kodiak bear)
L-Large Game		4	Cape Buffalo, elephant
XL-Extra Large Game		M	Match

\# Acceptable for use in pistols and revolvers also.
Bold type indicates Supreme® product line

*Intended for use in fast twist barrels (e.g., 1 in 7 to 1 in 9).
Slower twist barrels may not sufficiently stabilize bullet.

Cartridge	Symbol	Game Selector Guide	CXP Guide Number	Bullet Wt. Grs.	Bullet Type	Barrel Length (in.)	Muzzle	Velocity in Feet Per Second (fps) 100	200	300	400	500	Muzzle	Energy in Foot Pounds (ft-lbs.) 100	200	300	400	500	50	Trajectory, Short Range Yards 100	150	200	250	300	100	Trajectory, Long Range Yards 150	200	250	300	400	500
218 Bee	X218B	V	1	46	Hollow Point	24	2760	2102	1550	1155	961	850	778	451	245	136	94	74	0.3	0	-2.3	-7.2	-15.8	-29.4	1.5	0	-4.2	-12.0	-24.8	-71.4	-155.6
22 Hornet	X22H1	V	1	45	Soft Point	24	2690	2042	1502	1128	948	840	723	417	225	127	90	70	0.3	0	-2.4	-7.7	-16.9	-31.3	1.6	0	-4.5	-12.8	-26.4	-75.6	-163.4
22 Hornet	X22H2	V	1	45	Hollow Point	24	2690	2042	1502	1128	948	841	723	417	225	127	90	72	0.3	0	-2.4	-7.7	-16.9	-31.3	1.6	0	-4.5	-12.8	-26.4	-75.5	-163.3
22-250 Remington	S22250	V	1	52	Hollow Point Boattail	24	3750	3268	2836	2442	2082	1755	1624	1233	928	689	501	356	0.1	0	-0.7	-2.4	-5.1	-9.1	1.2	1.1	0	-2.1	-5.5	-16.9	-36.3
22-250 Remington	X222501	V	1	55	Pointed Soft Point	24	3680	3137	2656	2222	1832	1493	1654	1201	861	603	410	272	0.2	0.5	0	-1.6	-4.4	-8.7	2.3	2.6	1.9	0	-3.4	-15.9	-38.9
222 Remington	X222R	V	1	50	Pointed Soft Point	24	3140	2602	2123	1700	1350	1107	1094	752	500	321	202	136	0.5	0.9	0	-2.5	-6.9	-13.7	2.2	1.9	0	-3.8	-10.0	-32.3	-73.8
222 Remington	X222R1	V	1	55	Full Metal Jacket	24	3020	2675	2355	2057	1783	1537	1114	874	677	517	388	288	0.5	0.9	0	-2.2	-6.1	-11.7	2.0	1.7	0	-3.3	-8.3	-24.9	-52.5
223 Remington	X223RH	V	1	53	Hollow Point	24	3330	2882	2477	2106	1770	1475	1305	978	722	522	369	256	0.3	0.7	0	-1.9	-5.3	-10.3	1.7	1.4	0	-2.9	-7.4	-22.7	-49.1
223 Remington	X223R	V	1	55	Pointed Soft Point	24	3240	2747	2304	1905	1554	1270	1282	921	648	443	295	197	0.4	0.8	0	-2.2	-6.0	-11.8	1.9	1.6	0	-3.3	-8.5	-26.7	-59.6
223 Remington	X223R1	V	1	55	Full Metal Jacket	24	3240	2877	2543	2232	1943	1679	1282	1011	790	608	461	344	0.4	0.7	0	-1.9	-5.1	-9.9	1.7	1.4	0	-2.8	-7.1	-21.2	-44.6
223 Remington	X223R2	D	2	64	Power-Point	24	3020	2656	2320	2009	1724	1473	1296	1003	765	574	423	308	0.1	0.7	0	-2.1	-5.8	-11.4	1.7	1.6	0	-3.2	-8.2	-25.1	-53.6
223 Remington Match	S223M*	–	M	69	Hollow Point Boattail	24	3060	2740	2442	2164	1904	1665	1435	1151	914	717	555	425	-0.2	-0.9	-3.1	-6.8	-12.1	-20.8	1.6	1.4	0	-2.9	-7.4	-22.3	-46.7
225 Winchester	X2251	V	1	55	Pointed Soft Point	24	3570	3066	2616	2208	1838	1514	1556	1148	836	595	412	280	0.2	0.6	0	-1.7	-4.6	-9.0	2.4	2.8	2.0	0	-3.5	-16.3	-39.5
243 Winchester	X2431	V	1	80	Pointed Soft Point	24	3350	2955	2593	2259	1951	1670	1993	1551	1194	906	676	495	0.3	0.7	0	-1.8	-4.9	-9.4	2.6	2.9	2.1	0	-3.6	-16.2	-37.9
243 Winchester	X2432	D,O/P	2	100	Power-Point	24	2960	2697	2449	2215	1993	1786	1945	1615	1332	1089	882	708	0.5	0.9	0	-2.2	-5.8	-11.0	1.9	1.6	0	-3.1	-7.8	-22.6	-46.3
243 Winchester	X243	D,O/P	2	100	Soft Point Boattail	24	2960	2712	2477	2254	2042	1843	1946	1633	1363	1128	926	754	0.1	0	-1.3	-3.8	-7.8	-13.3	1.9	1.6	0	-3.0	-7.8	-22.0	-44.8
6mm Remington	X6MMR2	D,O/P	2	100	Power-Point	24	3100	2829	2573	2332	2104	1889	2133	1777	1470	1207	983	792	0.4	0.8	0	-1.9	-5.2	-9.9	1.7	1.5	0	-2.8	-7.0	-20.4	-41.7
25-06 Remington	X25061	V	1	90	Positive Expanding Point	24	3440	3043	2680	2344	2034	1749	2364	1850	1435	1098	827	611	0.3	0.6	0	-1.7	-4.5	-8.8	2.4	2.7	2.0	0	-3.4	-15.0	-35.2
25-06 Remington	X25062	D,O/P	2	120	Positive Expanding Point	24	2990	2730	2484	2252	2032	1825	2382	1985	1644	1351	1100	887	0.5	0.8	0	-2.1	-5.6	-10.7	1.9	1.6	0	-3.1	-7.5	-22.0	-44.8
25-20 Winchester	X25202	V	1	86	Soft Point	24	1460	1194	1030	931	858	798	407	272	203	166	141	122	0	-4.1	-14.4	-31.8	-57.3	-92.0	0	-8.2	-23.5	-47.0	-79.6	-175.9	-319.4
25-35 Winchester	X2535	D	2	117	Soft Point	24	2230	1866	1545	1282	1097	984	1292	904	620	427	313	252	0.6	0	-3.1	-9.2	-19.0	-33.1	2.1	0	-5.1	-13.8	-27.0	-70.1	-142.0
250 Savage	X2503	D,O/P	2	100	Silvertip®	24	2820	2467	2140	1839	1569	1339	1765	1351	1017	751	547	398	0.2	0	-1.6	-4.9	-10.0	-17.4	2.4	2.0	0	-3.9	-10.1	-30.5	-65.2
257 Roberts + P	X257P3	D,O/P	2	117	Power-Point	24	2780	2411	2071	1761	1488	1263	2009	1511	1115	806	576	415	0.8	1.1	0	-2.9	-7.8	-15.1	2.6	2.2	0	-4.2	-10.8	-33.0	-70.0
264 Winchester Mag.	X2642	D,O/P	2	140	Power-Point	24	3030	2782	2548	2326	2114	1914	2854	2406	2018	1682	1389	1139	0.5	0.8	0	-2.0	-5.4	-10.2	1.8	1.5	0	-2.9	-7.2	-20.8	-42.2
6.5 x 55 Swedish	X6555	D,O/P	2	140	Soft Point	24	2550	2359	2176	2002	1836	1680	2022	1731	1473	1246	1048	878	0	-1.5	-4.8	-9.8	-16.9	-2...	2.4	2	0	-3.9	-9.7	-28.1	-56.5
270 Winchester	X2705	D,O/P	2	130	Power-Point	24	3060	2902	2559	2329	2110	1904	2702	2267	1890	1565	1285	1046	0.4	0.8	0	-2.0	-5.3	-10.1	1.8	1.5	0	-2.8	-7.1	-20.6	-42.0
270 Winchester	X2703	D,O/P	2	130	Silvertip	24	3060	2776	2510	2259	2022	1801	2702	2225	1818	1472	1180	936	0.5	0.8	0	-2.0	-5.5	-10.4	1.8	1.5	0	-2.9	-7.4	-21.6	-44.3
270 Winchester	S270	D,O/P	2	140	Silvertip Boattail	24	2960	2753	2554	2365	2181	2006	2724	2358	2029	1739	1422	1256	0.1	-1.2	-3.7	-7.5	-12.7	1.8	1.5	0	-2.9	-7.2	-20.6	-41.3
270 Winchester	S270X	D,O/P,M	3	140	Fail Safe®	24	2920	2671	2435	2211	1999	1799	2651	2218	1843	1519	1242	1007	-0.2	0	-1	-3.4	-7.2	-12.6	1.7	1.5	0	-3	-7.8	-22.6	-46.4
270 Winchester	X2704	D,M	3	150	Power-Point	24	2850	2585	2336	2100	1879	1673	2705	2226	1817	1468	1175	932	0.6	1.0	0	-2.4	-6.4	-12.2	2.2	1.8	0	-3.4	-8.6	-25.0	-51.4
280 Remington	X280R	D,O/P	2	140	Power-Point	24	3050	2705	2428	2167	1924	1698	2799	2274	1833	1461	1151	897	0.5	0.8	0	-2.2	-5.8	-11.1	1.9	1.6	0	-3.1	-7.8	-23.1	-47.8
280 Remington	X280	D,O/P	2	150	Silvertip Boattail	24	2840	2637	2442	2256	2078	1909	2686	2316	1985	1692	1438	1213	0.1	0	-1.4	-4.1	-8.4	-14.3	1.9	1.7	0	-3.2	-7.9	-22.6	-45.4
284 Winchester	X2842	D,O/P,M	3	150	Fail Safe	24	2860	2595	2344	2108	1886	1680	2724	2243	1830	1480	1185	940	0.6	1.0	0	-2.4	-6.3	-12.1	2.1	1.8	0	-3.4	-8.5	-24.8	-51.0
7mm Mauser (7x57)	X7MM1	D	2	140	Power-Point	24	2660	2413	2180	1959	1754	1564	2199	1875	1530	1236	990	788	0.7	0	-1.5	-10.3	-17.5	1.1	0	-2.8	-7.4	-14.1	-34.4	-66.1
7mm Remington Mag.	S7MAGA	D,O/P,M,L	3	140	Silvertip Boattail	24	3110	2830	2568	2320	2085	1866	3007	2489	2046	1667	1350	1082	0.4	0.7	0	-1.9	-5.1	-9.7	1.7	1.5	0	-2.9	-7.0	-20.5	-42.1
7mm Remington Mag.	S7MAGX	D,O/P,M,L	3	150	Fail Safe	24	2920	2678	2449	2231	2025	1830	3006	2543	2130	1777	1465	1115	-0.2	0	-3.4	-7.1	-12.5	1.7	1.5	0	-2.9	-7.5	-22	-44.4
7mm Remington Mag.	X7MMR2	D,O/P,M	3	150	Power-Point	24	3090	2818	2561	2316	2085	1866	3181	2667	2196	1792	1448	1160	0.4	0.7	0	-1.9	-5.2	-9.9	1.6	1.5	0	-2.8	-7.0	-20.5	-42.1
7.62 x 39mm Russian	X76230	D,V	2	123	Soft Point	20	2365	2033	1731	1465	1248	1093	3178	2718	2313	1956	1644	1372	0.6	0	-2.3	-6.0	-11.3	2.0	1.7	0	-3.9	-9.7	-22.7	-45.8
30 Carbine #	X30M1	V	1	110	Hollow Soft Point	20	1990	1567	1236	1035	923	842	967	600	373	262	208	173	0.9	0	-4.5	-13.5	-28.3	-49.9	0	-4.5	-13.5	-35.0	-49.9	-118.6	-228.2
30-30 Winchester	X30301	D	2	150	Hollow Point	24	2390	2018	1684	1398	1177	1036	1902	1356	944	651	461	357	0.5	0	-2.6	-7.7	-16.0	-27.9	1.7	0	-4.3	-11.6	-22.7	-59.1	-120.5
30-30 Winchester	X30306	D	2	150	Silvertip	24	2390	2018	1684	1398	1177	1036	1902	1356	944	651	461	357	0.5	0	-2.6	-7.7	-16.0	-27.9	1.7	0	-4.3	-11.6	-22.7	-59.1	-120.5
30-30 Winchester	X30302	D	2	150	Silvertip	24	2390	2018	1684	1398	1177	1036	1902	1356	944	651	461	357	0.5	0	-2.6	-7.7	-16.0	-27.9	1.7	0	-4.3	-11.6	-22.7	-59.1	-120.5
30-30 Winchester	X30303	D	2	170	Silvertip	24	2200	1895	1619	1381	1191	1061	1827	1355	989	720	535	425	0.6	0	-3.0	-8.9	-18.0	-31.1	2.0	0	-4.8	-13.0	-25.1	-63.6	-126.7
30-30 Winchester	X30304	D	2	170	Hollow Point	24	2200	1895	1619	1381	1191	1061	1827	1355	989	720	535	425	0.6	0	-3.0	-8.9	-18.0	-31.1	2.0	0	-4.8	-13.0	-25.1	-63.6	-126.7
30-06 Springfield	X30062	D,O/P	2	125	Pointed Soft Point	24	3140	2780	2447	2138	1853	1595	2736	2145	1662	1269	953	706	0.4	0.8	0	-2.1	-5.6	-11.0	1.8	1.5	0	-3.0	-7.7	-23.0	-48.5
30-06 Springfield	X30063	D,O/P	2	150	Power-Point	24	2920	2580	2265	1972	1704	1485	2839	2217	1708	1296	967	734	0.6	1.0	0	-2.4	-6.6	-12.7	2.1	1.8	0	-3.5	-9.0	-27.0	-57.1
30-06 Springfield	S3006	D,O/P,M	3	165	Silvertip Boattail	24	2800	2597	2402	2216	2039	1869	2873	2471	2114	1799	1522	1280	0.1	0	-1.4	-4.3	-8.6	-14.6	2.1	1.8	0	-3.3	-8.2	-23.4	-47.0

30-06 Springfield	S3006XA	D,O/P,M	3	165	Fail Safe	24	2800	2540	2295	2063	1846	1645	2873	2365	1930	1560	1249	992	-0.1	0	-1.2	-3.9	-8.2	-14.4	2.0	1.7	0	-3.4	-8.6	-25.3	-52.3
30-06 Springfield	X30065	D,O/P	2	165	Pointed Soft Point	24	2800	2573	2357	2151	1956	1772	2873	2426	2036	1696	1402	1151	0.7	1.0	0	-2.5	-6.5	-12.2	2.0	1.8	0	-3.5	-8.7	-25.5	-49.6
30-06 Springfield	S3006X	D,O/P,M,L	3	180	Fail Safe	24	2700	2466	2243	2032	1833	1648	2913	2430	2010	1650	1343	1085	0.7	0	-4.1	-8.6	-14.9	2.1	1.8	0	-3.5	-8.7	-25.5	-51.8
30-06 Springfield	X30064	D,O/P,M	3	180	Power-Point	24	2700	2348	2023	1727	1466	1251	2913	2203	1635	1192	859	625	0.2	0	-1.8	-5.5	-11.2	-19.5	2.4	2.0	0	-3.5	-9.3	-27.7	-55.8
30-06 Springfield	X30066	D,O/P,M,L	3	180	Silvertip	24	2700	2469	2250	2042	1846	1663	2913	2436	2023	1666	1362	1105	0.2	0	-1.8	-5.2	-10.4	-17.7	2.4	2.0	0	-3.6	-8.9	-26.0	-51.8
30-06 Springfield	X30069	M,L	3	220	Silvertip	24	2410	2192	1985	1791	1611	1448	2837	2347	1924	1567	1268	1024	0.4	0	-3.5	-9.1	-17.2	-41.8	2.9	0	-6.2	-16.2	-30.9	-74.9	-137.5
30-40 Krag	X30401	D,M	3	180	Power-Point	24	2430	2099	1795	1525	1298	1128	2360	1761	1288	929	673	508	0.4	0	-3.5	-9.1	-17.2	-41.8	2.9	0	-6.2	-16.2	-30.9	-74.9	-137.5
300 Winchester Mag.	X30WM1	D,O/P	2	150	Power-Point	24	3290	2951	2636	2342	2068	1813	3605	2900	2314	1827	1424	1095	0.3	0.7	0	-1.8	-4.8	-9.3	1.5	1.3	0	-2.6	-6.5	-19.2	-40.5
300 Winchester Mag.	S30WMA	D,O/P,M	3	180	Silvertip Boattail	24	2960	2745	2540	2344	2157	1979	3501	3011	2578	2196	1859	1565	0	-1.3	-3.9	-7.8	-13.3	1.9	1.6	0	-3.1	-7.7	-21.9	-43.9
NEW 300 Winchester Mag.	S30WMX	D,O/P,M,L	3	180	Fail Safe	24	2960	2678	2412	2165	1928	1704	3501	2865	2326	1871	1484	1161	0.2	0	-3.8	-9.8	-16.9	2.1	1.7	0	-3.7	-9.3	-27.0	-55.1
300 Winchester Mag.	X30WM2	D,O/P,M	3	200	Silvertip	24	2825	2595	2376	2167	1970	1785	3545	2991	2508	2086	1722	1415	0.2	0	-1.6	-4.6	-9.0	-15.2	2.7	2.2	0	-3.7	-9.1	-26.1	-52.0
300 H & H Magnum	X300HHA	M,L	3	180	Silvertip Boattail	24	2880	2660	2450	2251	2060	1879	3315	2826	2401	2027	1697	1411	0	-1.8	-5.0	-10.0	-16.9	1.5	0	-2.8	-7.0	-12.9	-37.2	-73.0
300 H & H Magnum	X300HHX	M,L	3	180	Fail Safe	24	2880	2610	2354	2112	1884	1671	3315	2723	2215	1783	1419	1116	0.2	0	-3.9	-10.0	-17.2	2.3	1.9	0	-4.1	-10.3	-30.3	-62.9
300 Savage	X3001	D	2	150	Power-Point	24	2630	2311	2015	1743	1500	1295	2303	1779	1352	1012	749	558	0.3	0	-2.5	-7.4	-15.2	-26.9	2.8	2.3	0	-4.5	-11.5	-34.4	-73.0
300 Savage	X3003	D,O/P	2	150	Silvertip	24	2630	2354	2095	1853	1631	1434	2303	1845	1462	1143	886	685	0.4	0	-2.4	-6.9	-13.8	-23.7	2.7	2.2	0	-4.2	-10.7	-31.5	-65.5
300 Savage	X3004	D,M	3	180	Power-Point	24	2350	2025	1728	1467	1252	1098	2207	1639	1193	860	626	482	0.4	0	-3.3	-9.6	-19.2	-33.4	3.3	2.7	0	-5.0	-12.8	-37.9	-78.5
303 British	X3031	D,M	3	180	Power-Point	24	2460	2124	1817	1542	1311	1137	2418	1803	1319	950	687	517	0.4	0	-3.4	-9.5	-18.5	-32.0	3.0	2.5	0	-4.5	-11.7	-34.9	-71.7
307 Winchester	X3076	D,M	3	180	Power-Point	24	2510	2179	1874	1599	1362	1177	2519	1898	1404	1022	742	554	0.4	0	-3.4	-9.6	-18.8	-32.6	3.0	2.5	0	-4.5	-11.8	-35.1	-72.4
308 Winchester	S308	D,O/P,M	3	150	Silvertip Boattail	24	2820	2598	2386	2186	1996	1818	2648	2248	1896	1591	1327	1100	0	-1.5	-4.5	-9.3	-15.9	1.8	1.5	0	-2.8	-7.1	-20.8	-42.5
308 Winchester	X3082	D,O/P	2	150	Power-Point	24	2820	2533	2263	2009	1774	1560	2648	2137	1705	1344	1048	810	0.2	0	-1.8	-5.2	-10.4	-17.7	2.6	2.1	0	-3.5	-8.8	-25.7	-52.9
308 Winchester	X3086	D,O/P	2	180	Silvertip	24	2620	2393	2178	1974	1782	1604	2743	2288	1896	1557	1269	1028	0.2	0	-1.6	-4.8	-9.5	-15.9	2.6	2.1	0	-3.7	-9.1	-26.2	-51.5
308 Winchester Match	S308X	D,O/P,M	3	168	Hollow Point Boattail	24	2680	2493	2314	2143	1979	1823	2678	2318	1998	1713	1460	1239	0	-1.7	-5.0	-9.9	-16.9	1.6	0	-3.0	-7.7	-14.2	-40.7	-80.4

30-30 Winchester	X30WS	D	2	170	Silvertip	24	...
32 Win. Special	X32WS2	D	2	170	Power-Point	24	...
32-20 Winchester #	X32201	V	1	100	Lead	24	...
8mm Mauser (8 x 57)	X8MM	D	2	170	Power-Point	24	...
338 Winchester Mag.	X3381	M,L,XL	30	200	Power-Point	24	...
338 Winchester Mag.	S338XA	M,L,XL	30	225	Fail Safe	24	...
338 Winchester Mag.	X3382	M,L,XL	30	225	Power-Point	24	...
338 Winchester Mag.	S338X	M,L,XL	30	250	Silvertip	24	...
35 Remington	X35R1	D	2	200	Power-Point	24	...
356 Winchester	X3561	M,L	30	200	Power-Point	24	...
357 Magnum #	X357SP	D	2	158	Jacketed Soft Point	18	...
375 Winchester	X375W	D	2	200	Power-Point	24	...
375 Winchester	X375W1	M,L	30	250	Power-Point	24	...
NEW 375 H&H Magnum	S375HX	M,L,XL	30	300	Fail Safe	24	...
375 H&H Magnum	X375H	M,L,XL	30	300	Silvertip	24	...
38-40 Winchester #	X3840	D	2	180	Soft Point	24	...
38-55 Winchester	X3855	D	2	255	Soft Point	24	...
44 Remington Magnum #	X44MHSP	V,D	2	210	Silvertip Hollow Point	20	...
44 Remington Magnum #	X44MHSP2	D	2	240	Hollow Soft Point	20	...
44-40 Winchester #	X4440	D	2	200	Soft Point	24	...
45-70 Government	X4570H	D,M	3	300	Jacketed Hollow Point	24	...
458 Winchester Magnum	X4581	L,XL	30	510	Soft Point	24	...